Windows Development on NetWare® Systems

Windows Development on NetWare® Systems

Lori Gauthier
Sue Whitehead

Windcrest®/McGraw-Hill

New York San Francisco Washington, D.C. Auckland Bogotá
Caracas Lisbon London Madrid Mexico City Milan
Montreal New Delhi San Juan Singapore
Sydney Tokyo Toronto

The views expressed in this book are those of the authors
and do not necessarily reflect the views of Novell.

2 3 4 5 6 7 8 9 0   DOH/DOH   9 9 8 7 6 5 4

Library of Congress Cataloging-in-Publication Data
Gauthier, Lori.
   Windows development on NetWare Systems / by Lori Gauthier and Sue
Whitehead.
     p.   cm.
   Includes index.
   ISBN 0-8306-4559-4
     1. Windows (Computer programs)   2. NetWare (Computer file)
   I. Whitehead, Sue.   II. Title.
   QA76.76.W56G38   1993
   005.7'1369—dc20   93-36943
                                        CIP

Acquisitions editor: Jennifer Holt DiGiovanna
Editorial team: Bob Ostrander, Executive Editor
                John Baker, Book Editor
Production team: Katherine G. Brown, Director
                Ollie Harmon, Coding
                Susan E. Hansford, Coding
                Wendy L. Small, Layout
                Joan Wieland, Proofreading
                Stacey R. Spurlock, Indexer
Design team: Jaclyn J. Boone, Designer
              Brian Allison, Associate Designer   WK2
Cover design & marble paper by Margaret Karczewski, Vienna, Va   4498

⇨ Dedication

To all of the developers and administrators that have just wanted a little more information and a little more time.

 # Notices

Brain Share™	Novell, Inc.
DR DOS®	
Internetwork Packet Exchange™	
IPX™	
IPX/SPX™	
Link Support Layer™	
LSL™	
NetWare®	
NetWare Core Protocol™	
NetWare Directory Services™	
NetWare DOS Requester™	
Novell®	
Novell DOS®	
ODI™	
Open Data-Link Interface™	
Personal NetWare™	
Transactional Tracking System™	
TTS™	

©**NetWare Care**

©**NITQ.H**

©**NTT.H**

©**NWDIAG.H**

©**NWDIR.H**

©**NWDSACL.H**

©**NWDSASA.H**

©**NWDSBUFT.H**

©**NWDSDC.H**

©**NWDSDSA.H**

©**NWDSMISC.H**

Contents

⇨ Acknowledgments

We would like to acknowledge with gratitude the help and encouragement of our families and friends. In addition, several people deserve individual recognition. To Leslie Martinich for her encouragement and guidance during this project and several others. To Ross Hopson, Chip Webb, Peter Lohman, Cliff Ross, Jack Harris, Drex Dixon, and Bill Alexander through whom much knowledge and understanding were gained. To our husbands, Andy and Bob, for telling us to finish it and giving us the time to do so.

Introduction

This book is intended to help networking professionals and professional developers better understand the services provided by NetWare systems. Additionally, the powers of network computing and network distributed processing are to be exposed and explained.

How NetWare systems work, how to manage them, and how to take advantage of them are the aims and goals of the discussions in this book. If you have ever had something unexpected happen on a network, you know that networking knowledge still is priceless. Understanding what is happening is half of the battle to solving the challenges and problems on the network. With this book, detailed information on how a NetWare network works and what to expect will improve the process of using and managing the network.

This book is not intended to be an exhaustive reference manual on every NetWare application programming interface. The application interfaces discussed in this book were chosen to demonstrate distributed programming techniques and to give examples of items in which many developers have expressed an interest.

Getting an application that is faster or has more features than the competition is the key to software success. This book will help

developers understand the items necessary to make their applications NetWare systems-aware and take advantage of the power and performance of the number one network in the world. In the chapters of this book, you will find explanations of the protocols used in NetWare systems, of the bindery, of the new NetWare Directory, of file services, of print services, and of management and security services available to your application through NetWare systems. Additionally, you will learn how to take advantage of one or many of these services in combination to tap the processing power spread across the network on each desktop machine. Ideas on using these services are provided along with the in-depth discussions on how to use them.

The applications provided with this book are for teaching the concepts discussed and to provide working samples as reference. Additionally, these samples provide exercises for the reader to further develop an understanding of programming for NetWare. The applications discussed in chapters 5, 12, and 14 use the NetWare Client SDK for C. The applications in chapters 3, 8, and 10 use the NetWare C Interface for Windows. The Client SDK for C recently has replaced the C Interface for Windows. Chapter 16 explains the steps to port from the C Interface for Windows to the Client SDK for C. The porting of the applications in chapters 3, 8, and 10 are left to the reader as an exercise to follow chapter 16. The services provided by these applications remain the same. The applications can be run without rebuilding them, but the exercise is useful to increase the reader's knowledge of the software tools provided by Novell.

Editor's note: This book has icons next to the subheadings in the text. A icon is beside each major subheading, and a icon is next to each minor subheading.

Overview:
Windows, networking,
& NetWare systems

AS businesses face the realities of economics and getting the work done in the most efficient manner possible, they are turning to solutions that provide easy-to-use interfaces on economical systems. Using Microsoft Windows on Novell NetWare systems often fits as the solution to many business needs. Networking is changing the face of the computer industry by offering high-performance, low-cost solutions to sharing resources and sharing information. NetWare is the highest performance and most reliable networking solution available.

NetWare systems allow data and resources to be shared across heterogeneous desktop environments. Each user or business is able to choose the desktop system that they desire and communicate with other desktop systems. Many people are choosing Windows as the desktop solution. Using Windows provides a more intuitive graphical user interface (GUI). This interface allows people to learn to use new software more quickly and once learned, retain that knowledge more easily by using symbols, pictures, and assisting software to find and run applications. Both NetWare and Windows are good systems, but applications are needed that take advantage of the strengths of both. Applications that stretch the capabilities of NetWare and Windows are the beginning of the future of computing and will provide solutions to many business needs. The steps that you take here will lead you to windows of opportunity for NetWare systems-aware Windows applications.

Windows

The Windows operating system by Microsoft is a nonpreemptive operating system with a graphical user interface (GUI). This interface provides ease of use by organizing features in icons, menus, and application windows. Each application uses an icon to choose and run it, a menu to choose options from and a window for input and output.

With Windows, an individual often must develop an entirely new vocabulary. Included in this vocabulary are terms and acronyms such as dynamic link libraries (DLLs), instances, launching, focus, segment

management, definition files, imports, exports, ordinal numbers, import libraries (implibs), link files, symbol files, etc.

A *dynamic link library* is a library in which the link to the code it contains occurs at run time. Commonly referred to as a DLL, these libraries allow the same code to be used by several applications, thus reducing individual application sizes. Another advantage to DLLs is doing away with the need to relink an application every time an error is fixed in the library.

Instances refers to each time an application is executed. If an application is executed multiple times, multiple instances of the application exist. All Windows applications have an instance handle, which also is referred to as a task ID. When an application is executed, it is launched.

Focus is a term used to indicate which application or windows currently are active. The active window will have the processing focus.

Segment management is necessary for applications in the Windows architecture. Because applications run in protected mode, the code segments are read-only and data segments are read and write. The purposes of these segments are not the same. Therefore, data and code management also require decisions as to which segment they will exist in and what the characteristics of those segments will be. Segments can be defined as LOADONCALL, PRELOAD, FIXED, MOVEABLE, DISCARDABLE, MULTIPLE, and SINGLE. Segments are defined in the applications definition file. Also defined in the definition file are the program title, program type, import functions, and export functions.

Import functions are functions that the application knows exist elsewhere, either in another application or DLL. These functions are imported by specifying the source (application) name in the IMPORTS section of the definition file followed by a period and the name of the function. When functions are specified in the IMPORTS section, the linker doesn't look for them in the libraries at link time.

Export functions are functions exported by an application. Often, after they are specified by name, they are followed by an @ and a number. This number is called the ordinal number. *Ordinal numbers* allow the Windows system to quickly reference a function by number instead of scanning for the name in the source file. When the application IMPLIB.EXE is run on a definition file, an import library is created from the exports specified in the definition file. This library then can be used when linking an application to let the linker know where these calls can be found. Definition files are located on the link line for Windows applications or within the link files.

Link files define all the object files (.OBJs) that are to be linked into the executable or DLL. Linking a program generates a map file from which a symbol file is created. The application MAPSYM.EXE is run on the map file to convert it to a symbol file.

→ Windows application programming overview

Windows applications are message driven. A message-driven system is one in which applications take action based on a message sent to a message queue. In Microsoft Windows, moving the cursor, displaying a typed character, drawing a window, etc. are all done as the result of messages sent from the operating system to the application. The application decides which messages are required for it to operate and takes action on these messages. If the message in the queue is not one which the application is watching for, then the application must pass the message on. To do this, a Windows application will issue a TranslateMessage() and DispatchMessage() call pair.

Windows messages are data structures that indicate where the message came from and what its value is. A handle to these structures is moved from application queue to application queue. In this manner, each application is allowed to see the messages coming from the system. Microsoft provides a function, DefaultWindowsProc, to allow applications to process standard messages in a standard fashion. For example, if an application wants to treat only a certain character, it can pass all other keyboard messages to the default procedure. When

the cursor is moved by the mouse, this default procedure will move the cursor on the screen.

The application developer isn't required to learn all the functions necessary to move the cursor. Every hardware function on the computer will cause a message to be sent under the Windows system. Moving the mouse generates dozens of messages. To see how many messages are generated and what they are, Windows has provided a tool in the Software Development Kit (SDK) called SPY.

Because Windows is message driven, it is important to remember that Windows is nonpreemptive. In other words, Windows will not suspend the execution of an application, the application must relinquish control to the Windows operating systems. One programming construct that should be avoided in Windows is a tight loop. For example, when tight, while loop like the following one:

```
while(inUseFlag);
```

is used in a Windows application, it will cause that application to completely consume the CPU cycles. Control is never relinquished to the operating system and the application appears to have hung. In reality, with the tight loop in the program in control, no messages are able to be processed by any of the applications.

⇒ Windows application memory

Windows allows applications to make use of all the memory in the machine, not just that below 1Mb. The memory management scheme in Windows deals with movement of program segments from one location to another to have the largest free block of memory available. Thus, to take greatest advantage of the Windows operating system, an application should declare segments fixed only when absolutely necessary. Examples of when a fixed segment might be necessary include procedures accessed asynchronously as from a hardware interrupt or as from a Windows timer. A fixed segment might not be necessary if the application uses a MakeProcInstance for a procedure that needs to be called asynchronously. Such a procedure would be most optimal if its purpose was to send a message to the application to indicate what action should be taken.

In the Windows memory management scheme, program data can be
allocated from the local memory pool or the global memory pool. The
local memory pool is located on the program's heap. The global
memory pool is managed by the Windows operating system.

Under Windows, the same applications can be multiply executed.
Because of this, applications must either instance their data segment
by declaring it multiple or use a table to instance the data. However, a
dynamic link library (DLL) can have only one data segment and must
do one of three things: avoid global data, instance global data in
tables, or use data buffers passed from the application.

Windows uses handles to allow the memory allocated to be moved
and to still be accessible to the application. When memory is allocated
from the local heap or the global heap, it should be locked before it is
dereferenced. Otherwise, the variables might be changing as the
physical location of the data segment changes.

Windows modes

Three modes of operation exist in Windows 3.0: Enhanced, Standard,
and Real mode. Only two of these modes exist in Windows 3.1:
Enhanced and Standard. Real mode requires an 8087-based
computer or better.

Real mode runs in the real mode emulation on an 80286 or 80386
machine. In Real mode, DOS applications' memory and Windows
applications' memory all exist below the 1Mb memory boundary. This
is all the memory that can be referenced with segment:offset
addressing. When Windows applications are executing, the DOS
applications are not and vice versa. This mode will not be supported
in any version above Windows 3.0.

Standard mode requires at least an 80286 computer. This mode of
operation uses the 80286 instruction set. Windows applications run
in 80286 protected memory. Any application attempting to write to
memory that it doesn't own will experience an unrecoverable
application error or a general protection fault indicating a memory
protection violation. Again, as in Real Mode, when Windows

applications are executing, DOS applications aren't and vice versa. Throughout this book, Real mode and Standard mode are both referred to when Standard mode is mentioned due to the similarity of operation in both modes. Enhanced mode requires a minimum of an 80386 computer. This mode takes advantage of the 80386 instruction set and virtual machine capabilities.

Virtual machines

A *virtual machine* (VM) is a memory image and set of register values that, when executing, appears to be the entire computer but is one of several virtual machines all running at the same time or taking turns. The process of each virtual machine taking turns processing is called *time-slicing*. When the operating system manages each virtual machine getting these turns, the system is called *task switching*. Task switching indicates that the system switches from task to task.

A virtual machine is exactly that, virtual rather than physical. This principle of virtual machines has been used for a long time on mainframe computers, allowing many users to have access to physical system resources. The ability to have more than one virtual machine in computers based on the Intel CPU chips was not available until the 80386 chip was designed. This chip allows operating systems to be written that make use of principles such as virtual machines.

Under Windows, all Windows applications and the Windows kernel run in VM1 or the system VM. Each DOS prompt runs in a separate VM. For example, if you are running program manager in Windows and have two DOS programs running, each from a separate DOS prompt, then you have three virtual machines.

Virtual Machine Manager & the DOS Protected Mode Interface

Under Windows, DOS prompts run preemptively just as DOS does normally. This means that any process can be interrupted at any time that interrupts are enabled. To emulate the DOS environment from

Windows, input and output must be managed. To manage information input and output from the keyboard, the mouse, the screen, or other hardware, virtual devices are written. A virtual device is a device driver that runs at ring 0 in 386 protected mode. A virtual device runs below a layer of the Windows operating system called the Virtual Machine Manager (VMM).

The VMM enables Windows to virtualize interrupts, memory, and communications for each of the VMs. This virtualization is why each virtual machine runs as if it is a stand-alone process. Each of the virtual devices acts as a demultiplexing layer between applications in Windows and the physical devices in the computer. The virtual device allows all the applications to communicate to each device while avoiding collisions and deadlock situations. Information in a certain memory location in one virtual machine is not necessarily in the same place in another virtual machine. Therefore, a virtual device must be aware of which virtual machine is running and write the correct information to the correct location in memory for only that virtual machine.

Because Windows applications run in protected mode, an interface was written to allow them to communicate with drivers that are loaded before Windows that run in real mode (8088 mode). This interface is called the DOS Protected Mode Interface (DPMI). Under the DPMI, applications can allocate global DOS memory, allocate a call back entry point, allocate descriptors to refer to Global DOS memory, and simulate real mode calls with a far return stack frame or an interrupt return stack frame. The callbacks allocated under the DPMI are virtualized with a maximum of 16 per VM. Therefore, an application that is trying to be accessed from real mode asynchronously will need a virtual device, not a DPMI callback, because the correct VM might not be running at the time that the asynchronous callback is executed.

The Windows operating system is time slicing rather than multitasking. This means that all applications that can run in the background take turns on the CPU with the application running in the foreground. A DOS prompt that is marked as running only in the foreground will suspend all processing while it is in the background.

Background processing occurs when the application continues processing although it is not the currently active program.

Foreground processing occurs in an application in the context of the currently active window. The window that is foremost on the computer screen is the application that is running in foreground. A DOS prompt marked exclusive will not allow any other applications to execute in the background while it is running in the foreground. A DOS prompt should be marked Exclusive only if it is absolutely necessary for the application to run properly. No applications that process data asynchronously should be run at the same time as a DOS prompt running in exclusive mode.

When Windows loads, all resident applications (TSRs) loaded prior to Windows are considered global to all VMs. Anything loaded after Windows is running is local to that VM. To instance data contained in global devices, a virtual device must know where the data is located, know how much data is to be instanced, and issue the command to the Windows kernel to virtualize this memory location on initialization of Windows.

To build applications that will run in both Windows 3.0 and Windows 3.1, each C file must contain the #define WINVER 0x0300 definition. Additionally, the RC.EXE utility needs to be run with a v3.0 compatibility switch. For example:

```
rc -30 ipxchat.rc.
```

Networking

Networking allows users to share resources by allowing their desktop machines to communicate with one another and with the servers on the network. This communication is accomplished through a combination of hardware and software. The hardware consists of some kind of cabling between the machines and the use of network interface cards. These cards are responsible for communicating based on established communications protocols for ethernet, arcnet, token ring, etc. The software consists of drivers that pick up the packets from the network cards and put them together for the applications

and operating system running at the desktop. The networking software that runs at the desktop usually is referred to as the client. A machine located on the network that provides services or resources is referred to as the *server*. Later in this book, we will discuss when a client can also function as a server.

In networking, portions of the work done by applications occur at the client machines such as the information display and the calculations of the data and portions of the work occur at the server machines, such as saving the information to disk and printing. This division of labor between multiple machines each having their own central processing unit is called distributed processing. Centralized processing occurs when all the work is done in one place. A personal computer not on a network and a mainframe computer are two examples of centralized processing. Networks are based on distributed processing, whereas mainframe environments are based on centralized processing. Distributed processing with personal desktop machines costs less than the larger, multi-user machines necessary for centralized processing.

Windows users are predominantly located on networks. The software written to take advantage of these facts, by and large, will be preferred to software that is neither Windows based or network-aware.

NetWare systems

The single largest market share of the networking market is held by Novell, Inc.'s NetWare systems. NetWare networking software is considered an open platform due to support of the user's choice of hardware platform. Applications for NetWare systems currently are limited only by one's imagination.

NetWare Windows drivers

The NetWare Windows networking solution includes a set of standard calls that any Windows network driver should support. These functions are defined by Microsoft and found in the Windows Driver

Development Kit. These calls are to support calls the Windows
operating system makes to query the status of the network. For
NetWare clients, Novell wrote a driver called NETWARE.DRV. This
driver provides the interface required by Windows for networking
drivers. In addition, NETWARE.DRV provides an interface for
Windows applications to access the network and network
information. NETWARE.DRV is the NetWare driver for performing
network functions such as mapping drives, logging in to servers,
printing, and receiving network messages. This driver works in
conjunction with the shell (NETX.COM) or the NetWare DOS
Requester (VLM.COM) to maintain file server connections and other
information needed to access network resources. A list of the
software components comprising the NetWare Windows support is
found in Table 1-1.

Windows support provided for NetWare

Table 1-1

Driver	Version
NETWARE.DRV	2.00
VNETWARE.386	3.00
VIPX.386	1.40
VLM.COM	1.02
*.VLM	(supplied with VLM.COM)
NETX.COM	3.32
TBMI.COM	1.20
TASKID.COM	1.20
IPX.OBJ	3.10
IPXODI.COM	1.30
LSL.COM	2.00
TBMI2.COM	3.00

Two other drivers were written to virtualize communication with
IPX.COM and the shell or the NetWare DOS requester. These drivers
are VIPX.386 and VNETWARE.386, respectively. VNETWARE.386
virtualizes int 21h input from DOS prompts to the shell and ensures
that information is returned to the correct VM. VNETWARE.386 is a

386 Enhanced Mode Virtual Device Driver. In Enhanced mode
Windows, all Windows applications run in the same virtual machine,
VM1. When a DOS prompt is desired, the user switches to DOS.
Each DOS prompt opened by the user is a separate virtual machine.
Each virtual machine will have its own map of memory. For the
correct responses to be given to the appropriate virtual machine,
VNETWARE.386 maintains virtual machine information for each
request. When an application in a DOS prompt makes a request to
the network such as an Open File request, VNETWARE.386 will
capture that request and before passing it to the shell or requester
will record information such as the virtual machine ID. The request
then is passed to the shell or requester that, in turn, sends the
request to the server. After processing the request, the server sends
the reply to the workstation. The shell or requester then attempts to
return this information. For the information to be returned to the
correct virtual machine, VNETWARE.386 must activate the right
virtual machine, then copy the data. The software necessary to run
each mode of Windows is summarized in Table 1-2.

Table 1-2

**NetWare Windows drivers
and the modes where they are functional**

NetWare Drivers Windows:	Enhanced	Standard	Real
NETWARE.DRV	X	X	X
VNETWARE.386	X		
VIPX.386	X		
TBMI.COM*		X	X
TASKID.COM*		X	X
TBMI2.COM**	X	X	

* Windows 3.0 only

** Windows 3.0 and 3.1

NETWARE.DRV also offers an assembly interface to the network for
Windows applications. This interface is provided through a function
call, NetwareRequest, and is written to emulate calls normally using
an int 21h under DOS. These calls are used to communicate with the

NetWare file server using the NetWare Core Protocol (NCP). This is a synchronous protocol built on top of Novell's Internetwork Packet Exchange (IPX). NCP is a guaranteed delivery, connection-oriented protocol.

A request is sent by the NetWare shell or requester to the file server. The shell or requester then waits for a reply from the server. When this reply comes, the shell passes the information back to the application that issued the request. Requests are sent and received in packets on IPX. IPX is a connectionless datagram protocol. IPX is one of the fastest protocols on the market today. Because of this high performance, the shell or requester is able to communicate with NCP very quickly and efficiently. Once information is in the workstation's memory, the user can manipulate that information independent of the file server.

This is one of the great advantages to networking and distributed processing. With the proper tools and information, applications can be written to take advantage of the great power available in distributed processing on networks. These tools include the appropriate versions of the drivers and the NetWare C-Interface for Windows SDK. The principles discussed in this book are general NetWare programming concepts and can be applied to other platforms through the NetWare Application Programming Interface (API).

The NetWare Windows components include NETWARE.DRV, VNETWARE.386, VIPX.386, NETX.COM or VLM.COM, TBMI.COM or TBMI2.COM, TASKID.COM, IPX.COM, and the DLLs available for interfacing with the NetWare operating system. These DLLs might include NWIPXSPX.DLL, NWACCT.DLL, NWAFP.DLL, NWBIND.DLL, NWCONN.DLL, NWFILE.DLL, NWDIR.DLL, NWFSERV.DLL, NWQMS.DLL, NWSAP.DLL, NWDIAG.DLL, NWWORK.DLL, NWPSERV.DLL, NWCORE.DLL, NWMISC.DLL, and NWPRINT.DLL, or they might include NWIPXSPX.DLL, NWNETAPI.DLL, and NWPSERV.DLL. These DLLs comprise the NetWare C-Interface for Windows. Using the C-Interface calls in your applications will enable your applications to become NetWare-aware and take advantage of the services and power placed at your fingertips by NetWare. The DLLs alternatively could be provided

through the NetWare Client SDK. The DLLs provided by the client SDK are NWCALLS.DLL, NWNET.DLL, and NWIPXSPX.DLL. These DLLs shipped with support for NetWare 4.0 and currently are available from Novell.

⇨ VIPX

Under Windows Enhanced mode, memory is virtualized and the system takes advantage of all the memory in the computer. The memory used by the Windows applications usually is above the 1Mb boundary. IPX.COM on the other hand is a real mode TSR that can reference only memory below the 1Mb boundary.

To allow applications to use IPX from protected mode, VIPX was written. VIPX is responsible for copying event control blocks (ECBs) and packet buffers from the protected mode application to global DOS memory, for making sure that packets are copied back only when the right VM is active, and for translating the call to IPX from protected mode to virtual 86 mode. Virtual 86 mode is the mode that the computer runs in to allow DOS applications to process.

To save as much memory as possible in the global DOS memory pool, VIPX allocates low-memory buffers only on an as-needed basis. For send packets, the low-memory buffers are allocated immediately and freed as soon as the send completes. For listens, however, VIPX uses a late packet allocation process. This means that dozens of protected mode listens can be outstanding and not one byte will use up the global DOS memory pool until the listen actually is received by IPX.

When IPX receives a packet, it first checks to see if there are any outstanding listens posted on that socket queue. If there are no listen ECBs outstanding, IPX calls VIPX with a request for a listen buffer on the specified socket. If VIPX does have such a listen, memory is used from the global DOS pool VIPX allocates on start up and passed to IPX to receive the packet. The event service routine (ESR) in this ECB is set to VIPX's own routine.

When the listen is copied to the global buffer and the event service routine is called, VIPX then copies the information from the global memory buffer to the client application's buffers and frees the global memory buffer for use by other listens. Due to this algorithm, VIPX rarely has more than two or three global memory buffers outstanding at any one time. Thus, all calls to the NetWare Windows DLLs are processed through VIPX for enhanced mode. In Real and Standard modes a different solution is necessary because virtual devices run only in Enhanced mode.

 TBMI & TBMI2

The solution for Real and Standard modes is TBMI.COM or TBMI2.COM, the Task-switch Buffer Manager for IPX. This application is a DOS TSR that is loaded before Windows and buffers IPX/SPX packets for applications during task switching.

Application memory in a task that is not currently active is not available asynchronously in Standard mode. For example, if IPX tried to write to a buffer that was submitted from a Windows application while a DOS application is running from the Windows DOS prompt, that memory location would be corrupted. That memory is not owned by the application that was switched out and might even be the code segment of the currently executing DOS application.

The converse also is true when a DOS application using IPX/SPX is not the active task. To address this issue and buffer IPX/SPX traffic until the application was again active, Novell wrote TBMI.COM, TBMI2.COM, and TASKID.COM. Version 1.0 of TBMI supported IPX/SPX traffic from DOS prompts only. TBMI version 1.1 was modified to be used in conjunction with the NWIPXSPX.DLL for buffering of packets for Windows applications as well. TASKID is not needed if the user is running applications from Windows only. However, if the user ever plans to use a DOS prompt, then, prior to launching a Windows application that uses IPX/SPX, TASKID should be run in the DOS prompt and the user should switch back to Windows without closing the DOS prompt. This will enable TBMI to run properly and to recognize when the user has switched away from their Windows application. TBMI2.COM version 2.0 was written to

support Windows 3.1. TBMI2.COM version 3.0 supports both
Windows 3.0 and Windows 3.1. When running TBMI2.COM with
Windows 3.0 place Using Windows 3.0 = ON in the
NET.CFG file. You then will run TASKID.COM as described earlier.
With Windows 3.1, only TBMI2.COM is necessary. TBMI2 and its
interaction with NWIPXSPX.DLL will be further discussed in the
chapter on IPX. Throughout the remainder of this book, all
references will be to TBMI2 but will apply appropriately to both TBMI
and TBMI2.

NetWare C-Interface for Windows

The NetWare C-Interface for Windows provides a rich variety of
functionality for the applications developer. These DLLs are written
to provide access to the network for applications written in Windows.
This access is similar to that provided for DOS and is documented in
the Novell NetWare C-Interface for Windows Software Development
Kit. The applications discussed in this book were written using this
SDK and will explain how to use a number of calls contained in it.
For developers to find the functionality necessary to writing their
applications, Table 1-3 has been provided to indicate what
functionality is contained within which DLL.

Table 1-3   **NetWare DLLs and supported functionality**

DLL	Function
NWIPXSPX.DLL	IPX and SPX function calls
	Service Advertising function calls
	Diagnostic services function calls
NWNETAPI.DLL	Accounting services function calls
or	AFP services function calls
NWCALLS.DLL	Bindery services function calls
	Connection services function calls
	File system directory services function calls
	File system services function calls
	File Server Environment function calls

	Message services function calls
	Miscellaneous support function calls
	Name Space services function calls
	Print and QMS services function calls
	Synchronization services function calls
	Transaction Tracking System services function calls
	Work station services function calls
NWPSERV.DLL or NWPSRV.DLL	Print server services function calls

In the C-Interface for Windows SDK version 1.3, NWIPXSPX.DLL has the same functionality as NWSAP.DLL, NWDIAG.DLL, and NWIPXSPX.DLL. NWNETAPI.DLL has the same functionality as NWACCT.DLL, NWAFP.DLL, NWBINDRY.DLL, NWCONN.DLL, NWCORE.DLL, NWDIR.DLL, NWFILE.DLL, NWFSERVER.DLL, NWMESSAG.DLL, NWMISC.DLL, NWNAMESP.DLL, NWPRTQUE.DLL, NWSYNC.DLL, NWTTS.DLL, and NWWRKSTN.DLL. NWPSERV.DLL has the same functionality as before. In the Novell NetWare Client SDK v1.0, NWCALLS.DLL includes the functionality of NWNETAPI.DLL. NWIPXSPX.DLL is the same DLL with two additional calls. NWNET.DLL is a new DLL with support for NetWare Directory Services (new with NetWare version 4.0). NWPSERV.DLL has been replaced by the NWPSRV.DLL.

All DLLs use a version string format defined by Novell. This version format is able to be read by NetWare's VERSION.EXE program. The version format consists of a string containing the word version in mixed case followed by an equals sign and the version information. For example, the version string for NWIPXSPX.DLL would look like this:

```
versionString = "VeRsIoN=v. 1.30 NWIPXSPX.DLL".
```

Sample code that scans executable files for this version string is provided with the Novell NetWare C-Interface for Windows. Any application using this string can have its version read by VERSION.EXE. Any application implementing the code to find this string can check the versions of DLLs with an easy and standard method.

The applications in this book are a small sampling of the applications that can be written to take advantage of the power of NetWare operating systems and distributed computing. Additional applications that can be implemented include stand-alone accounting servers that charge network resource use to departments, an authorization server that controls the corporate approval process for electronic documents, E-mail services, printing services, fax servers using QMS or SPX, and any other application that can further automate the office.

Securing your network: bindery & trustee control

I N the press during the last three years, security hacking has made the headlines. Hackers have used back doors and security gaps on systems to access classified and sensitive information as well as corrupt important research data. Proper use of NetWare security features through the bindery will help network managers avoid security breaches that could compromise the company's data and intellectual rights.

Network security consists of three basic levels of controlling access to the file server. These levels consist of the bindery, login control, and file and directory access. Each of these levels, in conjunction with the others, can work together to make a network secure and safe from intrusion and data theft.

⇨ Bindery overview

The bindery is a special purpose database consisting of objects and properties for those objects. The bindery itself has security access levels to limit access to and information about security on the server. This security is called the *bindery access level*. An access level defines who can read the object information and who can write or modify the object information. The bindery access levels are defined in Table 2-1.

Table 2-1	**Bindery access levels**
	4 = Bindery or OS access
	3 = Supervisor access
	2 = Object access
	1 = Logged access

⇨ Bindery objects

The bindery APIs can be used to create objects, define their access level, and define characteristics of those objects. Object

characteristics are called *properties*. The bindery access level and
properties can be added to objects to limit access to owned resources
and programmatically verify the property values assigned. An object's
access level consists of read access and write access. When using the
bindery APIs, the read access level is defined by the low-order nibble
(0xXR) and the write access level is defined by the high-order nibble
(0xWX). For example, an object's name is LOGGED access. This is
necessary so that the object can be verified as existing before being
logged in. The write level can protect a property from being changed
by the wrong individual. This is true of the LOGIN_CONTROL
property. It has a write access of 3. This allows only the supervisor or
OS to change the login restrictions.

The read access level also can be used to protect a property. For
example, the PASSWORD property has a write access level of 2,
which allows the user to change his password. However, the read
level is 4. This requires the password to be changed through a
specific API that the OS has provided because only the OS can read
the encrypted password contained in the bindery. When changing the
password, the API must pass in the old password as well as the new
password. Therefore, when an object is logged in, the password can
be changed only by someone knowing the old password. This
protects the user's password from anyone, including the Supervisor.

Managing and creating objects can be done programmatically through
the use of bindery APIs. Additionally, the bindery APIs allow
applications to close the bindery to allow it to be archived and
subsequently reopen it, disable logins for individuals or all users, and
detect intruders.

When creating an object, an application must assign it a type and an
access level. Bindery objects have a name that is up to 48 characters
long including the null terminator. They also have a type that is
2 bytes and an access level that is one byte (0x31). Bindery objects
are created using the CreateBinderyObject call. When a bindery
object is created initially, it has no properties associated with it. To
be a proper object of the type defined, the object must have the
properties that are defined for that type of object. The properties for
the user determine what access the object has to resources and
information on the file server. This access can include directory

access and can even limit when the user is allowed to login to the file server. A user object is required to have the properties listed in Table 2-2 to be properly configured.

Table 2-2

USER object properties

GROUPS_I'M_IN	0x31 STATIC/SET
SECURITY_EQUALS	0x32 STATIC/SET
LOGIN_CONTROL	0x32 STATIC/ITEM
PASSWORD	0x24 STATIC/ITEM

A USER object also can have the properties listed in Table 2-3. Properties are created using the CreateProperty function. Values for the properties are set using the WritePropertyValue function call.

Table 2-3

Other USER object properties

IDENTIFICATION	0x31 STATIC/ITEM
OLD_PASSWORDS	0x24 STATIC/SET
NODE_CONTROL	0x32 STATIC/ITEM

To have the OLD_PASSWORDS property, the supervisor must require that the password be unique and require change periodically. When SYSCON receives this direction, it then creates the OLD_PASSWORDS property and the file server maintains it from there. The NODE_CONTROL property is created for controlling the workstations from which a user can login. The ACCOUNT_LOCKOUT property controls how many times attempts at logging in can be made.

Bindery properties are classified as either items or sets. An *item* can have a single value, and *sets* can have multiple values. A property is made up of one or more 128-byte segments. When a value is changed, the change must occur in the appropriate 128-byte segment. An item property will have at least a single segment, and a set property can have one or more segments as well. The properties also have bindery access levels like the object. Reading of the

property segments is done in sequence. The ReadPropertyValue function call has a flag that is set when no more segments exist for that property.

A bindery object can be static or dynamic. A *static object* is written to disk and is available even if a server has gone down. A *dynamic object* is a temporary object contained in the bindery when it is in memory but is not written to disk and, therefore, is lost when a file server goes down. Servers on the network are dynamic objects that are found and placed in the bindery through the NetWare Service Advertising Protocol (SAP).

⇨ Bindery object structure

The bindery consists of several files in the server's SYS:\SYSTEM directory. These files contain the bindery objects, properties, and the values for those properties. The logical structure of entries in these files is shown in Fig. 2-1.

Figure 2-1

Object Structure

Node Type:1	In Use
Object	
Name[48]	

⋮

Flags	Security
Link to First Property	
Hash Link	

The Bindery object structure.

23

The Node Type field of the object structure indicates whether or not the structure is being used for an object or for some other bindery construct. The In Use field indicates whether or not this node of the bindery is in use. The ID is the 4-byte bindery object ID. The Type field contains the value for the bindery object type. For type USER, this would be a 0x0001. The Name field contains the 48-byte bindery object name. The Flags field describes whether or not the object is static or dynamic, a set an item. The Security field is the bindery access level for the object. The Link to First Property is a pointer to the location of the first property structure that the object has. If this link is zero, then the object has no properties. The Hash Link is the link to the next node in the bindery database.

Other bindery objects include those found in Table 2-4.

Table 2-4

Bindery object types

OT_WILD	0xFFFF
OT_USER	0x0001
OT_USER_GROUP	0x0002
OT_PRINT_QUEUE	0x0003
OT_FILE_SERVER	0x0004
OT_JOB_SERVER	0x0005
OT_GATEWAY	0x0006
OT_PRINT_SERVER	0x0007
OT_JOB_QUEUE	0x000A
OT_ADMINISTRATION	0x000B
OT_REMOTE_BRIDGE_SERVER	0x0024
OT_ADVERTISING_PRINT_SERVER	0x0047

A bindery object type can be obtained for developer application programming use from Novell. This is administered by the developer relations program at Novell.

User objects & properties

The different properties of the user object define who and what the user is. Each property has a specific function.

 ## GROUPS_I'M_IN

The GROUPS_I'M_IN property defines what groups a user belongs to. GROUPS_I'M_IN is a STATIC/SET property. It contains the bindery object IDs of every group that the user belongs to. Groups are assigned trustee rights, security equivalence, etc. When a user is a member of a group, he or she is able to inherit all the rights that the group has. An example of this property and its values is in Fig. 2-2.

The GROUPS_I'M_IN property dump.

Figure 2-2

```
GROUPS_I'M_IN  STATIC/SET        SUPERVISOR WRITE/LOGGED READ

     EVERYONE
```

 ## SECURITY_EQUALS

The SECURITY_EQUALS property defines other groups or users that the object is equal to and can exercise rights as. This property is a STATIC/SET property. Security equivalence is granted only for another object and does not allow the user object to inherit the other objects' security equivalences as well. For example, if JOE has the object ID of the supervisor in his SECURITY_EQUALS property, he has all the rights of the supervisor. However, if MARY has JOE's object ID in her SECURITY_EQUALS property, she inherits only JOE's personal rights, not supervisor rights. A dump of the SECURITY_EQUALS property is found in Fig. 2-3.

The SECURITY_EQUALS property dump.

Figure 2-3

```
SECURITY_EQUALS STATIC/SET        SUPERVISOR WRITE/OBJECT READ

     EVERYONE
```

⇨ IDENTIFICATION

IDENTIFICATION is a STATIC/ITEM property. It can be set to any value the supervisor wishes but is intended to be descriptive of the individual assigned the user account. This property consists of a single segment. A dump of this property is shown in Fig. 2-4.

Figure 2-4 IDENTIFICATION STATIC/ITEM   SUPERVISOR   WRITE/LOGGED READ

```
4c 6f 72 69 20 47 61 75 74 68 69 65 72 00 1c 98   Lori Gauthier    . . .
1c 8b 1c 7b 1c 43 1c 11 1c fe 1b ed 44 10 4e 01   . . .{. C . . . D . N .
16 f2 9d 0e 00 f2 5d 5d 5d 5d 78 77 3c 7c 20 7c   . . . . .]]]]x w <|    |
00 02 08 00 04 7c 5c 00 44 53 46 72 6d 7e 06 00   . . . .| \.DSF r m~ . .
5d 5d ea 7b 55 01 8a 52 00 02 3c 7c 5d 5d 08 00   ] ]. { U..R..<| ] ] . .
20 7c 5d 5d 16 00 06 00 6d 7e 61 a2 61 o4 61 fa    |]] .. .. m~ a. a. a.
00 00 3c 7c 5d 5d 00 02 20 7c 5d 5d 2c c5 08 00   . .<| ]] .. |]] . . . .
2c da 2c df 2c a4 31 f5 30 c5 30 8b 2f 31 2f f3   . . . . .|. o.o. / | / .
```

The IDENTIFICATION property dump.

⇨ LOGIN_CONTROL

The LOGIN_CONTROL property is a STATIC/ITEM property. The LOGIN_CONTROL property can be used to secure the file server and to limit access to it at any time. The LOGIN_CONTROL property consists of bindery segments. Security checks of the system by the file server, using the LOGIN_CONTROL property, occur at ½-hour intervals. This allows the file server to force a user off the system if it is logged in past its allowed time or if its login control property has changed. Different offsets in this segment represent different information, and the values at these offsets determine the login access of the object that owns the property. The fields contained in the LOGIN_CONTROL property are displayed in Table 2-5.

LOGIN_CONTROL property

Table 2-5

Offset	Field	Size
0	Account Expiration Date	3 bytes
3	Account Disabled Flag	1 byte
4	Password Expiration Date	3 bytes
7	Grace Logins Remaining	1 byte
8	Password Expiration Interval	2 bytes
10	Grace Login Reset Value	1 byte
11	Minimum Password Length	1 byte
12	Maximum Concurrent Connections	2 bytes
14	Allowed Login Time Bitmap	42 bytes
56	Last Login Date And Time	6 bytes
62	Restriction Flags	1 byte
63	Unused	1 byte
64	Maximum Disk Usage in Blocks	4 bytes
68	Bad Login Count	2 bytes
70	Next Reset Time	4 bytes
74	Bad Login Address	12 bytes

Only the Minimum Password Length, Old Passwords, Login Times, and Allowed Login Stations restrictions affect the supervisor.

The Account Expiration Date field represents the date the account expires. The first byte is the year, the second byte represents the month, and the last byte is the day of the month. When each of these bytes is set to 0 the account will not expire.

The Account Disabled Flag is a boolean flag that represents whether or not the object has been disabled (00 = enabled, FFh = disabled). This field allows the supervisor to disallow access to the system without removing a user. This is especially useful for managing guest accounts or accounts in which the user is not currently accessing his account. This flag is checked by the system every half hour. If this flag has been set while the user is logged in, then a message is sent

to the user to logout. After five minutes, the connection is cleared and all logins will receive an error (0xDC) indicating the account is disabled. This flag doesn't have any effect on the supervisor user.

The Password Expiration Date indicates when a password will expire. This field is three bytes long and the date is contained in the same way as the Account Expiration Field. This value is reset when the password is changed by adding the number of days contained in the Password Expiration Interval to the date the password was changed—except in a special case discussed later in this section: when someone with supervisor rights changes the password, the date is set to Jan 1, 1985 to force the user to reassign his own password.

A Grace Login occurs when a user is allowed access to the server with an expired password. Grace Logins can be controlled from zero to many. Grace Logins Remaining indicates the number of times that a user can login without changing his or her password. This value is reset by the Grace Login Reset Value when a user changes his or her password, or it can be reset manually by the supervisor. When a system needs to be very secure, the Grace Login Values should be very low.

The Minimum Password Length field allows the supervisor to decrease the risk of accidental or break-in access to the system by increasing the minimum length a password must be. Security studies have shown that, when a password is 3 bytes or less, security can be breached easily.

The Maximum Concurrent Connections field allows control of the number of connections a user can have simultaneously. This facility allows the supervisor to control the user's number of connections to the number of workstations in an office. This also decreases the risk that a user will leave a logged in workstation unattended.

The Allowed Login Time Bitmap is an array of 42 bytes where each bit is equal to ½-hour intervals. The complete array represents the half hours that are in one week. This field allows the network manager the ability to limit the times when an object can login. When the bit is on, the user can access the server during the time specified. Using this functionality will allow the supervisor to limit login to times

when backups are not occurring as well as when a user shouldn't be at work whether due to needing a secure system where users don't leave their workstations logged in or to avoid overtime work.

The Last Login Date And Time contains the date and time of the object's last login. This field consists of year, month, day, hour, minute, and second. Each successful login to the file server generates an update to this field.

The Restriction Flags are eight bits that control the PASSWORD and OLD_PASSWORDS properties. If bit 0 is set (0x01), then only the supervisor can change the password. In this case, the Password Expiration Date is not set to January 1, 1985. If bit 1 is set (0x02), then the OLD_PASSWORDS property exists and needs to be updated. When a password is changed, this bit can be checked to determine whether or not the password must be unique. This bit is available because a user does not have access to the OLD_PASSWORDS property to even know if it exists.

The Maximum Disk Usage In Blocks field is the number of server disk blocks to which a user's disk space is limited. Unlimited disk space is indicated by 0x7FFFFFFF. Limiting disk space is an option that must be enabled during installation. Disk blocks in NetWare 2.x are 4K in size. The disk block limitation in 2.x is file server wide or the sum of all disk blocks on all volumes. Disk blocks in NetWare 3.x are configurable on installation. Disk block limitations on 3.x are on a per volume basis. This allows a network manager to limit disk space on volumes where it might be important but not on volumes where the limits are not necessary. If the user, including the supervisor, tries to write to disk after the limit has been reached, a DISK_FULL error will be received at the workstation. Applications that are NetWare aware should understand this error and indicate to the user that the error might be physical or virtual.

Unsuccessful login information is maintained by the LOGIN_CONTROL property as well as successful login information. The fields representing intruder detection in the LOGIN_CONTROL property are the Bad Login Count, Next Reset Time, and Bad Login Address. These fields are maintained only if the file server object for the file

server that it is on has the ACCT_LOCKOUT property. When that property is available, intruder detection information is tracked.

The Bad Login Count is a count of the number of bad login attempts since the value was reset. This value is reset to zero when a successful login occurs or when the number of reset minutes from the ACCT_LOCKOUT property expires. If an account has been disabled, this field is set to 0xFFFF.

The Next Reset Time is the number of seconds since Jan 1, 1985 that represents the time the Bad Login Count will be reset.

The Bad Login Address is the 12-byte internetwork address of the station where the failed login attempt came from. This field enables the network manager to track where intruders are attempting to login from.

PASSWORD

The PASSWORD property is a STATIC/ITEM property. It has a bindery access level of 0x24. Beginning with NetWare 2.15, the password was encrypted on the wire. The encryption algorithm used is nonreversible. The password then is stored in the bindery in its encrypted form. When a password given by the user is compared to the value contained in the PASSWORD property, it is done in the encrypted form. If the encryptions don't match, then the password is rejected.

OLD_PASSWORDS

The OLD_PASSWORDS property is a STATIC/ITEM property. It contains the last eight passwords that the object has used and the user name in encrypted format. This property is created to limit how often a password can be used. This property allows the file server to store the encrypted version of the previous password here when the user object changes passwords. The object name is stored here as well to increase security by not allowing the object to use its own name as a password.

NODE_CONTROL

The NODE_CONTROL property is a STATIC/ITEM. This property defines which node a user can login from. Login from any other node will cause the user to be refused. The property value consists of the network and node of the allowed location for login. The network address cannot be set to 00000000 or to FFFFFFFFh. If the node is set to FFFFFFFFFFFFh, then the user can login from any node on the specified network.

 # ACCT_LOCKOUT

The ACCT_LOCKOUT property is a STATIC/ITEM property. It is a property of the file server. It is used to compare with the Bad Login Count of the LOGIN_CONTROL property and to set the value for the Next Reset Time. This property is used for intruder detection and lockout. It consists of values for the number of *attempts* for a period of minutes. The *reset* value is the number of minutes necessary before the number of attempts is reset to 0. The *lockout* value is the number of minutes an account is locked if an intruder is detected. No login will be accepted while the account is locked. The structure of this property is in Table 2-6.

ACCT_LOCKOUT property   Table 2-6

OFFSET	Field	Size
0	Allowed Login Attempts	2 bytes
2	Reset Minutes	2 bytes
4	Lockout Minutes	2 bytes

If the Allowed Login Attempts are set to 0, intruder detection takes place with one unsuccessful login. An unsuccessful or bad login is defined to be when someone attempts to login with a missing or incorrect password. If an intruder is detected, the user object account is locked and no login attempt is accepted until the Lockout Minutes have expired since the last intruder was detected.

USER_DEFAULTS

The USER_DEFAULTS property is a special property of the supervisor object that contains the default values for any user object's LOGIN_CONTROL property. The USER_DEFAULTS property has a bindery access level of 0x31. This allows any logged in object to read the property and values but allows only the supervisor to change the property.

Server objects & properties

File servers are contained in the bindery as a type 4 bindery object. File server objects fall into two classes. The *static file server object* is the object entry that any file server has in its bindery for itself. The *dynamic file server objects* are the file servers whose information is gathered and maintained dynamically in the bindery through the Service Advertising Protocol (SAP) method. A static server object will have properties that describe what kind of options are available on the file server concerning intruder detection, accounting, and file server console operators. These properties can include OPERATORS, ACCT_LOCKOUT, ACCOUNT_SERVERS, DISK_STORAGE, REQUESTS_MADE, CONNECT_TIME, BLOCKS_WRITTEN, and BLOCKS_READ. The static file server object, like all the dynamic file server objects, always will have the NET_ADDRESS property. The NET_ADDRESS property contains the network and node of the file server specified by the object name.

Bindery Objects can be of many different types, and any bindery object can have any additional optional properties that an application finds pertinent for managing the object properly within the scope of that application. Bindery objects can be created to maintain copyright or site license information as well as the current status of their disk use. The possible uses for the bindery and its objects and properties are only limited by software implementation.

File & directory access

In addition to the bindery and its login control, the file server can limit access to files and directories. NetWare 2.*x* and NetWare 3.*x* have the concepts of trustee rights, directory and file access rights, and inheritance. A *trustee* is an object that is assigned certain access rights to a directory in NetWare 286 and to a directory or file in NetWare 386. Trustee rights that can be assigned in NetWare 286 include Parental, Read, Write, Open, Search, Delete, and Modify rights. Trustee rights that can be assigned in NetWare 386 are Supervisor, Read, Write, Create, Erase, Modify, Scan, and Access Control. Table 2-7 shows how these rights correspond to each other.

Trustee rights mappings in NetWare 286 and 386 Table 2-7

NetWare 286	NetWare 386
Parental	Access Control
Read	Read
Write	Write
Open	n/a
Search	Scan
Delete	Erase
Modify	Modify
Write/Open	Create
n/a	Supervisor

Note: NetWare 286 needs OPEN with READ or WRITE to read from or WRITE to a file

These rights will allow a user to do the specified actions. With NetWare 386, the concept of assigning someone to have Supervisor rights over a portion of a directory tree was introduced. Trustee rights are assigned to bindery objects.

Directory and file access rights limit what can be done to a specified file or directory. While trustee rights are assigned to bindery objects,

access rights are assigned to a directory in NetWare 2.x and to a directory or a file in NetWare 3.x. It is the intersection of the trustee rights and directory/file access rights that indicates what actions can be taken on each file or directory.

To simplify the management of a server and not force rights to be explicitly assigned to every file and directory for every user, NetWare uses inheritance. Inheritance means that trustee rights assigned at a node of a directory tree are in effect for any of its children nodes until explicit trustee rights are assigned. The access that a user has to a file or directory can be understood as the intersection of the lowest defined trustee rights in the path and the directory access rights of the directory or file. Figure 2-5 illustrates an example of inheritance. If Scan rights are assigned to all the volumes on server STEALTH, this right will be inherited by all the subdirectories that don't have rights assigned. However, in the cases of CLIBS and LOGIN, the rights are explicitly declared.

The bindery and file system security would have particular application in programming archive servers, site setup programs, management utilities, and alternate security hardware including thumbprint login systems and retinal scanners right out of Star Trek. The next chapter demonstrates how to use the bindery and bindery APIs to get and set the information contained in the bindery.

Figure 2-5

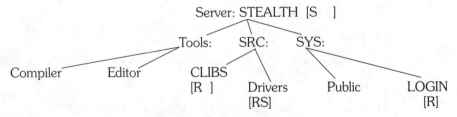

Directory entries and inheritance.

Bindery application:
finding users & servers

T HE bindery is manipulated by the SYSCON utility provided with NetWare systems. Additionally, the bindery can be manipulated programmatically. This programmatic manipulation of the bindery is commonly used to create, find, and modify users and service providers, as well as being an easy method of licensing software. The programming steps explained in this chapter are only one way to retrieve and set information about the bindery and the objects that it contains. The bindery calls can be combined in any order required to get the information to display.

The sample program shows one way to get and display information about bindery objects. Through the use of only four bindery functions, this application produces a large amount of information that can be used to profile the users on a particular server.

Finding objects

Finding objects in the bindery is useful for determining who has access rights to specific information in the bindery and on the network. Additionally, this method can be used to find service providers on the network and their addresses to take advantage of the service they provide.

ScanBinderyObject

To find all bindery objects of any and all types, use the ScanBinderyObject call. The ScanBinderyObject call searches the bindery for all the objects fitting the search object name and the search object type descriptions. This call can accept wildcard values for both the search object name and the search object type fields. You don't need to have made other function calls or obtained information previous to calling this function. Simply use all of the wildcard input values available. The variables used by this function are as follows:

```
char     searchObjName[48], objName[48];
WORD     searchObjType, objType;
```

```
DWORD objectID;
BYTE     objectHasProperties, objFlag, objSecurity;.
```

Assign the searchObjName and searchObjType a wildcard value:

```
lstrcpy (searchObjName, "*");
searchObjType = OT_WILD;   /* or -1 if you would rather */
```

To begin a search, you need to assign the objectID a value of −1 and pass the address of that variable into the function. This will initialize the function and indicate that the call is being made for the first time with current search values. The function will assign a new object ID to this variable on return from the function call. Then, the function will use that same value the next time that it is called. Put the function in a loop and continue scanning until a completion code other than SUCCESSFUL, or 0, is returned. This is demonstrated in the code sample in Fig. 3-1.

Sample code to search the bindery for objects.   Figure 3-1

```
do
{
    sboCode =  ScanBinderyObject (searchObjName, searchObjType,
    &objectID, objectName, &objectType,
    &objectHasProperties, &objFlag, &objSecurity);

    //  Here you can display information such as objectName and its' type...

}while (!sboCode);
```

⇨ GetBinderyObjectName

Another function call used to obtain an object's name is the GetBinderyObjectName. This function primarily is used when you need only one objectName and you already have the object's ID. This function will not allow wildcards, and you can't use it as an iterative call in a loop beginning with a −1 as the object ID. You must specify a valid object ID. The function will return the name and type of the object corresponding to the given object ID:

```
gbonCode = GetBinderyObjectName (0x00000001, objName, &objType);
```

 GetBinderyObjectID

By knowing an object's name and type, you can retrieve the object's ID by calling GetBinderyObjectID. This call is made by passing in the object name and the object type. The bindery object ID is returned:

```
gbonCode = GetBinderyObjectID (objName, objType, &objectID);
```

 # Finding & reading object properties

Once you have scanned the bindery object, you can dig a little deeper and find out whether that object has any properties associated with it and what these properties are. By checking the value of the objectHasProperties variable upon return of the ScanBinderyObject call, you can determine whether the object has any associated properties. The value is 0 if the object has no properties and nonzero if it does. If the bindery object does have associated properties, the next step in this application is to find what those properties are.

 # ScanProperty

To find out what the properties are, call the ScanProperty function and pass the bindery object name and type obtained from one of the other calls explained in the section "Finding objects," a wildcard ("*") as the search property name, and a −1 as the sequence number. This call should be in a loop and repeated until the more properties variable is returned as a 0. This loop is demonstrated in the sample code in Fig. 3-2.

Figure 3-2   *Getting the properties for a bindery object.*

```
do
{
    ccode = ScanProperty (objName, objType, "*", &sequence,
                          propertyName, &propertyFlags, &propertySecurity,
                          &propertyHasValue, &moreProperties);

    // Display property name here

}while (moreProperties);
```

Property characteristics

Now that you know the propertyName, you can check the
propertyHasValue parameter and determine whether it's nonzero. If
the propertyHasValue parameter is nonzero, determine what its value
is by calling ReadPropertyValue. You also will want to examine the
propertyFlags parameter. This parameter indicates whether the
property is a SET or an ITEM. This determines how you interpret the
value of the property. If it's a SET property, then the value will be an
array of object IDs corresponding to the property. If it's an ITEM
property, then the value will have some other format. For example, if
the propertyName was IDENTIFICATION, the propertyFlags would
be of type ITEM and the value would be an ASCII string that has
been assigned to the objectName. It can be something like the
following:

objectName	DB-PROGRAMMERS
objectType	OT_GROUP
propertyName	IDENTIFICATION
propertyFlags	BF_ITEM
propertyValue	"Programmers working on database products"

An example of a SET property is the property GROUPS_I'M_IN. If
you want to get the object names corresponding to the object IDs in
this property, you first would swap the bytes of the object IDs
because they are returned in HI-LO format. Then, you would call
GetBinderyObjectName:

```
objID = LongSwap (*((DWORD far *) &propertyValue[0]));
GetBinderyObjectName (objID, objName, &objType);
```

As you can see, a lot of the bindery functions build on top of each
other. Let's now look at how to create objects and set information
about objects in the bindery.

Creating objects & setting information

Objects and properties in the bindery have some well-known definitions but also can be defined by an individual application. To create custom objects, an application programmer should call the Developer Relations program at Novell and reserve some object types. Some not-so-well-known objects that can be custom crafted include license objects and custom service providers.

Creating a user object

To create a new object in the bindery, you must have a security equivalence of SUPERVISOR. The following steps provide a guideline for adding a new user to the bindery. You can create a user with or without a password. To begin, you will need to make a call to CreateBinderyObject:

```
ccode = CreateBinderyObject ("NewUserName", OT_USER, BF_STATIC,
                     BS_SUPER_WRITE | BS_LOGGED_READ);
```

Whether the user is going to have a password or not, you need to create a password property and assign a password or a NULL password. This is done by making the following call:

```
password[0] = '\0';
ChangeBinderyObjectPassword ("NewUserName", OT_USER, NULL, password);
```

Creating user object properties

User objects are well-defined objects used to login and manage access to the file server. These objects have a set of properties for the user object to be recognized by the NetWare utilities as a legitimate object. These properties must all be created properly for the user to be able to login to the server. For a list of these properties, see the chapter explaining the bindery. One of the most important properties is the LOGIN_CONTROL property. Next, you will want to create and initialize the new user's LOGIN_CONTROL property:

```
CreateProperty ("NewUserName", OT_USER, "LOGIN_CONTROL",
                BF_STATIC | BF_ITEM, BS_SUPER_WRITE |
                BS_OBJECT_READ);
```

Now, read the Supervisor's USER_DEFAULTS property for the initial values that correspond to the LOGIN_CONTROL and ACCOUNT_BALANCE properties:

```
ReadPropertyValue ("SUPERVISOR", OT_USER, "USER_DEFAULTS", 1,
                   &userDefaults, (BYTE far *) NULL, (BYTE far *)
NULL);
```

The property value is returned in userDefaults where userDefaults is a structure type with the fields defined in Fig. 3-3.

```
typedef struct UserDefaults_t
{
    BYTE        yearAccountExpires;
    BYTE        monthAccountExpires;
    BYTE        dayAccountExpires;
    BYTE        restrictionFlags;
    WORD        changePasswordInterval;
    BYTE        graceReset;
    BYTE        minimumPasswordLength;
    WORD        maxConcurrentConnections;
    BYTE        loginTimeMap[42];
    DWORD       balance;
    DWORD       creditLimit;
    DWORD       maxDiskBlocks;
    BYTE        createHomeDir;
    BYTE        reserved;
    BYTE        filler[64];
} UserDefaults_t;
```

Figure 3-3

The structure for the User Defaults property.

Once you have the user defaults, fill the default values into the LOGIN_CONTROL properties of the new user. The LOGIN_CONTROL property has the form described by the structure in Fig. 3-4.

After setting the default values, make the following call:

```
WritePropertyValue ("NewUserName", OT_USER, "LOGIN_CONTROL", 1,
                    &loginControl, 0);
```

Once the LOGIN_CONTROL property has been created, check to see if accounting is installed on the file server. If accounting is installed, create and set the ACCOUNT_BALANCE property for the user object. To set the ACCOUNT_BALANCE property, see the code in Fig. 3-5.

Figure 3-4   *The structure for the Login Control property.*

```
typedef struct LoginControl_t
{
     BYTE        yearAccountExpires;
     BYTE        monthAccountExpires;
     BYTE        dayAccountExpires;
     BYTE        accountExpired;
     BYTE        yearPasswordExpires;
     BYTE        monthPasswordExpires;
     BYTE        dayPasswordExpires;
     BYTE        haveGraceLogins;
     WORD        changePasswordInterval;
     BYTE        graceReset;
     BYTE        minimumPasswordLength;
     WORD        maxConcurrentConnections;
     BYTE        loginTimeMap[42];
     BYTE        lastLoginDate[6];
     BYTE        restrictionFlags;
     BYTE        reserved;
     DWORD       maxDiskBlocks;
     WORD        badLoginCount;
     DWORD       nextResetTime;
     BYTE        badStationAddress[12];
} LoginControl_t;
```

If the restriction flags of the USER_DEFAULTS property have bit 1 set, then create the OLD_PASSWORDS property and set the value of the old password to the user's name or to null. Again, the necessary calls would be CreateProperty and WritePropertyValue.

Once the user's security has been initialized, create the new user's GROUPS_I'M_IN and SECURITY_EQUALS properties:

```
CreateProperty ("NewUserName", OT_USER, "GROUPS_I'M_IN", BF_STATIC
                   | BF_SET, BS_SUPER_WRITE | BS_LOGGED_READ);
CreateProperty ("NewUserName", OT_USER, "SECURITY_EQUALS", BF_STATIC
                   | BF_SET, BS_SUPER_WRITE | BS_LOGGED_READ);
```

When creating these properties, the values of the property must be set to the object IDs of the groups or users to the property set and by adding the newly created user object ID to the set properties of the other objects. So, now add the new user to the list of members of the user group EVERYONE:

```
AddBinderyObjectToSet ("EVERYONE", OT_USER_GROUP,
                    "GROUP_MEMBERS", "NewUserName", OT_USER);
```

Setting the Account Balance property.   Figure 3-5

```
sequenceNumber = -1;
ccode = ScanProperty ("FileServerName", OT_FILE_SERVER,
                      ACCOUNT_SERVERS", &sequenceNumber,
                      (char far *)NULL, (char far *)NULL, (char far *) NULL,
                      (char far *) NULL, (char far *) NULL);
switch (ccode)
{
    case 0:
            /* Accounting is installed, so set the account balance and credit
            limit to the default values we previously obtained in the
            userDefaults structure.  Then create and write the
            property value. */

            CreateProperty ("NewUserName", OT_USER,
                            "ACCOUNT_BALANCE", BF_STATIC |
                            BF_ITEM, BS_SUPER_WRITE |
                            BS_OBJECT_READ);
            WritePropertyValue ("NewUserName", OT_USER,
                                "ACCOUNT_BALANCE", 1, &accountBalance, 0);
            break;

    case 251:
            /* NO_SUCH_PROPERTY.  This means accounting is not
            installed on the file server. */
            break;

    default:
            break;
}
```

and add the group name EVERYONE to the list of groups that the
new user is in:

```
AddBinderyObjectToSet ("NewUserName", OT_USER, "GROUPS_I'M_IN",
                       "EVERYONE", OT_USER_GROUP);
```

Also, the SECURITY_EQUALS property of the new user property
must be updated as membership in a group gives the user security
equivalence to that group:

```
AddBinderyObjectToSet ("NewUserName", OT_USER, "SECURITY_EQUALS",
                       "EVERYONE", OT_USER_GROUP);
```

This programming example should enable you to make use of the
bindery in gaining access rights to the file server. As your application
needs to grant access to services, find service providers, login to the
server, or create custom objects, you will find this information to be
extremely valuable.

NetWare Directory
Services

W ITH NetWare v4.0 comes a new feature that will change networking permanently. This feature is NetWare Directory Services (NDS). NetWare Directory Services provides a distributed global name service and a network authentication service. In NetWare versions previous to v4.0, a user was required to login to each server individually and enter a password for each one. With NetWare v4.0 and NetWare Directory Services, the user now can login once to the network and be authenticated by applications in the background to each additional service.

All the servers on the network can become services whose access is administered from a single entity, the Directory. When a user is added to the Directory, it is added to the network. This alleviates the repetition of creating the same user on each server as with bindery-based servers. The Directory also allows easier location of services in a large internet or in a wide-area network. With all the services and their locations contained in the Directory, applications can query the Directory for the location of a particular server offering a specific service. If the service has used the Directory to implement authentication, the application can also authenticate to the service through the Directory.

⇨ Directory structure

The Directory consists of *objects*. Each object has properties called *attributes*. The Directory structure is logically that of a tree with a root, branches, and leaves. When drawn, the tree is inverted with the root at the top. From the root come the branches or container objects. Each container object, just like the branches of a tree, can hold many leaf objects or other container objects. An example of a simple Directory structure is found in Fig. 4-1. Traversing the branches of the tree to find the information an application requests is referred to as tree walking. As you can see from Fig. 4-1, the root of the database has a special object, [ROOT]. [ROOT] is a special nonaccessible object used by NDS as the origin of the tree. Every object in the Directory is subordinate to [ROOT]. The database that contains all the Directory data is called the Directory Information Base (DIB).

Figure 4-1

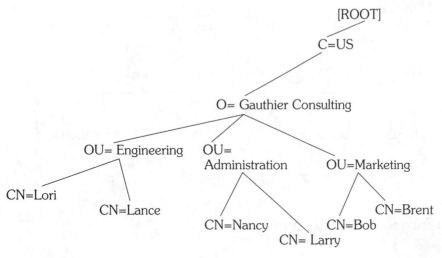

A sample directory tree. Novell, Inc.

Partitions & replicas

To speed access to the Directory, it is implemented as a distributed database. Sections of the Directory tree can have their master copies on different NetWare v4.0 servers. Each of these sections is called a *partition*. Figure 4-2 shows how a tree might be partitioned. All the partitions together perform as one service through a referral system built in to NDS. By locating the master of the partition on a server in the area where that section of the tree is accessed most heavily, synchronization and access times are optimized. If the partitions on any one server do not contain the information necessary to service a request, the server will refer the Directory client to another server that possibly will have that information. To optimize access to other partitions, read-write and read-only copies can be kept on various servers throughout the network. Copies of each partition are called *replicas*. This replication of partitions on the network will improve access to information on the network by decreasing the time spent in referrals and remote tree walking.

This partitioning and replication of the Directory on the network also introduces an added measure of safety and reliability by increasing its fault tolerance. If one server goes down, any other server with

Figure 4-2

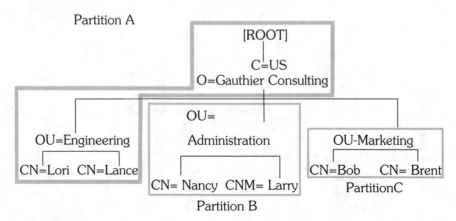

Partition A

[ROOT]
C=US
O=Gauthier Consulting

OU=Engineering

CN=Lori CN=Lance

OU=
Administration

CN= Nancy CNM= Larry

Partition B

OU-Marketing

CN=Bob   CN= Brent
PartitionC

A directory tree in three partitions. Novell, Inc.

replicas of the partitions from that server is able to service requests for the information. The client will find the location of the right replica through the referrals from the Directory servers. All replicas of a partition keep themselves synchronized. The master replica of a partition is the only replica that you can use to change the structure of the Directory tree. If you want to move a partition to a different place in the tree or join it with another partition, you must perform these actions on the master replicas.

⇨ Partition & replica management APIs

A list of the partition and replica management APIs appears in Fig. 4-3. These functions allow you to manage your partitions and replicas by providing lists of current partitions, adding new partitions or replicas, and splitting, joining, or removing existing ones.

⇨ Directory context

To specify where a partition is in relation to the [ROOT], you specify the path from the [ROOT] to the container object that is at the top of the partition. This path through the tree is part of the Directory context. Other parts of the Directory context include flags, reference scope, transport type, and confidence level, all of which

Prototypes for the NDS partition and replica management APIs. Novell, Inc.

Figure 4-3

```
NWDSCCODE NWFAR NWPASCAL NWDSAddPartition
(
    NWDSContextHandle       context,
    char            NWFAR *server,
    char            NWFAR *partitionRoot,
    int32           NWFAR *iterationHandle,
    uint8                   more,
    Buf_T           NWFAR *objectInfo
);

NWDSCCODE NWFAR NWPASCAL NWDSAddReplica
(
    NWDSContextHandle       context,
    char            NWFAR *server,
    char            NWFAR *partitionRoot,
    uint32                  replicaType
);

NWDSCCODE NWFAR NWPASCAL NWDSChangeReplicaType
(
    NWDSContextHandle       context,
    char            NWFAR *replicaName,
    char            NWFAR *server,
    uint32                  newReplicaType
);

NWDSCCODE NWFAR NWPASCAL NWDSJoinPartitions
(
    NWDSContextHandle       context,
    char            NWFAR *subordinatePartition,
    uint32          flags
);

NWDSCCODE NWFAR NWPASCAL NWDSListPartitions
(
    NWDSContextHandle       context,
    int32           NWFAR *iterationHandle,
    char            NWFAR *server,
    Buf_T           NWFAR *partitions
);

NWDSCCODE NWFAR NWPASCAL NWDSRemovePartition
(
    NWDSContextHandle       context,
    char            NWFAR *partitionRoot
);

NWDSCCODE NWFAR NWPASCAL NWDSRemoveReplica
(
    NWDSContextHandle       context,
    char            NWFAR *server,
```

Figure 4-3 *Continued.*

```
     char           NWFAR *partitionRoot
);

NWDSCCODE NWFAR NWPASCAL NWDSSplitPartition
(
     NWDSContextHandle    context,
     char           NWFAR *subordinatePartition,
     uint32              flags
);
```

assist APIs in making decisions as to what type of processing to
perform. The key values for these context items are found in
Table 4-1.

Table 4-1   **Directory context key names and corresponding values**

Key name	Value
DCK_FLAGS	1
DCK_CONFIDENCE	2
DCK_NAME_CONTEXT	3
DCK_TRANSPORT_TYPE	4
DCK_REFERRAL_SCOPE	5

Any object can be specified relative to a Directory context. Directory
contexts can be maintained by an application, relieving a user of the need
to remember the entire path from the [ROOT] of the Directory to where
his object resides. The Directory context for partition C in Fig. 4-4 is:

```
O=Gauthier Consulting.C=US
```

The context for the object Bob in the tree is

```
.OU=Marketing.O=Gauthier Consulting.C=US
```

and could be used by the application along with the object's common
name (CN) to indicate the specific object in the Directory tree.

The context also contains flags that indicate to other functions in
NDS the appropriate steps to take during processing. These flags are

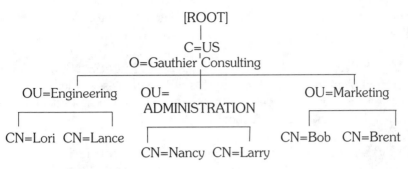

Figure 4-4

A sample directory tree.

set in context by API calls. The flags are defined in Table 4-2 with their corresponding values.

Directory context flags and corresponding values   Table 4-2

Flag	Value
DCV_DEREF_ALIASES	0x00000001L
DCV_XLATE_STRINGS	0x00000002L
DCV_TYPELESS_NAMES	0x00000004L
DCV_ASYNC_MODE	0x00000008L
DCV_CANONICALIZE_NAMES	0x00000010L

❋ **DCV_CANONICALIZE_NAMES** The DCV_CANONICALIZE _NAMES flag indicates to other APIs the names passed to them are not canonicalized (explained in the section "Abbreviating, canonicalizing, and normalizing"). The API then will be responsible for the canonicalizing of the name.

❋ **DCV_DEREF_ALIASES** The DCV_DEREF_ALIASES flag requires that each API dereference a common name that is an alias to its appropriate object before performing the rest of the operations of the call on the object.

❋ **DCV_XLATE_STRINGS** The DCV_XLATE_STRINGS flag indicates to the API that all names and strings passed to it use characters from the

local code page. The API will need to translate or convert all strings to UNICODE before placing them in packets to send to the server.

※ **DCV_TYPELESS_NAMES**   The DCV_TYPELESS_NAMES flag means that all names passed to the APIs will be typeless names and must be treated accordingly. Typeless names are explained in more detail in the Typed and Typeless Names section.

※ **DCV_ASYNC_MODE**   Although not fully implemented in the current release of the NetWare Directory Services APIs, the DCV_ASYNC_MODE flag determines whether the API function should return to the calling application immediately after sending the request or if it should wait until the response is received before returning to the API. Currently, the APIs all wait for the response, then return to the application. When this functionality is fully implemented, the application will have the responsibility of managing asynchronous communications and of knowing when the receive buffers contain valid data.

⇨ Directory Context APIs

The Directory Context APIs allow you to create, delete, duplicate, get and set contexts in order to navigate the directory. The prototypes for the Directory Context APIs can be seen in Fig. 4-5. The NWDSCreateContext function must be called first to create an initial context. Using the context returned from this call, other context APIs, or NDS calls can be used. If the application wants to use abbreviated names, then the DCV_CANONICALIZE_NAMES flag needs to be on. The DCV flags are set using the NWDSSetContext API with the key value set to DCK_FLAGS, and the value set to all the desired flags ORed together.

Once a context is allocated, the application will need to initialize it for use with the specific function that is to be performed. This is done by calling the NWDSInitBuffer call with the appropriate flag.

Prototypes for the directory context APIs. Novell, Inc.

Figure 4-5

```
NWDSContextHandle NWFAR NWPASCAL NWDSCreateContext
(
     void
);

NWDSContextHandle NWFAR NWPASCAL NWDSDuplicateContext
(
     NWDSContextHandle oldContext
);

NWDSCCODE NWFAR NWPASCAL NWDSFreeContext
(
     NWDSContextHandle       context
);

NWDSCCODE NWFAR NWPASCAL NWDSGetContext
(
     NWDSContextHandle       context,
     int                     key,
     void            NWFAR *value
);

NWDSCCODE NWFAR NWPASCAL NWDSSetContext
(
     NWDSContextHandle       context,
     int                     key,
     void            NWFAR *value
);
```

⇨ Distinguished names & relative distinguished names

Specifying objects in the Directory is done in either of two fashions. One is to use the distinguished name. The distinguished name is the unique name of the object from the common name of the object to [ROOT]. For example, in the Directory tree in Fig. 4-4, the Bob object would have the distinguished name (DN) of:

```
CN=Bob.OU=Marketing.O=Gauthier Consulting.C=US
```

A second way to specify the object is relative to a Directory context. This is the relative distinguished name (RDN). If the Directory context is:

```
OU=Marketing.O=Gauthier Consulting.C=US
```

then the relative distinguished name for the Bob object is CN=Bob. In NDS, each object value in a name is separated from the next with a period or dot.

Typed & typeless names

Two types of names are accepted by the Directory: typed and typeless. Typed names consist of each value in the name preceded by the value type. For example:

```
CN=Bob.OU=Marketing.O=Gauthier Consulting.C=US
```

is a typed name. A typeless name for the same object would be:

```
Bob.Marketing.Gauthier Consulting.US
```

Typeless names are interpreted according to a set of default containment rules specifying which objects can contain specified types of objects. Containment and the rules governing it are explained in more detail in the "Schema" section of this chapter.

Abbreviating, canonicalizing, & normalizing

A canonicalized name is one that is both distinguished and has the attribute type specification for each part of the name. An application can use a name in an abbreviated form that might or might not be typeless but is assumed to be relative to the Directory context. To convert between abbreviated and canonicalized names, two APIs are supplied: NWDSCanonicalizeName and NWDSAbbreviateName.

✳ **NWDSCanonicalizeName** The NWDSCanonicalizeName function will convert a name to its canonicalized form according to the flags set in the context. If the DCV_TYPELESS_NAMES is set in the context, the function will accept a typeless abbreviated name as input and convert it to a typed distinguished name. If the DCV_TYPELESS_NAMES value is not set

in the context, the function will expect a typed RDN and will convert it to a distinguished name. Thus:

```
.CN=Bob
```

would be converted to

```
CN=Bob.OU=Marketing.O=Gauthier Consulting.C=US
```

If a typeless name `Bob` were passed in, the result would be the same.

✳ **NWDSAbbreviateName**   The NWDSAbbreviateName function will convert a name passed in according to the DCV_TYPELESS_NAMES and the DCV_CANONICALIZE_NAMES flags. If both flags are set, only the common name without a type specifier will be returned as the abbreviated name. If only the DCV_TYPELESS_NAMES flag is set in the Directory context, then only the types will be stripped from the name string passed in and the result returned as the abbreviated name. If only the DCV_CANONICALIZE_NAMES flag is set in the context, then the output would be the common name with the type specifier. Table 4-3 demonstrates the input and output of each of the possibilities.

NWDS AbbreviateName input and output   Table 4-3

Name Input	Flags	Name output
CN=Bob.OU=Marketing.O=Gauthier Consulting.C=US.	Typeless/canonicalize	Bob
CN=Bob.OU=Marketing.O=Gauthier. Consulting.US		
Bob.Marketing.Gauthier Consulting.C=US	Typeless	
CN=Bob.OU=Marketing.O=Gauthier Consulting.C=US..CN=Bob	Canonicalize	

✳ **Normalizing directory names**   Directory names can have all the extra white space stripped out. White space is not considered to be a unique differentiating character in NDS. Normalizing a name allows it to be properly compared to the names as they are stored in the Directory.

 # Schema

All objects in the Directory follow rules that define what attributes are required and how the objects must be named. These rules are contained in the data dictionary called the schema. The schema defines the syntax for every attribute and value representation in the Directory. The schema defines rules for what attributes the objects in the Directory consist of as well. These attribute rules are class definitions. All objects in the Directory belong to classes.

 # Classes & super classes

Classes are definitions of what attributes an object is required to have. These are an object's mandatory attributes. An object cannot be created in the Directory that does not have all its mandatory attributes. A class also can define optional attributes. These attributes do not have to be set to create an object of a specified class. Some of the classes in the schema can be instantiated as objects. These are effective classes. Other classes function only as super classes. Super classes are classes from which other classes inherit attributes. Table 4-4 lists the standard classes available in the NetWare Directory and their types. Custom classes also can be defined.

Table 4-4   **The standard object classes in the NetWare directory schema**

Class	Object type
AFP Server	Leaf
Alias	Leaf
Bindery	Leaf
Bindery Queue	Leaf
Computer	Leaf
Country	Container
Directory Map	Leaf
Group	Leaf
Locality	Container

NetWare Server	Leaf
Organization	Container
Organizational Role	Leaf
Organizational Unit	Container
Print Server	Leaf
Printer	Leaf
Profile	Leaf
Queue	Leaf
SMS	Leaf
Top	Container
Unknown	Leaf
User	Leaf
Volume	Leaf

Novell, Inc.

Syntax definitions

Syntax definitions define the structures that attribute values can have. All attribute values use these definitions. Custom syntaxes cannot be defined and added to the schema. The directory code would not be able to compare something that it had not been programmed to understand. When comparing two attributes of the same syntax, the Directory uses three matching rules—equality, substrings, and ordering. Each syntax definition defines which of the matching rules apply to it, if any.

Objects & attributes

Objects in the Directory are defined according to the classes contained in the schema. The object class definitions for the standard classes are found in Figs. 4-6 through 4-33. Each attribute that an object class contains is defined within the schema. Attributes are defined according to their name and what type of value they have (string, integer, etc.). Attributes can be multivalued, having many values of the same type. The attribute syntax is defined according to

Figure 4-6   *The AFP server.*

Super Classes	Top
Mandatory Attributes	
Optional Attributes	Serial Number
	Supported Connections

Figure 4-7   *Alias.*

Super Classes	Top
Mandatory Attributes	Aliased Object Name
Optional Attributes	

Figure 4-8   *Bindery object.*

Super Classes	Top
Mandatory Attributes	Bindery Object Restriction
	Bindery Type
	Common Name
Optional Attributes	

Figure 4-9   *Bindery queue.*

Super Classes	Queue
Mandatory Attributes	Bindery Type
Optional Attributes	Common Name

Figure 4-10   *Certification authority.*

Super Classes	Top
Mandatory Attributes	Authority Revocation
	Certificate Revocation
Optional Attributes	CA Operator
	CA Private Key
	CA Public Key
	Cross Certificate Pair

Figure 4-11   *Computer.*

Super Classes	Device
Mandatory Attributes	
Optional Attributes	Operator
	Server
	Status

Country.

Super Classes	Top
Mandatory Attributes	Country Name
Optional Attributes	Description

Device.

Super Classes	Top
Mandatory Attributes	Common Name
Optional Attributes	Description
	Locality Name
	Network Address
	Organization Name
	Organizational Unit
	Owner
	See Also
	Serial Number

Directory map.

Super Classes	Resource
Mandatory Attributes	
Optional Attributes	Path

Group.

Super Classes	Top
Mandatory Attributes	Common Name
Optional Attributes	Description
	GID
	Locality Name
	Member
	Organization Name
	Organizational Unit Name
	Owner
	See Also

Locality.

Super Classes	Top
Mandatory Attributes	
Optional Attributes	Description
	Locality Name
	See Also
	State or Province Name
	Street Address

Figure 4-17 *NCP server.*

```
Super Classes              Server
Mandatory Attributes
Optional Attributes        Operator
                           Supported Services
```

Figure 4-18 *Organization.*

```
Super Classes              Top
Mandatory Attributes       Organization Name
Optional Attributes        Description
                           EMail Address
                           Facsimile Telephone Number
                           Locality Name
                           Login Script
                           Login Intruder Limit
                           Physical Delivery Office Name
                           Postal Address
                           Postal Code
                           Postal Office Box
                           Print Job Configuration
                           Printer Control
                           See Also
                           State or Province Name
                           Street Address
                           Telephone Number
```

Figure 4-19 *Organizational person.*

```
Super Classes              Person
Mandatory Attributes
Optional Attributes        Email Address
                           Facsimile Telephone Number
                           Locality Name
                           Organizational Unit Name
                           Physical Delivery Office Name
                           Postal Address
                           Postal Code
                           Postal Office Box
                           State or Province Name
                           Street Address
                           Title
```

Organizational role.

Figure 4-20

```
Super Classes              Top
Mandatory Attributes       Common Name
Optional Attributes        Description
                           Email Address
                           Facsimile Telephone Number
                           Locality Name
                           Organizational Unit Name
                           Physical Delivery Office Name
                           Postal Address
                           Postal Code
                           Postal Office Box
                           Roll Occupant
                           See Also
                           State or Province Name
                           Street Address
                           Telephone Number
```

Organizational unit.

Figure 4-21

```
Super Classes              Top
Mandatory Attributes       Organizational Unit Name
Optional Attributes        Description
                           Email Address
                           Facsimile Telephone Number
                           Locality Name
                           Login Script
                           Login Intruder Limit
                           Physical Delivery Office Name
                           Postal Address
                           Postal Code
                           Postal Office Box
                           Print Job Configuration
                           Printer Control
                           See Also
                           State or Province Name
                           Street Address
                           Telephone NumberÆPT1Ø
```

Partition.

Figure 4-22

```
Super Classes              Top
Mandatory Attributes       Convergence
                           Partition Creation Time
                           Replica
Optional Attributes        Inherited ACL
                           Received Up To
                           Synchronization Interval
                           Synchronized Up ToÆPT1Ø
```

Figure 4-23   *Person.*

```
Super Classes            Top
Mandatory Attributes     Common Name
                         Surname
Optional Attributes      Description
                         See Also
                         Telephone Number
```

Figure 4-24   *Print server.*

```
Super Classes            Server
Mandatory Attributes
Optional Attributes      Operator
```

Figure 4-25   *Printer.*

```
Super Classes            Device
Mandatory Attributes
Optional Attributes      Cartridge
                         Default Queue
                         Host Device
                         Print Server
                         Memory
                         Network Address Restriction
                         Notify
                         Operator
                         Page Description Language
                         Printer Configuration
                         Queue
                         Status
                         Supported Typefaces
```

Figure 4-26   *Profile.*

```
Super Classes            Top
Mandatory Attributes     Common Name
                         Login Script
Optional Attributes      Description
                         Locality Name
                         Organization Name
                         Organizational Unit Name
                         See Also
```

Queue.

Figure 4-27

Super Classes   Resource
Mandatory Attributes   Queue Directory
Optional Attributes   Device
                       Network Address
                       Operator
                       Server
                       User

Resource.

Figure 4-28

Super Classes   Top
Mandatory Attributes   Common Name
                       Host Server
Optional Attributes   Description
                       Host Resource Name
                       Locality Name
                       Organization Name
                       Organizational Unit Name
                       See Also

Server.

Figure 4-29

Super Classes   Top
Mandatory Attributes   Common Name
Optional Attributes   Description
                       Host Device
                       Locality Name
                       Network Address
                       Organization Name
                       Organizational Unit Name
                       Private Key
                       Public Key
                       Resource
                       See Also
                       Status
                       User
                       Version

Top.

Figure 4-30

Super Classes   Top
Mandatory Attributes   Unknown Object Restriction
Optional Attributes

Unknown.

Figure 4-31

Super Classes   Top
Mandatory Attributes   Unknown Object Restriction
Optional Attributes

Figure 4-32   *User.*

Super Classes	Organizational Person
Mandatory Attributes	
Optional Attributes	Account Balance
	Allow Unlimited Credit
	Group Membership
	Home Directory
	Language
	Last Login Time
	Locked By Intruder
	Login Allowed Time Map
	Login Disabled
	Login Expiration Date
	Login Grace Limit
	Login Intruder Address
	Login Intruder Attempts
	Login Intruder Reset Time
	Login Maximum Simultaneous
	Login Script
	Login Time
	Message Server
	Minimum Account Balance
	Network Address
	Network Address Restrictions
	Password Allow Change
	Password Expiration Interval
	Password Expiration Time
	Password Minimum Length
	Password Required
	Password Unique Required
	Passwords Used
	Print Job Configuration
	Private Key
	Profile
	Public Key
	Security Equals
	Server Holds
	Type Creator Map
	UID

Figure 4-33   *Volume.*

Super Classes	Resource
Mandatory Attributes	
Optional Attributes	Network Address
	Status

the flags in Table 4-5. This syntax allows the Directory to properly constrain the object attribute values and to properly match attribute values between two objects.

The Directory attribute definite information

Table 4-5

Flag	Value	
DS_STRING	0x0001	/* string, can be used in names */
DS_SINGLE_VALUED	0x0002	
DS_SUPPORTS_ORDER	0x0004	
DS_SUPPORTS_EQUAL	0x0008	
DS_IGNORE_CASE	0x0010	/* Ignore case */
DS_IGNORE_SPACE	0x0020	/* Ignore white space */
DS_IGNORE_DASH	0x0040	/* Ignore dashes */
DS_ONLY_DIGITS	0x0080	
DS_ONLY_PRINTABLE	0x0100	
DS_SIZEABLE	0x0200	

Novell, Inc.

Managing the schema

The schema APIs allow an application to manage the schema by getting information from the schema. The schema can be queried for class definitions. Additionally, the schema APIs allow applications to create new class definitions. The schema APIs are found in Fig. 4-34.

Accessing the Directory

The Directory is accessed to create, read, modify, and delete objects and their attribute values. When creating an NDS object, you must pass the full definition of the entire object and all its mandatory attribute values to the create call. No object can be created a piece at a time as this would not be an object according to its class definitions. To properly access an object, the application must use the Buffer

Figure 4-34   *NDS schema management APIs.* Novell, Inc.

```
NWDSCCODE NWFAR NWPASCAL NWDSDefineAttr
(
    NWDSContextHandle      context,
    char            NWFAR *attrName,
    Attr_Info_T     NWFAR *attrDef
);

NWDSCCODE NWFAR NWPASCAL NWDSDefineClass
(
    NWDSContextHandle      context,
    char            NWFAR *className,
    Class_Info_T    NWFAR *classInfo,
    Buf_T           NWFAR *classItems
);

NWDSCCODE NWFAR NWPASCAL NWDSListContainableClasses
(
    NWDSContextHandle      context,
    char            NWFAR *parentObject,
    int32           NWFAR *iterationHandle,
    Buf_T           NWFAR *containableClasses
);

NWDSCCODE NWFAR NWPASCAL NWDSModifyClassDef
(
    NWDSContextHandle      context,
    char            NWFAR *className,
    Buf_T           NWFAR *optionalAttrs
);

NWDSCCODE NWFAR NWPASCAL NWDSReadAttrDef
(
    NWDSContextHandle      context,
    uint32                 infoType,
    uint8                  allAttrs,
    Buf_T           NWFAR *attrNames,
    int32           NWFAR *iterationHandle,
    Buf_T           NWFAR *attrDefs
);

NWDSCCODE NWFAR NWPASCAL NWDSReadClassDef
(
    NWDSContextHandle      context,
    uint32                 infoType,
    uint8                  allClasses,
    Buf_T           NWFAR *classNames,
    int32           NWFAR *iterationHandle,
    Buf_T           NWFAR *classDefs
);

NWDSCCODE NWFAR NWPASCAL NWDSRemoveAttrDef
(
```

```
    NWDSContextHandle      context,
    char              NWFAR *attrName
);

NWDSCCODE NWFAR NWPASCAL NWDSRemoveClassDef
(
    NWDSContextHandle      context,
    char              NWFAR *className
);
```

Figure 4-34

Management APIs to create a buffer and place each attribute name and value in the buffer with APIs. When modifying an object, you first read the object, change the values you want to change, then call the modify call with the full object definition. Deleting attribute values qualifies as modifying the object. It also is possible to search the Directory for an object. The NWDSSearch call also requires the application to build a filter for the search.

The Directory access and buffer management APIs are found in Figs. 4-35 and 4-36 respectively. As you put each item in the buffer in preparation to send the packet to the Directory service, the function call will check the context. If the context flags are set for DCV_CANONICALIZE and DCV_XLATE_STRINGS, the API function will canonicalize the names and translate the strings to UNICODE before placing the value in the buffer. If these context flags are not set, then the application is responsible for the canonicalization and translation before passing the string to the API.

⇨ Access control

Access to the Directory is controlled through the granting of access rights to objects to access the various locations in the Directory tree. Each object has an Access Control List (ACL). The ACL consists of entries each composed of three values. These values are the name of the protected attribute, the name of the subject receiving rights to the object, and the set of privileges granted to the subject.

Figure 4-35   *NDS directory access APIs.* Novell, Inc.

```
NWDSCCODE NWFAR NWPASCAL          NWDSAddObject
(
     NWDSContextHandle      context,
     char           NWFAR *objectName,
     int32          NWFAR *iterationHandle,
     uint8                 more,
     Buf_T          NWFAR *objectInfo
);


NWDSCCODE NWFAR NWPASCAL NWDSBackupObject
(
     NWDSContextHandle      context,
     char           NWFAR *objectName,
     int32          NWFAR *iterationHandle,
     Buf_T          NWFAR *objectInfo
);


NWDSCCODE NWFAR NWPASCAL NWDSCompare
(
     NWDSContextHandle      context,
     char           NWFAR *object,
     Buf_T          NWFAR *buf,
     uint8          NWFAR *matched
);


NWDSCCODE NWFAR NWPASCAL          NWDSGetPartitionRoot
(
     NWDSContextHandle      context,
     char           NWFAR *objectName,
     char           NWFAR *partitionRoot
);


NWDSCCODE NWFAR NWPASCAL NWDSList
(
     NWDSContextHandle      context,
     char           NWFAR *object,
     int32          NWFAR *iterationHandle,
     Buf_T          NWFAR *subordinates
);


NWDSCCODE NWFAR NWPASCAL NWDSMapIDToName
(
     NWDSContextHandle      context,
     NWCONN_HANDLE          conn,
     uint32                 objectID,
     char           NWFAR *object
);


NWDSCCODE NWFAR NWPASCAL NWDSMapNameToID
(
     NWDSContextHandle      context,
     NWCONN_HANDLE          conn,
```

```
        char            NWFAR *object,
        uint32          NWFAR *objectID
);

NWDSCCODE NWFAR NWPASCAL NWDSModifyObject
(
        NWDSContextHandle       context,
        char            NWFAR *objectName,
        int32           NWFAR *iterationHandle,
        uint8                 more,
        Buf_T           NWFAR *changes
);

NWDSCCODE NWFAR NWPASCAL NWDSModifyDN
(
        NWDSContextHandle       context,
        char            NWFAR *objectName,
        char            NWFAR *newDN,
        uint8                 deleteOldRDN
);

NWDSCCODE NWFAR NWPASCAL NWDSModifyRDN
(
        NWDSContextHandle       context,
        char            NWFAR *objectName,
        char            NWFAR *newDN,
);

NWDSCCODE NWFAR NWPASCAL NWDSMoveObject
(
        NWDSContextHandle       context,
        char            NWFAR *objectName,
        char            NWFAR *destParentDN,
        char            NWFAR *destRDN
);

NWDSCCODE NWFAR NWPASCAL NWDSRead
(
        NWDSContextHandle       context,
        char            NWFAR *object,
        uint32                infoType,
        uint8                 allAttrs,
        Buf_T           NWFAR *attrNames,
        int32           NWFAR *iterationHandle,
        Buf_T           NWFAR *objectInfo
);

NWDSCCODE NWFAR NWPASCAL NWDSReadObjectInfo
(
        NWDSContextHandle       context,
        char            NWFAR *object,
        char            NWFAR *distinguishedName,
        Object_Info_T   NWFAR *objectInfo
);
```

Figure 4-35   *Continued.*

```
NWDSCCODE NWFAR NWPASCAL NWDSRemoveObject
(
     NWDSContextHandle        context,
     char            NWFAR *object
);

NWDSCCODE NWFAR NWPASCAL NWDSRestoreObject
(
     NWDSContextHandle        context,
     char            NWFAR *objectName,
     int32           NWFAR *iterationHandle,
     uint8                  more,
     uint32                 size,
     uint8           NWFAR *objectInfo
);

NWDSCCODE NWFAR NWPASCAL NWDSSearch
(
     NWDSContextHandle        context,
     char            NWFAR *baseObjectName,
     int                    scope,
     uint8                  searchAliases,
     Buf_T           NWFAR *filter,
     uint32                 infoType,
     uint8                  allAttrs,
     Buf_T           NWFAR *attrNames,
     int32           NWFAR *iterationHandle,
     int32                  countObjectsToSearch,
     int32           NWFAR *countObjectsSearched,
     Buf_T           NWFAR *objectInfo
);

NWDSCCODE NWFAR NWPASCAL NWDSOpenStream
(
     NWDSContextHandle        context,
     char            NWFAR *objectName,
     char            NWFAR *attrName,
     uint32                 flags,
     int             NWFAR *fileHandle
);

NWDSCCODE NWFAR NWPASCAL NWDSWhoAmI
(
     NWDSContextHandle        context,
     char            NWFAR *objectName
);

NWDSCCODE NWFAR NWPASCAL NWDSGetServerDN
(
     NWCONN_HANDLE          conn,
```

```
    char            NWFAR *serverDN
);

NWDSCCODE NWFAR NWPASCAL NWDSGetServerAddresses
(
    NWDSContextHandle       context,
    NWCONN_HANDLE           conn,
    uint32          NWFAR *countNetAddress,
    Buf_T           NWFAR *netAddresses
);
```

Directory buffer management APIs. Novell, Inc.

Figure 4-36

```
NWDSCCODE NWFAR NWPASCAL NWDSAllocBuf
(
    size_t                  size,
    Buf_T   NWFAR * NWFAR   *buf
);

NWDSCCODE NWFAR NWPASCAL NWDSComputeAttrValSize
(
    NWDSContextHandle       context,
    Buf_T           NWFAR *buf,
    uint32                  syntaxID,
    uint32          NWFAR *attrValSize
);

NWDSCCODE NWFAR NWPASCAL NWDSFreeBuf
(
    Buf_T           NWFAR *buf
);

NWDSCCODE NWFAR NWPASCAL NWDSGetAttrCount
(
    NWDSContextHandle       context,
    Buf_T           NWFAR *buf,
    uint32          NWFAR *attrCount
);

NWDSCCODE NWFAR NWPASCAL NWDSGetAttrDef
(
    NWDSContextHandle       context,
    Buf_T           NWFAR *buf,
    char            NWFAR *attrName,
    Attr_Info_T     NWFAR *attrInfo
);

NWDSCCODE NWFAR NWPASCAL NWDSGetAttrName
(
    NWDSContextHandle       context,
    Buf_T           NWFAR *buf,
    char            NWFAR *attrName,
    uint32          NWFAR *attrValCount,
```

Figure 4-36   *Continued.*

```
        uint32          NWFAR   *syntaxID

);

NWDSCCODE NWFAR NWPASCAL NWDSGetAttrVal
(
    NWDSContextHandle       context,
    Buf_T           NWFAR   *buf,
    uint32                  syntaxID,
    void            NWFAR   *attrVal
);

NWDSCCODE NWFAR NWPASCAL NWDSGetClassDef
(
    NWDSContextHandle       context,
    Buf_T           NWFAR   *buf,
    char            NWFAR   *className,
    Class_Info_T    NWFAR   *classInfo
);

NWDSCCODE NWFAR NWPASCAL NWDSGetClassDefCount
(
    NWDSContextHandle       context,
    Buf_T           NWFAR   *buf,
    uint32          NWFAR   *classDefCount
);

NWDSCCODE NWFAR NWPASCAL NWDSGetClassItem
(
    NWDSContextHandle       context,
    Buf_T           NWFAR   *buf,
    char            NWFAR   *itemName
);

NWDSCCODE NWFAR NWPASCAL NWDSGetClassItemCount
(
    NWDSContextHandle       context,
    Buf_T           NWFAR   *buf,
);

NWDSCCODE NWFAR NWPASCAL NWDSGetObjectCount
(
    NWDSContextHandle       context,
    Buf_T           NWFAR   *buf,
    uint32          NWFAR   *objectCount
);

NWDSCCODE NWFAR NWPASCAL NWDSGetObjectName
(
    NWDSContextHandle       context,
    Buf_T           NWFAR   *buf,
    char            NWFAR   *objectName,
```

```
     uint32          NWFAR   *attrCount,
     Object_Info_T   NWFAR   *objectInfo
);

NWDSCCODE NWFAR NWPASCAL NWDSGetPartitionInfo
(
     NWDSContextHandle        context,
     Buf_T           NWFAR   *buf,
     char            NWFAR   *partitionName,
     uint32          NWFAR   *replicaType
);

NWDSCCODE NWFAR NWPASCAL NWDSGetServerName
(
     NWDSContextHandle        context,
     Buf_T           NWFAR   *buf,
     char            NWFAR   *serverName,
     uint32          NWFAR   *partitionCount
);

NWDSCCODE NWFAR NWPASCAL NWDSGetSyntaxCount
(
     NWDSContextHandle        context,
     Buf_T           NWFAR   *buf,
     uint32          NWFAR   *syntaxCount
);

NWDSCCODE NWFAR NWPASCAL NWDSGetSyntaxDef
(
     NWDSContextHandle        context,
     Buf_T           NWFAR   *buf,
     char            NWFAR   *syntaxName,
     Syntax_Info_T   NWFAR   *syntaxDef
);

NWDSCCODE NWFAR NWPASCAL NWDSInitBuf
(
     NWDSContextHandle        context,
     uint32                   operation,
     Buf_T           NWFAR   *buf
);

NWDSCCODE NWFAR NWPASCAL NWDSPutAttrName
(
     NWDSContextHandle        context,
     Buf_T           NWFAR   *buf,
     char            NWFAR   *attrName
);

NWDSCCODE NWFAR NWPASCAL NWDSPutAttrVal
(
     NWDSContextHandle        context,
     Buf_T           NWFAR   *buf,
     uint32                   syntaxID,
```

Figure 4-36   *Continued.*

```
        void            NWFAR    *attrVal
);

NWDSCCODE NWFAR NWPASCAL NWDSPutChange
(
    NWDSContextHandle        context,
    Buf_T           NWFAR    *buf,
    uint32                   changeType,
    char            NWFAR    *attrName
);

NWDSCCODE NWFAR NWPASCAL NWDSPutClassItem
(
    NWDSContextHandle        context,
    Buf_T           NWFAR    *buf,
    char            NWFAR    *itemName
);

NWDSCCODE NWFAR NWPASCAL NWDSBeginClassItem
(
    NWDSContextHandle        context,
    Buf_T           NWFAR    *buf
);
```

Granting access through the ACL

To grant access rights, an entry needs to be created in an object's ACL attribute. The ACL is a multivalued attribute. This will allow multiple entries in the list. Each entry in the ACL specifies an attribute by name that is to be protected. A subject for the ACL is specified. The subject is the Directory object to be granted the access privileges. There are two special subjects, [Public] and [Inheritance Mask]. [Public] access gives rights to all objects in the tree for the attribute in the entry.

Additionally, rights can be inherited through the tree by having been assigned to a container object above the object in question. To have sections of the tree inherit rights, the subject in the ACL needs to specify [Inheritance Mask] in an entry and define the access rights for the attribute specified. The intersection of the assigned access rights and the inherited rights defines the access one object has to another object. Access rights can be reduced as well as augmented by use of the [Inheritance Mask] subject.

Object & attribute access rights

Three sets of rights can be placed in the ACL. These sets are the
[Entry Rights], the [Attribute Rights], and [SMS
Rights]. [Entry Rights] deal with the entire object and consist
of Browse, Add, Delete, Rename, and Supervisor. [Attribute
Rights] protect individual attributes. These rights include Compare,
Read, Write, Self, and Supervisor. [SMS Rights] are defined for
backing up and restoring the object information. These rights consist of
Scan, Backup, Restore, Rename, Delete, and Admin.

Directory access is dependent upon the proper access rights. Each of
the Directory Access APIs might fail if the object access rights do not
permit the operation by the object performing the operation.

ACL APIs

The access control APIs are found in Fig. 4-37. These APIs are for
specifically getting or listing the rights to an object and its attributes.
The ACL is an optional attribute of any object in the Directory. The
ACL is created, modified, and deleted using the attribute Directory
access APIs.

Directory access control APIs. Novell, Inc.

Figure 4-37

```
NWDSCCODE NWFAR NWPASCAL NWDSGetEffectiveRights
(
    NWDSContextHandle       context,
    char            NWFAR *subjectName,
    char            NWFAR *objectName,
    char            NWFAR *attrName,
    uint32          NWFAR *privileges
);


NWDSCCODE NWFAR NWPASCAL NWDSListAttrsEffectiveRights
(
    NWDSContextHandle       context,
    char            NWFAR *objectName,
    char            NWFAR *subjectName,
    uint8                 allAttrs,
    Buf_T           NWFAR *attrNames,
    int32           NWFAR *iterationHandle,
    Buf_T           NWFAR *privilegeInfo
);
```

⇨ Authentication

Authentication services provided by the NetWare Directory make use of public/private key encryption technology. This technology involves mathematical algorithms to produce encryption keys, signatures, and proofs. Items encrypted with the private key are decrypted with the public key and vice versa. The authentication service is never required to send the encryption keys over the network, thus increasing the security of the network and the Directory.

The authentication services APIs are found in Fig. 4-38. These APIs allow the application to connect and authenticate to the network with NWDSLogin and NWDSAuthenticate. After using these two APIs, the workstation can perform background authentication to any other service it connects to for Directory information as well as other services that take advantage of the authentication services. An application can change a password, verify a password, generate a public and private key pair, and logout from the network. When an application logs out of the network with NWDSLogout, any connections to the Directory have the lock counts set to zero and can be reused by the workstation but the connections are not completely removed from the connection table.

The NetWare Directory Service provides a hierarchical, global naming service. This service can be accessed to find, describe, and use resources anywhere on the network. The Directory allows for easier network management and network access. A manager can administer all the users from one location. The users can access the network and all their network resources with one login, not several. The next chapter will provide examples and information on programming for the NetWare Directory Services environment.

Authentication APIs. Novell, Inc.   Figure 4-38

```
NWDSCCODE NWFAR NWPASCAL NWDSAuthenticate
(
    NWCONN_HANDLE              conn,
    uint32                     optionsFlag,
    NWDS_Session_Key_T NWFAR  *sessionKey
);

NWDSCCODE NWFAR NWPASCAL NWDSChangeObjectPassword
(
    NWDSContextHandle     context,
    uint32                optionsFlag,
    char           NWFAR *objectName,
    char           NWFAR *oldPassword,
    char           NWFAR *newPassword
);

NWDSCCODE NWFAR NWPASCAL NWDSGenerateObjectKeyPair
(
    NWDSContextHandle     contextHandle,
    char           NWFAR *objectName,
    char           NWFAR *objectPassword,
    uint32                optionsFlag
);

NWDSCCODE NWFAR NWPASCAL NWDSLogin
(
    NWDSContextHandle     context,
    uint32                optionsFlag,
    char           NWFAR *objectName,
    char           NWFAR *password,
    uint32                validityPeriod
);

NWDSCCODE NWFAR NWPASCAL NWDSLogout
(
    NWDSContextHandle     context
);

NWDSCCODE NWFAR NWPASCAL NWDSVerifyObjectPassword
(
    NWDSContextHandle     context,
    uint32                optionsFlag,
    char           NWFAR *objectName,
    char           NWFAR *password
);
```

5

Directory Services
programming sample

CHAPTER 5

W ITH NetWare v4.0, NetWare Directory Services (NDS) was introduced. NDS provides a new paradigm to the developer as well as to the network administrator. For developers, this paradigm largely affects the way that an application locates services on the network and connects or authenticates to those services. As a distributed object data base, the directory contains the information for the network necessary for a client to connect and access the services provided across the network. The directory itself stores this information in UNICODE. UNICODE is the 16-bit encoding of most of the written scripts for the languages of the world. This allows the servers connected within a directory and the information within the directory to be accessed from servers using languages from all over the world.

Programming to NDS requires the application to be aware of international issues. It also imposes increased security on server access while allowing a wider and more robust service for locating and accessing those services.

➡ Programming preliminaries

To properly use NWNET and the NetWare Directory Services APIs, the application must initialize the UNICODE tables for the locale it is running in. The locale is detected using the NWLlocaleconv function call. This call is based on the ANSI standard llocaleconv function but, with some additions to the structure returned, supplying additional locale information. Using the country_id and the code_page values returned from this call, the application makes a call to NWInitUnicodeTables. The application is now ready to make calls to the NWNET library.

Once the application has completed processing, it should shut down properly. This is done by calling NWFreeUnicodeTables. The application can then safely exit to Windows. Sample code demonstrating both the initialization and deinitialization sequences is found in Fig. 5-1.

Initialization and deinitialization sequences for using NWNET.   Figure 5-1

```
int SetupToUseNWNET(void)
{
    int err2;
    LCONV NWFAR *lconv, NWFAR *lconv2;

    lconv = (LCONV NWFAR *)malloc(sizeof(LCONV));

    /* Find the locale */
    if ((lconv2 = NWLlocaleconv(lconv)) != NULL)
        /* Init Unicode tables */
        err2 = NWInitUnicodeTables(lconv->country_id, lconv->code_page);

    free(lconv);
    return err2;

}
int DeinitNWNET(void)
{
    int err;

    err = NWFreeUnicodeTables();
    return err;
}
```

Now that the application is initialized, a buffer needs to be allocated
to receive information from NDS. These buffers are allocated and
initialized by calling NWDSAllocBuf and passing in the size of the
buffer to be allocated. The default size can be chosen by using the
DEFAULT_MESSAGE_LEN define. Code demonstrating this
allocation is found in Fig. 5-2.

⇨ Context: walking the tree

In addition to having an NDS buffer, the application must create a
context to use with the rest of the NDS functions. This context is
created using the NWDSCreateContext call. This call returns a
context handle to be passed in on subsequent calls. When you create
the context, it contains the default name context for your
workstation. The default context for your workstation is the path
through the Directory from [ROOT] to the container holding the
object you logged in as. The context can be changed by calling
NWDSSetContext. The contents of the context can be retrieved with
the NWDSGetContext call.

Figure 5-2   *Buffer allocation under NetWare Directory Services.*

```
            .
            .
            .
    case IDM_LIST:
        List();
        wsprintf(str, "Check results in file sample.out");
        MessageBox(GetFocus(), str,
                "DS List...", MB_ICONASTERISK | MB_OK);
        break;
            .
            .
            .


void List()
{
    NWDS_BUFFER NWFAR *subordinates;
    NWDSCCODE err;

    stream = fopen("sample.out", "w");
    err = SetupToUseNWNET();
    if (!err)
    {
        err = NWDSAllocBuf(DEFAULT_MESSAGE_LEN, &subordinates);
        if (err)
        {
            fprintf(stream, "Error in Alloc Buff: %x",err);
            goto cleanup;
        }
        err = MainDSCode(subordinates);
        if (err)
        {
            fprintf(stream, "Error in Sample: %x",err);
            goto cleanup;
        }
        err = DeinitNWNET();
        if (err)
        {
            fprintf(stream, "Error in Deinit: %x",err);
            goto cleanup;
        }
    }
    else
        fprintf(stream, "Error in Setup: %x",err);

cleanup:
    fclose(stream);
}
```

Once you have a context and an NDS buffer, you can make a call to
NWDSListSubordinates, as demonstrated in Fig. 5-3. Listing the
subordinates will give you a list of all the objects subordinate to the

Listing the subordinates and getting them from the buffer.   Figure 5-3

```
int MainDSCode(NWDS_BUFFER NWFAR *subordinates)
{
    NWDSContextHandle context;
    NWDSCCODE err;
    NWDS_ITERATION iteration = NO_MORE_ITERATIONS;
    char objectName[MAX_DN_BYTES + 2];
    NWCOUNT count, attrCount;
    NWOBJECT_INFO NWFAR *objInfo;

    objInfo = (NWOBJECT_INFO NWFAR *)malloc(sizeof(NWOBJECT_INFO));

    /* Create Context */
    context = NWDSCreateContext();

    /* List Subordinates */
    err = NWDSList(context, "", (NWDS_ITERATION NWFAR *)&iteration,
                subordinates);

    if (err == 0)
    {
        err = NWDSGetObjectCount(context, subordinates,
            (NWCOUNT NWFAR *)&count);
        for (;count > 0; count--)
        {
            err = NWDSGetObjectName(context, subordinates, objectName,
                                &attrCount, objInfo);
            fprintf(stream, "%s\r\n", objectName);
        }
    }
    return err;

}
```

context you pass into the function. Using the names returned for the subordinates, you are able to walk through the directory tree by getting the current context, adding a subordinate container to it, and setting it. Traversing the tree in this fashion allows an application to see at least all objects with [PUBLIC] rights. Additionally, the application can see all items it has access to. This is one method of locating all the objects of a given type on the network. Another way to do this is to perform an NWDSSearch function. This function is discussed later in the chapter.

83

NDS buffers: unpacking the information

All the buffers used in NDS are opaque buffers. This opacity is due to the UNICODE and encryption features of NDS. The buffers can be allocated, initialized, unpacked, and freed through the use of APIs. A set of functions exists for unpacking the number of items in the buffer, NDS object names, and object attributes from the buffer. To know how much information is in a particular buffer, the application should call NWDSGetObjectCount. The sample application subsequently gets all the names out of the subordinates buffer by making calls to NSDSGetObjectName from within a loop controlled by the object count value returned from the previous call. For each of the object names returned from the NWDSList call, the application can get a list of all the attributes that the objects have.

NWDSRead & object attributes

To get all the information about a specific object, an application should use the NWDSRead function call with a buffer that has been initialized to DS_READ. Once the objInfo buffer returns from the function call, the application can use a combination of NWDSGetAttrCount, NWDSGetAttrName, and NWDSGetAttrValue to read the information that defines that object from the buffer. The sample code in Fig. 5-4 shows how to read an object from the directory. Attributes for objects in the directory include information for managing a user's access to the network, information for managing servers, and location of servers and the services that they provide.

NWDSLogin & NWDSAuthenticate

To gain access to the network, an application can implement a login and authentication sequence. If the application is the first network

Reading a directory object.   Figure 5-4

```
objInfo = (NWOBJECT_INFO NWFAR *)malloc(sizeof(NWDS_BUFFER));

/* Create Context */
context = NWDSCreateContext();

err = NWDSAllocBuf(DEFAULT_MESSAGE_LEN, &objAttrs);
if (err)
      return err;
err = NWDSInitBuf(context, DS_READ, objAttrs)

err = NWDSRead(context, ".O=GauthierCons", (NWDS_TYPE)1, TRUE,
      NULL, (NWDS_ITERATION NWFAR *)&iteration, objAttrs);

if (err == 0)
{
    err = NWDSGetAttrCount(context, objAttrs,
          (NWCOUNT NWFAR *)&count);
    for (;count > 0; count--)
    {
          err = NWDSGetAttrName(context, objAttrs, attrName,
                              &attrValCount, &syntaxID);
          fprintf(stream, "%s\r\n", attrName);
    }
}
return err;
```

software to run a machine, then, like LOGIN.EXE, it needs to execute an NWDSLogin function call. This call requires a user name and password. It establishes the connection to the network and caches all the authentication information for subsequent calls to NWDSAuthenticate.

After the NWDSLogin call or if a workstation already has a connection to the network, applications can call NWDSAuthenticate to properly authenticate to any server in the tree. Calling NWDSAuthenticate for a new connection is the process referred to as background authentication. This means that the application can cause the workstation to authenticate in the background without requiring the user to enter a user name or password.

 # NWDSSearch

To locate an object of a specific name, with specific attributes, or of a specific type, the application should call NWDSSearch. The NWDSSearch call uses a filter buffer built using the NWDSAddFilterToken call. These filter tokens include FTOK_ANAME (attribute name) and FTOK_AVAL (attribute value). If the application were searching for all objects with names beginning with A, it would be looking for objects with an FTOK_ANAME = Common Name and an FTOK_AVAL = "A*".

When the search is performed using the search filter, one of the flags passed to the call determines the scope of the search. The values for this flag are found in Table 5-1. If the application wants to search the entire directory, the base object specified should be [ROOT].

Table 5-1 | **The search scope flag values and meanings**

0	DS_SEARCH_ENTRY	Only search the object specified
1	DS_SEARCH_SUBORDINATES	Search subordinates of the object specified
2	DS_SEARCH_SUBTREE	Search the subtree beginning at the object specified

This chapter has demonstrated how to make the basic NetWare Directory Services calls and the necessary initialization and deinitialization. At least 50 more calls exist that can be used by an application to create new object definitions in the schema, to control the security auditing on the directory, to manage the directory, and to manage the network through the directory.

File, directory, &
synchronization services

T HIS chapter blends a discussion of the NetWare file system and the services provided by the file, directory, and synchronization APIs. Considerations for file operations on a multi-user environment are also discussed with some tips for using the synchronization APIs in that environment.

NetWare file system

Before discussing the service groups, let's look at the NetWare file system. The NetWare file system is organized by volumes, directories, subdirectories, and files. Every NetWare file server has at least one volume, and each volume has a root directory that might or might not have subdirectories and files under it. These subdirectories also can have more subdirectories and files. Each directory, with the exception of the root directory, has a parent subdirectory.

In the example in Fig. 6-1, SYS: is a volume on the file server named FILE_SERVER and also is the root directory for the volume. All of the directories under SYS: have a parent directory. For example, the directory DIR_141 has a parent directory named DIR_14, and DIR_14's parent directory is the root directory SYS:.

Figure 6-1

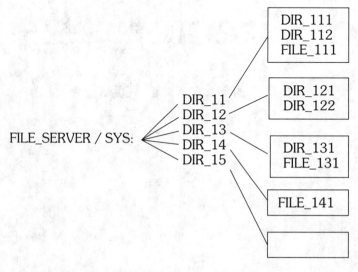

An example of a directory structure.

File system entry table

NetWare systems keep track of all of the directories and files through many tables. The one of most interest in this discussion is the file system entry table. This file entry table consists of an array of arrays of entries. In other words, each entry in the table is itself a 128-byte entry containing information on files, directories, and other NetWare file system specific information. Some types of information contained in an entry from this table are a file's name, attributes, creation date and time, and so on. Figure 6-2 gives a visual idea of how the file system entry table is set up.

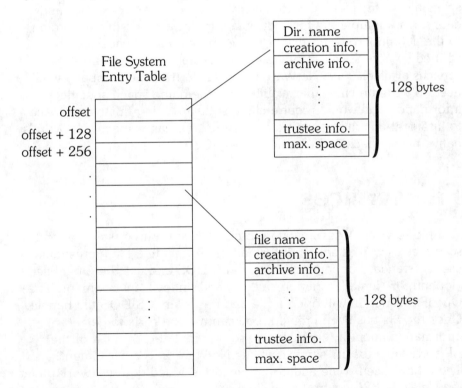

Figure 6-2

The file system entry table.

Name spaces

The NetWare file system also has the concept of name spaces. Different client file systems use different conventions for naming files. Novell supports five such conventions through name spaces. A name space consists of a NetWare Loadable Module (NLM) loaded at the file server and space on each volume to store name space information that is enabled on a per volume basis. The five name spaces currently supported by NetWare systems are DOS, OS/2, Macintosh, NFS, and FTAM. Each name space follows the naming conventions for the client platform that it supports. For example, the Macintosh name space allows for filenames to have 32 characters and resource and data forks. Multiple file forks or data streams are possible according to the definition of a particular name space. Name spaces can be defined by non-Novell software companies by using the name space services available with NetWare v4.0. To do this, the company would need to write an NLM that would store the name space specific information and would require client software using this name space to interpret the data structure defined for the name space. NetWare's native name space is the same as the DOS name space.

File services

The file services APIs allow you to copy, erase, purge, salvage, and scan files as well as set file information. To create a file, you should use the standard open() function call for DOS and use the OpenFile(), _lopen(), or _lcreat() function call for the Windows environment. The OpenFile function will open a file and return an MS-DOS file handle. Once the file has been created, you can use the APIs to get information about it, erase it, and so on. Table 6-1 is a list of the APIs available for file services in the NetWare 286 environment. There have been some additional functions added that will work under the NetWare 386 environment.

| The file services APIs | | Table 6-1 |

API function	What environment it works in
EraseFiles	286 and 386
FileServerFileCopy	286 and 386
GetExtendedFileAttributes	286, 386 doesn't return the complete attributes
PurgeAllErasedFiles	286 only
PurgeErasedFiles	286 only
RestoreErasedFile	286 only
ScanFileInformation	286 and 386
SetExtendedFileAttributes	286 and 386 won't set the complete attributes
SetFileInformation	286 and 386
PurgeSalvagableFile	386 only
RecoverSalvagableFile	386 only
ScanFileEntry	386 only
ScanFilePhysical	386 only
ScanSalvagableFiles	386 only

Novell, Inc.

 # Directory handles

Many of the file services APIs require you to have some information to indicate which file you want action taken on. For example, to delete a file, you use the EraseFiles API. This function requires that you know three things about the files to be deleted. These three things are the directoryHandle, the filePath, and the searchAttributes.

Most of the file services APIs require the directory handle and path in some combination. The directoryHandle and filePath go hand-in-hand. The directoryHandle is nothing more than an index number into a table stored in the file server's memory. This index number points to a volume name or directory name on a file server as indicated in Figure 6-3.

Figure 6-3

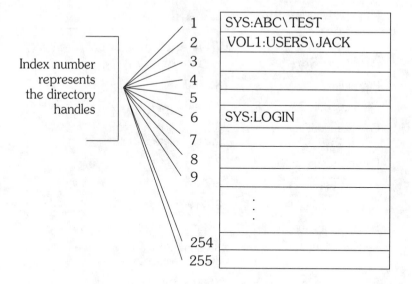

Note The file server maintains a directory handle
table for each connection.

The file server's directory handle table.

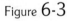 # Obtaining a directory handle

To obtain a directory handle, you can make one of a few calls in the
directory services APIs that will return a directoryHandle. If you
already have a drive letter assigned to a directory such as
F:=SYS:LOGIN, then you can make the function call
GetDirectoryHandle and pass the driveNumber corresponding to the
letter F (5) into the function. See Fig. 6-4. The function call returns
the directoryHandle associated with the drive letter F.

Other function calls that return a directoryHandle are
AllocPermanentDirectoryHandle or AllocTemporaryDirectoryHandle.
In these functions, you decide which drive letter you want to
correspond to a directory path that you specify.

One note about the allocation of directory handles: they must be
deallocated when you're finished using them. Deallocate them by

Drive Letter vs. Drive Number   Figure 6-4

A B C D E F G ...   V W X Y Z   *The drive letter vs. the drive*
                                                number.

0 1 2 3 4 5 6 ...   21 22 23 24 25

calling DeallocateDirectoryHandle. If this call isn't made, you might
use all of your handles and cause other functions to fail. Most often,
the GetDirectoryHandle call will provide the directory handle,
avoiding an allocation and deallocation of a new directory handle.

⇨ File paths

The filePath is exactly that: an ASCII-character string that identifies
the file and its path relative to the directory handle. For example, you
can have a directoryHandle that points to a directory path that is not
quite the complete path for your file *plus* a file path that has the rest
of the directory path and filename in it. For example, if you have a
directoryHandle (5) that points to the directory, SYS:USERS\JACK,
but your file that you want to manipulate is in the directory
SYS:USERS\JACK\WORKDIR\FILE.TXT, then you would pass the
directoryHandle (5) *plus* the filePath WORKDIR\FILE.TXT into the
function. You also can specify a complete path in the filePath
parameter and pass 0x00 as the directoryHandle. Now, the API will
know how to get to the file that you want to act on. The last
parameter, searchAttributes, is a byte indicating what type of file to
erase. This byte can be one of the following 4 values: 0x00 for
normal files, 0x02 for normal and hidden files, 0x04 for normal and
system files, and finally 0x06 for normal, hidden, and system files.

⇨ Erased files

A couple of the file services APIs sometimes are confusing to the user.
These are the EraseFiles, PurgeAllErasedFiles, and PurgeErasedFiles.
The EraseFiles function marks a file or files for deletion. If you were to
do a DIR after making this call, the file marked for deletion would not
show up. However, you can salvage this file because it is not actually
deleted but is placed in a *holding* area until the user does another delete

or create file call. Because the files are still on disk, no disk space is immediately freed after making this call. To actually free disk space from files that have been deleted, you need to purge them. The difference between the two purge functions is that PurgeErasedFiles permanently deletes only the files that a workstation has marked for deletion. The PurgeAllErasedFiles permanently deletes all files that have been marked for deletion. To make the latter call, you must have console operator rights. If not, an error will be returned indicating as much.

The functions that we just talked about are the ones used for NetWare 286. There are equivalent functions for NetWare 386, which are listed in Table 6-1. The file system in NetWare 386 uses a least recently used algorithm for use of space occupied by erased or deleted files. This algorithm is an improvement on NetWare 286 because it allows file activity to continue on the server and does not reuse the deleted file space until all other space is consumed.

File attributes

Two fields stored in the file system entry table are the DOS attribute byte and the NetWare attribute byte. They are both defined in Fig. 6-5.

A few more fields stored in the file system entry table and that are returned by ScanFileInformation, ScanFileEntry (386), ScanFilePhysical (386), ScanDirectoryInformation, and ScanDirEntry are the dates and times of various events such as creation, archiving, and updating of files and directories. These fields are sometimes tricky to decipher, so the following example shows how to parse the output from these functions. The functions return the date and time in the standard DOS format. This format is shown in Fig. 6-6.

Example 1

If we make a call to scan information about a file . . .

```
ScanFileInformation (directoryHandle, filePath,
        searchAttributes, &sequenceNumber, fileName,
        &fileAttributes, &extendedFileAttributes, &fileSize,
        &creationDate[0], &lastAccessDate[0],
        &lastUpdateDateAndTime[0],
        &lastArchiveDateAndTime[0], &fileOwnerID);
```

File Attributes Byte

Figure 6-5

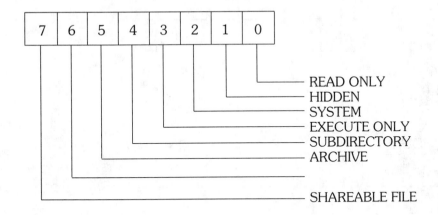

| 7 | 6 | 5 | 4 | 3 | 2 | 1 | 0 |

READ ONLY
HIDDEN
SYSTEM
EXECUTE ONLY
SUBDIRECTORY
ARCHIVE

SHAREABLE FILE

READ ONLY	-Set if file can be read but not written to
HIDDEN	-Set if file is a hidden file, can't be seen with DIR
SYSTEM	-Set if file is a system file, can't be seen with DIR
EXECUTE ONLY	-Set if file is to be loaded for execution only
SUBDIRECTORY	-Set if not a file, but a directory
ARCHIVE	-Set if file has been modified since last archived
SHAREABLE FILE	-Set if file can be shared

NetWare Extended Attribute Byte

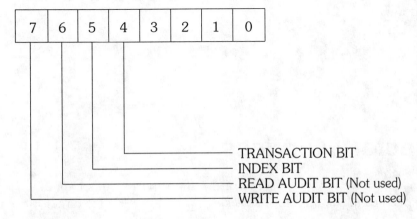

| 7 | 6 | 5 | 4 | 3 | 2 | 1 | 0 |

TRANSACTION BIT
INDEX BIT
READ AUDIT BIT (Not used)
WRITE AUDIT BIT (Not used)

The file attributes byte and NetWare extended attribute byte.

Figure 6-6   DOS Date and Time Format

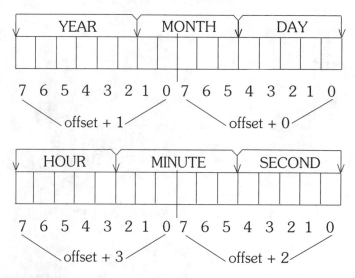

The DOS date and time format.

and want to parse the date and time from the lastArchiveDateAndTime field, here is how we would do it. First, typecast the lower two bytes to be a word and assign this to a temporary variable:

```
date = *(WORD *)lastArchiveDateAndTime[0];
time = *(WORD *)lastArchiveDateAndTime[2];
```

Now, use the bitwise operator to shift right the number of bits for the desired field:

```
year = date >> 9;
month = (date & 0x01E0) >> 5;
day = date & 0x001F;
hour = time >> 11;
minute = (time & 0x07E0) >> 5;
second = time & 0x001F;
```

Directory services

Now that we have looked at some of the file services, let's look at some specifics in the directory services. All of the APIs for directory services are available to use in both the DOS and Windows environment. There a few points of interest that we will touch on, namely the necessary information for the creation and deletion of a directory, the concept of trustees, maximum rights mask, inherited rights mask, and some differences between the NetWare 286 and 386 directory specifics.

Directory access rights in NetWare 286

To create and delete a directory using the C Interface APIs, you would use the CreateDirectory and DeleteDirectory functions. These functions require you to know the directory handle and path as well as the maximum rights mask. The directory path and handle were discussed at the beginning of this chapter in the file services section. The *maximum rights mask* is a byte that determines the rights that any trustee to a directory can have. A maximum rights mask is associated with each directory. To modify the maximum rights mask of a directory, the requesting workstation must have parental rights to the directory or to a parent of the directory. The *trustee rights mask* also is a byte that is assigned by the owner of the directory and, along with the maximum rights mask, determines a user's access to a directory.

The actual access rights that a user has to a directory are called the *effective rights*. The effective rights to a directory can be determined by the intersection of the trustee rights mask with the maximum rights mask of the directory in question. Programmatically, this is accomplished by ANDing the two masks together. Figure 6-7 shows a diagram of the rights byte associated with a directory.

Directory access rights in NetWare 386

NetWare 386 uses a slightly different concept for determining rights and trustees to directories and files. In NetWare 386, the maximum rights mask is no longer used. Instead, there is an inherited rights

Figure 6-7

RIGHTS MASK BYTE

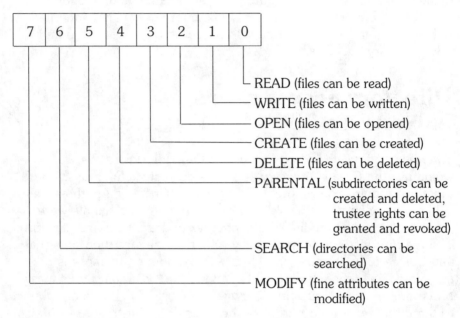

The rights mask byte.

mask that is similar in some ways to the maximum rights mask. Now, instead of having only rights and possible trustees to directories, you also can have rights and trustees to files. This gives you more control over directory and file access. When examining the bits in the trustee rights for NetWare 386, there are a few differences. One is that the trustee rights mask is no longer a byte, but a word. There is an added field in the second byte that is the Supervisor bit. If this bit is set, then all of the rights are granted. Second, the open file right is no longer necessary but is implicit in the read and write access rights.

Synchronization services

Now that we have looked at the features of the file and directory services, let's examine the Synchronization Services and how they relate to the other two services.

Synchronization Services APIs allow applications to coordinate the sharing of resources. One example of why this coordination is useful occurs if two applications are trying to update one file on the network at the same time. Using synchronization services, they can update the file in a manner that is not disastrous to the integrity of the file. Some examples of resources that might need to be shared are CPU time, files, printers, and modems. Without the synchronization of resources, a simple updating of a network file by two applications can result in data loss.

One way NetWare Systems enable applications to synchronize network resources is through the Synchronization Services APIs. Synchronization of resources can be accomplished through the use of logging files, locking files, and semaphores. The general idea is to log a file or set of files into a table, then lock that file or set of files so that no other application can access them while you have them locked. Next, through the use of semaphores, you can keep track of how many applications are using which resource, how many resources are left, and so on. First, let's examine the logging aspect of the APIs.

 # Logging files or records

Before you can lock your files or records, you need to have a place to put information about the files or records that you want to lock. This information includes the name of the file if you are logging an entire file, or the location and size of a record if you are logging only a record or portion of a file. The place this information is preserved is called a log table and is located on the file server. It is associated with the task on the requesting workstation. The API functions that let an application log records and files are LogFile, LogLogicalRecord, and LogPhysicalRecord.

 # Files versus records

When you log and lock data, you can do so on a file or a record. The simplest lock is that of an entire file. The problem with logging and locking the entire file can show up if the application is one in which a

lot of users will be trying to access and update data at the same time. If you log and lock the entire file, then it might cause quite an inconvenience for the users who didn't get to the file first. This is why there are ways to log and lock only portions of a file. This is done through the use of records. If you access data through a record, it can be a logical or physical record. A physical record is one that is on the disk, where a logical record is one that is maintained in memory.

⇨ Locking files or records

Once the file or record is logged in the log table, it can be locked. NetWare systems, by default, set the attributes on a file to be nonshareable read/write. This can be seen by using the FLAG utility. You also can modify the rights through the FLAG utility. File attributes can be modified programmatically through the SetFileInformation function in the File Services APIs. To lock a file or record programmatically, you can use LockFileSet, LockLogicalRecordSet, and LockPhysicalRecordSet.

⇨ Deadlock & how to avoid it

When one of these functions is made, the file server will take the files or records in the log table as a set and try to lock all of them. If any one of these files or records already has been locked by another workstation, the request will fail. This is a prime candidate for a *deadlock* situation.

An example of a deadlock might be if workstation A has three files that it wants to lock and has a program to do it (not using the Synchronization APIs) and workstation B has five files it wants to lock. They both have used some type of conditional such as "while locked, wait 5 seconds and try again." Both workstation A and B have a couple of files in common that each wants to lock (for instance file1, file2, and file3). Workstation A is executing its program and it finds file1 and locks it, but when it gets to file2 it has to wait 5 seconds because workstation B already has file2 locked. Meanwhile, workstation B has locked file2; however, when it gets to file1 it has to wait 5 seconds and try again because workstation A has file1 locked.

As you can see, the two applications are in an infinite loop of waiting and retrying, hence a deadlock.

A way of preventing a deadlock is to have a time out period specified that will tell the application to try locking the file again for this period of time and, if it still can't lock it, to fail the call. In this case, none of the files will be locked. Using the synchronization services APIs allows applications to put the burden of locking and retrying on NetWare systems rather than requiring the application do the work.

Logical versus physical records

Logical record locks sometimes are more convenient to use than physical record locks. Instead of being actual bytes that are being locked, a logical record lock is one that locks only a name that represents the data. The same techniques of logging, locking, releasing, and clearing record locks are used with logical record locks, but an important difference is that, when a logical record is locked, it is only the name that represents the data that is being locked. For this reason, an application needs to be consistent when using locks.

The logical record locks are more for keeping track of devices rather than for security tasks. If another workstation really wants to access the data that is logically locked, it can do so by knowing the data's address. Because physical record locks access bytes of data, they will override logical record locks. For this reason, you don't want to mix physical and logical record locking techniques.

Unlocking files & records

Now that you have the records locked and understand how the time out value works, you might want to remove some locks or remove some of the logged records from the log table. This is done through the use of other APIs. The APIs that deal with the releasing of records and files are ReleaseFile, ReleaseFileSet, ReleaseLogicalRecord, ReleaseLogicalRecordSet, ReleasePhysicalRecord, and Release-PhysicalRecordSet. When one of these functions is called, the file, physical record, or logical record will be released or unlocked. It will

remain in the log table and will be grouped with the other files or records in the table for the next lock call that is made. You can unlock one or all of the files or records that a workstation has locked by selecting the appropriate API function. For example, ReleaseFile releases only the file specified where ReleaseFileSet releases all files the workstation has locked.

By releasing the files and records, you don't remove them from the log table. To do this, you need to make a call to one of the clear functions. These functions include ClearFile, ClearFileSet, ClearLogicalRecord, ClearLogicalRecordSet, ClearPhysicalRecord, and ClearPhyscialRecordSet. When these functions are called, they actually remove the files or records from the log table.

⇨ Semaphores

Semaphores and their associated information are maintained in a table on the file server. They are another mechanism provided by NetWare systems to allow resources to be shared. The APIs provided for manipulating semaphores are OpenSemaphore, ExamineSemaphore, SignalSemaphore, WaitOnSemaphore, and CloseSemaphore. Semaphores are similar to logical record locks in that they are a way of coordinating network resources. NetWare semaphores are ASCII strings up to 127 characters in length with an associated value that can be from −127 to 127.

A good example of how semaphores might be used is illustrated by two modems that are being accessed by four different workstations. An initial value of two might be assigned to the semaphore value and the semaphore name would be MODEM_ACCESS. The value of two means there are two resources (modems) available for use. Each time a workstation accesses a modem, the value must be decremented. If the value is negative, this indicates that all resources are being used and the requesting workstation has to wait. Figure 6-8 illustrates this situation.

When OpenSemaphore is called, a semaphore name and an initial value are specified and returned to the caller as a semaphore handle and an open count. The semaphore handle is a pointer to the

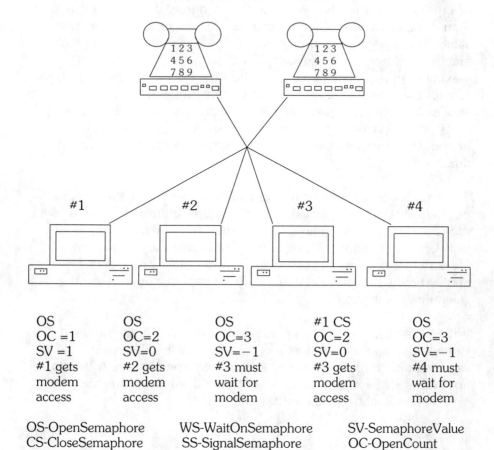

INITIAL SEMAPHORE VALUE = 2   Figure 6-8

#1	#2	#3	#4	
OS	OS	OS	#1 CS	OS
OC =1	OC=2	OC=3	OC=2	OC=3
SV =1	SV=0	SV=−1	SV=0	SV=−1
#1 gets modem access	#2 gets modem access	#3 must wait for modem	#3 gets modem access	#4 must wait for modem

OS-OpenSemaphore   WS-WaitOnSemaphore   SV-SemaphoreValue
CS-CloseSemaphore   SS-SignalSemaphore   OC-OpenCount

Semaphores and modem access.

semaphore. It needs to be used in other semaphore calls. The open count returned is a number indicating how many other processes have the semaphore open. When OpenSemaphore is called, this open count value is incremented. If a semaphore doesn't exist when this call is made, then one is created.

Once the semaphore is opened, you can change the semaphore value by calling SignalSemaphore or WaitOnSemaphore. The first of these two increments the semaphore value. This is called once a workstation or application has finished using the resource. The other,

WaitOnSemaphore, decrements the semaphoreValue and is called when the application wants to use the resource. If the value is greater than or equal to zero after this call has decremented the semaphore value, the application can gain access to the resource. If not, the function will hold off or queue the requesting application for a maximum time period specified in the time out limit parameter. If the semaphore value still is less than zero, the function removes the application from the queue and increments the semaphore value back to its original value. If the value is 0 or greater during the time out period, then the application can gain access to the resource at that time.

The ExamineSemaphore function can be called at any time to check on the status of a semaphore. Once an application has finished using the resource and no longer needs to keep the semaphore open, it calls CloseSemaphore. This call will decrement the open count to indicate that one less process has the semaphore open. If this application is the last one to have the semaphore open, then the semaphore is deleted.

With the methods described earlier, synchronizing network resources is made possible, straightforward, and easy to use. Use of the file services, directory services, and synchronization services APIs allows applications to access and manipulate the most basic shared resource on a network: data stored in files and directories.

Introduction to queue services

W HAT are Queue Services? The Queue Services make available the NetWare Queue Management System (QMS) to developers through the Queue Services APIs. QMS is simply a way of keeping track of a group of jobs and servicing them in a specified order. It's a way of organizing data. QMS allows for placement of jobs in a queue as well as servicing those jobs simultaneously. QMS originally was developed to support Novell's Print Services and, therefore, meets the requirements of the print services as well as many other applications. Many types of distributed processing applications could take advantage of QMS; however, it is not the best solution for all types of applications. Some of the different types of services that you could implement using QMS and the APIs available are print, compile, batch job processing, file copying, archiving, and E-mail servers. When deciding what type of queuing mechanism to use or whether to implement your own, you should keep the advantages and the disadvantages of QMS in mind.

➪ QMS advantages

There are a number of advantages to using QMS. These advantages include the following:

➤ QMS already is implemented and supported by NetWare systems. The distribution and synchronization protocols are defined and available for use. If it's used, it provides a built-in backout feature.

➤ QMS is great for batch mode operations such as a batch server that compiles source code.

➤ QMS was designed to handle large amounts of data.

➤ QMS has a high level of security because it was built to take advantage of NetWare bindery security features.

➤ QMS provides a way for the client and server to communicate with each other.

➤ QMS allows multiple requests without slowing down the job flow.

 # QMS disadvantages

Unfortunately, there also are some disadvantages to using QMS. These disadvantages include the following:

➢ QMS works best in a nontimed critical environment to be efficient. It's not fast enough for applications needing real-time response such as database applications. It's not well-suited for transferring small amounts of data rapidly.

➢ If portability is a concern, QMS might not be the best decision because it is NetWare systems specific.

➢ NetWare 2.2 is limited to 250 jobs in the queue at one time. This limit changed in NetWare v3.11 where up to 1000 jobs can be placed in the queue at one time. This could limit some applications.

 # Queues

A *queue* is a set of jobs that need servicing or a list of jobs destined for some type of batch server. Jobs are processed as an entry in a file. An analogy of a queue is a line of people waiting at a movie theater. Each person standing in line to go into the movie can be considered a queue job. A queue user can place a job in the queue, just as a person wanting to go to a movie can get in line. A job entry is moved to the top of the queue as jobs are serviced, deleted, rearranged. A job server takes the jobs from the queue and services them. QMS then removes those jobs from the queue. Likewise, when the ticket attendant takes the ticket from a customer, he is servicing a queue of people. As he services the queue of people, the line gets shorter. If a person wants to go into the movie, he must go to the end of the line. This is how a queue normally works. It's a first in first out (FIFO) queue. When a new job is put into the queue, it *normally* is put at the end of the list of queue jobs. However, if the priority of the queue job is higher than the ones already in the queue, the job will be placed at the front of the queue. QMS does not interpret the data held in queue jobs. It provides a method only for storing and

distributing data. Only the applications that submit and service the jobs in a queue job interpret it.

Queue jobs

You can have up to 25 job servers servicing any given queue. However, a single job server is not limited to the number of queues it attaches to. A queue can hold up to 250 jobs in NetWare v2.2 and up to 1000 jobs in NetWare 3.11. The job numbers associated with the job range from 1 to 999 even though only 250 can be in the queue at once. For NetWare versions greater than 3.0 the job numbers can range from 1 to 0xFFFFFFFF.

Creating a queue

When a queue is created, it has an object name, object type, object ID, and Q_DIRECTORY, Q_USERS, Q_OPERATORS, and Q_SERVERS properties associated with it. The object ID is assigned at the time of creation. The queue name, type, ID, and properties associated with it are stored in the bindery. QMS guarantees that only authorized users can access, modify, or view the contents of the queue because the queue name is defined as an object in the bindery. QMS provides control over who can access the queue and how they can use it by adding specific objects to the Q_USERS, Q_OPERATORS, and Q_SERVERS properties.

Queue properties

Let's take a closer look at the properties mentioned earlier. When a queue is created, a bindery object with the four previous properties is created. All of these properties have a security access associated with them. The Q_DIRECTORY property has a security access level of read supervisor/write supervisor. This means that only the supervisor can read or write to this property. The other three properties are created with a security access level of read logged/write supervisor. Therefore, any logged object can read these properties, but only the supervisor can modify them.

 Q_DIRECTORY

When a queue is created, a directory path must be specified. The directory specified is where the system files associated with the queue and the files associated with the jobs in the queue are stored. SYS:SYSTEM is a commonly used directory path for a queue directory, but you can specify any path that you want as long as it is less than 118 characters in length. When the queue is created, the object ID is added to the directory path name so that, if multiple queues are created, they can be uniquely identified. For example, if two queues named BATCH and PRINT were created with the directory SYS:SYSTEM as the path name and the object IDs 0x12345678 and 0x87654321 were returned, then the queue files associated with BATCH would be in the SYS:SYSTEM\12345678 directory and the queue files associated with PRINT would be in the SYS:SYSTEM\87654321 directory. In NetWare 386, an additional extension is added to the end of the object ID. This extension is .QRD and is there so that you can glance at the directory and know that it is a queue directory. Because of this extension, the maximum length for your directory path can be 114 characters instead of 118. Each queue can have only one Q_DIRECTORY property because it is an item property.

Q_USERS

The Q_USERS property is a set property, so there can be multiple object IDs associated with it. This is how QMS keeps track of who can place jobs in the queue. The object IDs within the Q_USERS property are of those who can add jobs to the queue. These object IDs can be either a user's or a group's object ID. For example, if the object ID for the PROGRAMMERS group is one of the Q_USERS' object IDs, then any user who is in the group PROGRAMMERS can place jobs in the queue. If you don't care who can add a job to the queue, you can either specify the group's object ID for EVERYONE or you can delete the Q_USERS property altogether.

 # Q_SERVERS

As with the Q_USERS property, QMS keeps track of who can service a queue through the Q_SERVERS set property. This property contains a list of object IDs of bindery objects who can attach to and service queue jobs.

With reference to our movie theater example, the Q_SERVERS could be any movie theater employee. Just because all of the employees are in this group, doesn't mean that they will all service the queue of people. It only means that they *can* service the line of people. When a job is submitted to a queue, QMS goes out and searches for a job server that meets the specification given by the submitter of the job. It will check to see if the target server ID matches the requesting server. If it does match, QMS will let that job server service the job. If the target server ID field had a −1 in it, that means that the requesting server doesn't care who services its job. In that case, QMS will try to match the job type field between the requesting node and the job server. One thing to keep in mind is that, if you put a −1 in the job type field for your job server, it will cause your job server to try to service any type of job. This could cause problems if you are setup for a print job server but get a request for a file copying job server.

 # Q_OPERATOR

An object in the Q_OPERATOR property is very powerful with respect to the queue. An object that is in the Q_OPERATOR set property can change contents of job entries in the queue, change the status of the queue, add a job, delete a job, change its position, keep servers from taking jobs out of the queue, prevent servers from attaching to the queue, and prevent jobs from being placed into the queue.

 # Clients & servers

A simple way to think of the QMS process is to consider the three main steps involved in the queuing process:

➤ CLIENT or USER (Submit request to queue for processing)

➤ JOB SERVER (Service job request)

➤ QMS (Remove job from queue)

⇨ Job entry structure

When a job is submitted to a queue, it has to give some information
with it. This information is contained in a job entry structure. The job
entry structure is the JobStruct structure type defined in the QMS
header file in the NetWare C-Interface for Windows SDK v1.3. In
Fig. 7-1, is a list of the fields in the JobStruct structure and an
explanation of each field. The names of these fields might vary
slightly from the actual releases, but the definitions for them are the
same.

The QMS job structure. Novell, Inc.

Figure 7-1

```
typedef struct
{
    BYTE       reserved[10];           Reserved for future QMS needs
    DWORD      clientStation;          Client workstation connection number
    DWORD      clientTaskNumber;       Client process task number
    DWORD      clientIDNumber;         Client object ID
    DWORD      targetServerIDNumber;   Target server's bindery object ID
    BYTE       targetExecutionTime[6]; Earliest execution start time
    BYTE       jobEntryTime[6];        Time job was placed in queue
    DWORD      jobNumber;              Job number assigned by QMS
    WORD       jobType;                Job type number (3-print job)
    WORD       jobPosition;            Position in queue where 1 is the first
                                       job in the queue
    WORD       jobControlFlags;        Bit wise job control flags
                                       QF_AUTO_START       (0x08)
                                       QF_SERVICE_RESTART  (0x10)
                                       QF_ENTRY_OPEN       (0x20)
                                       QF_USER_HOLD        (0x40)
                                       QF_OPERATOR_HOLD    (0x80)
    char       jobFileName[14];        Job file name contained in the queue
                                       subdirectory
    BYTE       jobFileHandle[6];       NetWare OS file handle
    DWORD      serverStation;          Job server's connection number
    DWORD      serverTaskNumber;       Job server's process task number
    DWORD      serverIDNumber;         Job server's bindery object ID
    char       textJobDescription[50]; User defined text job description
    BYTE       clientRecordArea[152];  User defined job information
} JobStruct;
```

 # Target execution time

The targetExecutionTime is the earliest time that a job can be serviced. If a −1 is placed in this field, then the job can be serviced immediately or at the soonest possible time.

 # Job control flags

The jobControlFlags contain five bitwise flags indicating the current status of the queue job. The QF_AUTO_START flag can be set so that, if the job server has to abort your job for some reason, it automatically will place your job in the queue and try it later. The QF_SERVICE_RESTART flag can be set to tell QMS that, if the server goes down for some reason, to place your job in the queue when the server is restored.

The QF_ENTRY_OPEN flag is used by QMS and tells QMS whether a client has released the queue job for servicing or not. If it is set, the queue job has not been released; when the client releases the queue job for servicing, QMS clears this field.

The QF_USER_HOLD flag can be set by the user to tell QMS not to process a job. If set, the queue job will be advanced through the queue as always; however, when it reaches the first position, it will not be serviced. It will remain at the beginning of the queue until the flag has been cleared. The QF_OPERATOR_HOLD flag is the same as the QF_USER_HOLD flag except it can be set only by an object that is a member of the Q_OPERATORS property.

Setting job entry structure fields

Tables 7-1 through 7-5 list the fields that the queue user fills in before a job is created, fields filled in by QMS when a job is created, fields user or operators can change, fields checked by QMS before request to service is granted, and fields changed by QMS when a job is released for servicing.

The job-entry structure fields that queue users must fill in before a job is created

Table 7-1

clientStation	(connection number)
clientTaskNumber	
clientIDNumber	(bindery or directory object ID)
targetServerIDNumber	(bindery or directory object ID)
	−1 is any target server
targetExecutionTime	fill with −1 is soonest possible time
jobEntryTime	
jobNumber	
jobType	0 <= value <= 255
jobPosition	
jobControlFlags	bit ORed flag, 0 is typical
QF_AUTO_START	(0x08)
QF_SERVICE_RESTART	(0x10)
QF_ENTRY_OPEN	(0x20)
QF_USER_HOLD	(0x40)
QF_OPERATOR_HOLD	(0x80)
jobFileName	
jobFileHandle	
serverStation	(connection number)
serverTaskNumber	
serverIDNumber	(bindery or directory object ID)
textJobDescription[50]	Not interpreted by QMS, string description
clientRecordArea[152]	Not interpreted by QMS, user data

The job-entry structure fields that are filled in by QMS when a job is created

Table 7-2

clientStation	(connection number)
clientTaskNumber	
clientIDNumber	(bindery or directory object ID)

113

Table 7-2	**Continued**	
	targetServerIDNumber	(bindery or directory object ID)
	targetExecutionTime	
	jobEntryTime	
	jobNumber	
	jobType	0 <= value <= 255
	jobPosition	
	jobControlFlags	bit ORed flag, 0 is typical
	QF_AUTO_START	(0x08)
	QF_SERVICE_RESTART	(0x10)
	QF_ENTRY_OPEN	(0x20)
	QF_USER_HOLD	(0x40)
	QF_OPERATOR_HOLD	(0x80)
	jobFileName	
	jobFileHandle	
	serverStation	(connection number)
	serverTaskNumber	
	serverIDNumber	(bindery or directory object ID)
	textJobDescription[50]	
	clientRecordArea[152]	

Table 7-3	**The job-entry structure fields that users or operators can change**	
	clientStation	(connection number)
	clientTaskNumber	
	clientIDNumber	(bindery or directory object ID)
	targetServerIDNumber	(bindery or directory object ID)
	targetExecutionTime	
	jobEntryTime	
	jobNumber	
	jobType	

jobPosition

jobControlFlags

    QF_AUTO_START   (0x08)

    QF_SERVICE_RESTART   (0x10)

    QF_ENTRY_OPEN   (0x20)

    QF_USER_HOLD   (0x40)

    QF_OPERATOR_HOLD   (0x80)

jobFileName

jobFileHandle

serverStation   (connection number)

serverTaskNumber

serverIDNumber   (bindery object ID)

textJobDescription[50]

clientRecordArea[152]

The job-entry structure fields that are checked by QMS before a request to service is granted	Table 7-4
clientStation (connection number)	
clientTaskNumber	
clientIDNumber (bindery or directory object ID)	
targetServerIDNumber (bindery or directory object ID)	
targetExecutionTime	
jobEntryTime	
jobNumber	
jobType pass –1 to API, or else must match exactly	
jobPosition	
jobControlFlags	
QF_AUTO_START (0x08)	
QF_SERVICE_RESTART (0x10)	
QF_ENTRY_OPEN (0x20)	
QF_USER_HOLD (0x40) all three flags must not be set	
QF_OPERATOR_HOLD (0x80)	

Table 7-4	**Continued**	
jobFileName		
jobFileHandle		
serverStation	(connection number)	
serverTaskNumber		
serverIDNumber	(bindery or directory object ID) is 0 if not being serviced	
textJobDescription[50]		
clientRecordArea[152]		

Table 7-5	**The job-entry structure fields that are changed by QMS when job is released for servicing**	
clientStation	(connection number)	
clientTaskNumber		
clientIDNumber	(bindery or directory object ID)	
targetServerIDNumber	(bindery or directory object ID)	
targetExecutionTime		
jobEntryTime		
jobNumber		
jobType		
jobPosition		
jobControlFlags		
QF_AUTO_START	(0x08)	
QF_SERVICE_RESTART	(0x10)	
QF_ENTRY_OPEN	(0x20)	
QF_USER_HOLD	(0x40)	
QF_OPERATOR_HOLD	(0x80)	
jobFileName		
jobFileHandle		
serverStation	(connection number)	
serverTaskNumber		
serverIDNumber	(bindery or directory object ID)	

textJobDescription[50]

clientRecordArea[152]

 **QMS APIs & security**

Table 7-6 shows API function names associated with the queue services. It also shows what security group an object needs to be in to be able to make those function calls.

The QMS security groups and what calls they can make	Table 7-6

Supervisor	CreateQueue
	DeleteQueue
	AddBinderyObjectToSet
	(Add members to queue groups, bindery function call)
	DeleteBinderyObjectFromSet
	(Delete members from a queue group, bindery function call)
	ScanProperty
	(View members of a queue group)
Q_USERS	CloseFileAndStartQueueJob
	ChangeQueueJobEntry
	(Set QF_USER_HOLD)
	CreateQueueJobAndFile
	GetQueueJobList
	GetJobsFileSize
	ReadQueueJobEntry
	RemoveJobFromQueue
	ReadQueueCurrentStatus
	ReadQueueServerCurrentStatus
Q_OPERATOR	ChangeQueueJobEntry
	(Set QF_OPERATOR_HOLD)
	ChangeQueueJobPosition
	GetQueueJobList

Table 7-6	Continued	
	GetJobsFileSize	
	ReadQueueJobEntry	
	RemoveJobFromQueue	
	ReadQueueCurrentStatus	
	ReadQueueServerCurrentStatus	
	SetQueueCurrentStatus	
Q_SERVERS	AbortServicingQueueJobAndFile	
	AttachQueueServerToQueue	
	ChangeToClientRights	
	DetachQueueServerFromQueue	
	FinishServicingQueueJobAndFile	
	ReadQueueJobEntry	
	RestoreQueueServerRights	
	ServiceQueueJobAndOpenFile	
	SetQueueServerCurrentStatus	

 # AbortServicingQueueJobAndFile

Just a little warning about using the AbortServicingQueueJobAndFile function call. If your job server has finished servicing or if something is not right with the queue job being serviced, you don't want to abort the queue job with the previously mentioned API. If you do abort with this API and the QF_SERVICE_RESTART flag is set, the queue job is left at its current position in the queue and the job server attempts to service it again. As you can see, if this logic is continued, your job server will get into an infinite loop of aborting and retrying to service a queue job. Instead, use the FinishServicingQueueJobAndFile function call. You should use the abort function call when there is some type of temporary problem that will be fixed readily (like a paper jam). However, if the QF_SERVICE_RESTART flag is not set and the abort function is called, then QMS removes the job entry from the queue and deletes the queue job's associated file.

The next chapter demonstrates how to write applications using the Queue Services APIs.

Client-server programming
with QMS

T HE latest revolution in application development is the client-server programming model. A resource can be located in one location and be managed by a server. The server receives requests from the clients for some type of processing to occur. If the resource is a printer, the processing is printing. If the resource is a database, the processing is accessing the data. Controlling the access or having a single point of access through a server allows multiple clients to share the resource without endangering the integrity or usability of the resource.

QMS application design

The application in this chapter will demonstrate how to use Queue Management Services (QMS) to create a queue-based client-server application. This application is modeled as an employee database access application. When searches need to be made, the client side of the application sends off a request for the search to be performed by the server with the parameters of the search. The search will then return the requested information. Each action the server performs has a unique request identification.

Q.EXE

The application Q.EXE consists of two sets of functionality: that of the server and that of the client. It runs on one workstation as both a client and a server. A real-world application typically runs on two workstations: one for the client and one for the server. Using QMS to create a queue-based client-server application manages the queue and incoming requests to the server for the developer. The developer can concentrate on the specifics of the service being provided and returning the information to the appropriate location. The design of the application requires the developer to make the following decisions:

➤ Where will the server and resources reside?

➤ How many queues will the server process or need to process?

➤ Will the service be one large process or several smaller processes?

➤ What format of the job record gives the server the information it needs?

➤ Where will the data be placed on completion and how is the client to be notified?

⇨ Location of client & server

The client and server portions of the application must be delineated. Where the client ends and the server begins determines where to place the code for creating jobs and processing requests. The client in the example, Q.EXE, is responsible only for presenting of the choices available to the user, translating the user's choice into a request to the server, and presenting the results. The server does all the work in opening and closing the data files and in searching, adding, modifying, and deleting the entries.

Different services would locate the processing differently. Some database services are available as NLMs. Print services often use an NLM or a dedicated workstation as a print server, but the printing is performed by remote machines on demand from the print server. Each method of locating all or some of the processing is determined by the needs of the service. To require all a company's printers to be in one location and directly connected to the print server might be a requirement for one company. However, another company might require all printers to be located in the departments that purchase them and connected directly to the network. One database server might need to have complete control of its data files and another will use distributed files. Typically, these decisions are made based on efficiency and maintaining data integrity. Some can be configured by the user, others are preset and cannot be changed. How to distribute a process is discussed in more detail in chapters 11 and 13. A typical QMS application uses the queues to centralize access to the service, then distributes the back-end service to as many machines as necessary. Print services using a remote printer as a back-end distribution location is a typical example.

Frequency & scope of processing

A service application needs to determine the frequency with which it checks the queues and how many queues to use for processing. Jobs can be prioritized within a queue or queues can be prioritized. A higher priority queue would require the service to check it more often than a lower priority queue. Queues also can be used to demultiplex the type of processing. This is useful for dividing up large requests into smaller pieces. The job type in the job control structure also can be used for the same purpose. Whichever methods are chosen, they affect the number of queues a service must process and how often each queue must be processed.

Distribution of processing

Distributing a service to remote processors and gathering it back to convey the results to the client can be useful in off-loading an individual machine of all the processing. However, this also greatly complicates error recovery and flow control. More than one server or a dedicated server often will keep a single machine from being a bottleneck to job processing efficiency. Printing is a good process to distribute to multiple locations. Each print job can be sent to a different location according to the type of printer and its priority. Database access, on the other hand, often will consist of one server controlling access to an individual database. Multiple servers easily could threaten data integrity if the service was not designed initially for distributed access.

Job format

The format of the job control structure allows user configurable information to be placed in the client record area. This information can consist of file location information or user name. The format of the queue file itself will control the job to be performed. This format is defined in the design process and mutually understood by the client and the server.

Notification of job completion & results

Notification of job status can be done throughout processing the job if the application chooses to do so. Completion of the job by the job server raises two decisions:

➤ Is the user to be notified programmatically that the job is complete?

➤ Where are the results of the job to be found?

With a print service, the job server can choose to send a message back to the user programmatically informing him of the completion of his job, or the completed job on the printer makes the same statement. In printing, the location of the results also is a simple decision—they are on the printer. In the case of a database server, the location of the results is more involved. The job server could place the results in another queue that the user takes them from, the job server could place the results in a separate data file per client, or the results could be sent back dynamically using some type of communications protocol. A data file per client with notification by the server of the job completion would be most useful for a batch processing environment. In the sample application, we used memory shared by the client and the server that are running as the same application. This easily could be replaced with a file write by the server, an IPX or SPX notification by the server, and a file read by the client.

Running the sample

In running the sample application, the proper actions need to be made in sequence for the application server and client to successfully communicate with each other. First, the queue needs to be set up by choosing the `Create` option from Queue menu item. When entering the queue name and directory name, do so in uppercase. The directory is an existing path under which the queue directory will be created. Most applications use the SYS:SYSTEM directory.

Next, the server needs to be initialized. This is accomplished by choosing the Attach option from the Server menu item. The queue server periodically will check the queue for jobs. If a job is present it will process it, remove it from the queue, and send a message to the client piece of the application.

The next step consists of choosing an option from the Client menu item. The first option, List all employees, is the option implemented as a demonstration. The rest of the options can be completed as an exercise by the reader.

Once the user has completed these steps, deinitialization and cleanup are completed by first choosing Detach from the Server menu item, then choosing Destroy from the Queue menu item. Finally, choose Exit from the menu.

Now that you have seen the application running, let's discuss the individual steps, how the application implements them, and why they are necessary.

Queues

Queues are centralized locations for the job files that are passed between the client and server. Before the client and server can communicate using the Queue Management System, a queue must exist. The first step in either the installation or the configuration of a QMS based application is to create a queue.

Creating queues

To create a queue, the user must be logged in to the server where the queue is created as SUPERVISOR or a SUPERVISOR-equivalent user. If a queue does not already exist, the user will need to create one before he/she can use the job server and client. The creation and setup of a queue consists of three steps. These steps are demonstrated in the sample code in Fig. 8-1.

Sample code for creating and destroying a queue.   Figure 8-1

```
BOOL FAR PASCAL CreateDestroyDlgProc (HWND hDlg, WORD message,
        WORD wParam, LONG lParam)
{

    switch (message)
    {
        case  WM_INITDIALOG:
            return (TRUE);

        case WM_COMMAND:
            switch (wParam)
            {
                case IDOK:
                    /*-- Retrieve information from edit boxes --*/
                    GetDlgItemText (hDlg, IDE_QCNAME, szQName, 48);
                    switch (function)
                    {
                        case CREATE:
                            GetDlgItemText (hDlg, IDE_QCDIR, szQDir, 118);
                            ccode = CreateQueue (szQName, OT_JOB_QUEUE, 0,
                                    szQDir, &qID);
                            wsprintf (errMsg, "ccode for CreateQueue =  %04X",
                                    ccode);

                            /*-- Here we add EVERYONE to the queue's
                                Q_SERVERS property.  This way any object
                                can attach itself to the queue and service
                                the queue if it knows how.  This was done
                                for example purposes.  If we didn't want
                                all objects to be able to attach to the
                                queue, we could assign specific object IDs
                                or group names to this property. --*/

                            MessageBox (hDlg, errMsg, "STATUS", IDOK);
                            ccode = AddBinderyObjectToSet (szQName,
                                    OT_JOB_QUEUE, "Q_SERVERS", "EVERYONE",
                                    OT_USER_GROUP);
                            wsprintf (errMsg, "ccode AddBindObjToSet =  %04X",
                                    ccode);
                            MessageBox (hDlg, errMsg, "STATUS", IDOK);

                            ccode = AddBinderyObjectToSet (szQName,
                                    OT_JOB_QUEUE, "Q_USERS", "EVERYONE",
                                    OT_USER_GROUP);
                            wsprintf (errMsg, "ccode AddBindObjToSet =  %04X",
                                    ccode);
                            MessageBox (hDlg, errMsg, "STATUS", IDOK);
                            EndDialog (hDlg, TRUE);
                            break;

                        case DESTROY:
                            ccode = GetBinderyObjectID (szQName,
                                    OT_JOB_QUEUE, &qID);
```

Figure 8-1   *Continued.*

```
                      wsprintf (errMsg, "ccode for GetBinderyObjID = %04X",
                              ccode);
                      MessageBox (hDlg, errMsg, "STATUS", IDOK);
                      ccode = DestroyQueue (qID);
                      wsprintf (errMsg, "ccode for DestroyQueue =  %04X",
                              ccode);
                      MessageBox (hDlg, errMsg, "STATUS", IDOK);
                      EndDialog (hDlg, TRUE);
                      break;
                }
                return (TRUE);

            case IDCANCEL:
                EndDialog (hDlg, FALSE) ;
                return TRUE ;
        }
        break ;
    }
    return FALSE ;
}
```

The first step in setting up a queue is to create the queue itself. Use the CreateQueue call to do this. The CreateQueue call requires four input parameters: the queue name, the queue type, the directory path specified by the directory handle, and the path from the handle. The full path specified by the path from the handle must already exist. If the directory handle is zero, then the path must include the full path to be used including the volume name.

To protect the queue files, queues typically are created in the SYS:SYSTEM directory. However, the application can create the queue files in any location on the server that exists. On successful completion of this call, the return code is equal to zero and the qID parameter has been set to the bindery object ID of the queue that was created. If the low byte of the return code is in the range of 0x90–0x9F, an error relating to the directory path has occurred. These errors are not all documented in the CreateQueue call in the SDK reference manuals.

Setting up servers

If the CreateQueue call is successful, then the application takes the second and third steps, setting up the Q_SERVERS and Q_USERS

properties. In the example program, we add EVERYONE to the queue's Q_SERVERS property. This way, any object can attach itself to the queue and service the queue if it knows how. In a production application, this property would contain the list of job servers installed on the network. If an installation detected that a queue already existed, it would need only to add the name of the server being installed to the Q_SERVERS for the second step of the setup. The server being installed is added to the Q_SERVERS property by specifying the name of the bindery object the server will login as and adding it using the AddBinderyObjectToSet call. This call requires input parameters consisting of the name of the queue, the type of the queue, the name of the property to add the object to, the object name to be added, and the type of the object to be added.

⇨ Setting up users

To complete the third step of the queue setup process, the call from the second step is repeated for the Q_USERS property. This step differs from the last in the objects that are to be added to the property. The members of this set property consist of the objects allowed to submit jobs to this queue to be serviced by the objects in the Q_SERVERS property.

⇨ Destroying queues

Once a queue is no longer needed, then the queue can be destroyed. Two steps are necessary to destroy the queue. First, the application calls GetBinderyObjectID to get the ID of the queue to be destroyed. The parameters to this call are the queue name and the queue's bindery object type. Next, the application calls, then calls DestroyQueue with the ID returned from the GetBinderyObjectID. The sample code demonstrating these steps also can be found in Fig. 8-1.

QMS flow control

The flow of jobs from the clients to the server can be controlled through QMS. The use of QMS itself controls the flow of jobs to the application by queueing them. The server then goes on to process the next job as it completes the current one. The application is not required to queue up all the requests or to manage network traffic. Additionally, the flow can be controlled through the queues or through the job control structure.

High priority queues can be defined by the application by giving them a different bindery type on creation. Jobs with higher priorities can be placed in high priority queues. The server then would always process any jobs in the high priority queue first. The application also can use the job type to prioritize the processing order of jobs. In this situation, all the jobs of one type are processed before any jobs of the next type are processed.

QMS servers

Servers can process requests through QMS. To do so, the server must be attached to the queue to which jobs will be submitted. Once the server is attached to the queue, it can open queue jobs, process them, remove them from the queue, or abort them.

Attaching to the queue

When the application starts as a server, it needs to attach to the queue. The sample code in Fig. 8-2 demonstrates the steps necessary to attach to the queue as a queue server. First, to attach to or detach from the queue, the application always calls GetBinderyObjectID to get the bindery object ID for the queue specified. In the sample application, the queue is specified by user input when the attach is chosen. In a production application, the name for the queue could be resolved in the same way or it could be resolved at installation, at

Sample code for attaching to and detaching from a queue.   Figure 8-2

```
BOOL FAR PASCAL AttachDetachDlgProc (HWND hDlg, WORD message,
        WORD wParam, LONG lParam)
{
    static BOOL  timerSet = FALSE;

    switch (message)
    {
        case WM_INITDIALOG:
            return (TRUE);

        case WM_COMMAND:
            switch (wParam)
            {
                case IDOK:
                    /*-- Retrieve information from edit box --*/
                    GetDlgItemText (hDlg, IDE_QNAME, szQName, 48);
                    ccode = GetBinderyObjectID (szQName, OT_JOB_QUEUE, &qID);
                    switch (function)
                    {
                        case ATTACH:
                            connection = GetConnectionNumber ();
                            GetConnectionInformation (connection, szJobServer,
                                    &jobServerObjType, &jobServerObjID,
                                    loginTime);
                            ccode = AttachQueueServerToQueue (qID);
                            wsprintf (errMsg, "ccode AttachQServerToQ =  %04X",
                                    ccode);
                            MessageBox (hDlg, errMsg, "STATUS", IDOK);
                            if (!ccode)
                            {
                                PostMessage (hParent, SERVICE_JOB_MSG, NULL,
                                        (DWORD) NULL);
                                SetTimer (hParent, SERVICE_JOB_TIMER,
                                        TWO_SECONDS, NULL);
                                timerSet = TRUE;
                            }
                            break;

                        case DETACH:
                            ccode = DetachQueueServerFromQueue (qID);
                            wsprintf (errMsg, "ccode DetachQServerFromQ =  %04X",
                                    ccode);
                            MessageBox (hDlg, errMsg, "STATUS", IDOK);
                            if (!ccode)
                            {
                                KillTimer (hParent, SERVICE_JOB_TIMER);
                            }
                            break;
                    }

                    EndDialog (hDlg, TRUE) ;
                    return TRUE ;
```

Figure 8-2   *Continued.*

```
                case IDCANCEL:
                    EndDialog (hDlg, FALSE) ;
                    return TRUE ;
            }
            break ;
    }
    return FALSE ;
}
```

start-up, through a configuration parameter in a .INI file or through a hard coded value.

Next, the application gets the connection number from the server where the queue resides using the GetConnectionNumber call. With this connection number, the application queries the server for its bindery object name, bindery object ID, bindery object type, and the login time using the GetConnectionInformationCall. The first three values are saved. These values will be used later when servicing a job.

Once the application has the necessary information, it attaches to the queue using the AttachQueueServerToQueue call. On successful completion of the attach call, a Windows timer is started using SERVICE_JOB_TIMER to identify which timer sent the WM_TIMER message. The timer sends the WM_TIMER message to the main message loop, notifying the application when to check for jobs in the queue.

Once the server is attached to the queue, it must periodically check the queue for jobs to service. The sample code in Fig. 8-3 demonstrates the timer case that sends the message to the application to service the job. The SERVICE_JOB_TIMER case calls the TryToServiceJob function. The steps necessary to process a queue job are found in the sample code in Fig. 8-4.

The TryToServiceJob function checks the queue specified in the attach for jobs using the ServiceQueueJobAndOpenFile function call. If this call returns successfully, a job structure and file handle are returned to the server application. When this call is made, the server specifies the type of job to open. This type can be a wildcard but, if specified, must correspond to the job type set in the job control

Sample code for checking the queue of a Windows timer message.   Figure 8-3

```
#define SERVICE_JOB_MSG          (WM_USER + 1)
    .
    .
    .

    case WM_TIMER :              // Posts a message to service the queue.
        PostMessage (hwnd, SERVICE_JOB_MSG, NULL, (DWORD) NULL);
        break;

    case SERVICE_JOB_MSG :       // See if there is a job to service.
        TryToServiceJob (hParent);
        break;
    .
    .
    .
```

Sample code for service queue jobs.   Figure 8-4

```
/*------------------------------------------------------------------------
    This function is where we actually get the job out of the queue and
    examine it, determine what request has been made, service that request,
    and then remove the job from the queue.
    ---------------------------------------------------------------------*/
BOOL FAR PASCAL TryToServiceJob (HWND hParent)
{
    DWORD dwLength;
    int num, newNum;

    ccode = ServiceQueueJobAndOpenFile (qID, IntSwap(EMPLOYEE_JOB_TYPE),
            &job, &fHandle);
    if (ccode == 0xD5 || ccode != 0)  /* 0xD5 = no queue jobs to be serviced.*/
    {
        return (FALSE);
    }
    else
    {

        ccode = ChangeToClientRights (qID, job.jobNumber);
        if (ccode)
            return (FALSE);

        /*-- Here is where we look at the file to determine what request is
             being made and how to process it. --*/

        dwLength = GetFileLength (fHandle);
        _lread (fHandle, szRequestBuff, dwLength);

        /*-- When we parse the request buffer, we will obtain the request the
             user wants to make, the employee name for some requests, and the
             data base file name that contains the information. --*/
        ParseRequest (szRequestBuff);
        GetDataFile ((char far *)&fileName[0]);
```

131

Figure 8-4   *Continued.*

```
switch (request)
{
    case IDM_LISTALL:
        /*-- Use a list control to display a list of all of the
            employees --*/
        displayBuf = GetEmployeeListing ();
        PostMessage (hParent, DISPLAY_LIST_MSG, NULL, (DWORD) NULL);
        break;

    case IDM_SEARCH:
    case IDM_ADD:
    case IDM_REMOVE:
    case IDM_MODIFY:
        PostMessage (hParent, DISPLAY_INFO_MSG, NULL, (DWORD) NULL);
        break;
}

ccode = RestoreQueueServerRights ();
if (ccode)
    return (FALSE);
ccode = FinishServicingQueueJobAndFile (qID, job.jobNumber, 0, fHandle);
if (ccode)
    return (FALSE);
return (TRUE);
    }
}
```

structure created by the client. The value passed to this call is the
swapped version of the value set in the job control structure. If jobs
are available, the server will then process them.

Assuming the client's rights

To process the job, the server needs to assume the same level of access
rights and privileges held by the client making the request. This prevents
the client from making requests for information or services that they
haven't been granted access to. The server assumes this privilege level
by making the ChangeToClientRights function call. See Fig. 8-4.

Processing the job

To process the jobs, the server next parses the queue file to discover
which request is to be made, which data file should be used in the
request, and if applicable to the request, which employee name to use

in the request. After the request is parsed, the data file is opened. If the data file is on the network, the server will be able to open it only if the client had rights to it.

The request will determine which action we perform. When the request has been serviced successfully, the server calls RestoreQueueServerRights to restore its rights. The job then is removed from the queue using FinishServicingQueueJobAndFile.

If the job cannot be completed successfully, the application can call the AbortServicingQueueJob function in place of the RestoreQueueServerRights and FinishServicingQueueJobAndFile calls. This function will leave the job in the queue in a good state for another attempt to service. This call should be used only if the server's state prevents it from servicing the job. If the job control structure itself is in error, then the server should call RestoreQueueServerRights and FinishServicingQueueJobAndFile calls to delete the job from the queue.

Returning the information

In the sample application, the server copies the information requested to the display buffer and simply sends a message to the main message loop for the information to be displayed. This simple solution to the return of the data is possible because the client and the server are running on the same workstation. A more typical method of returning information electronically would be to create a file on the network and send a message to the client that the information is there. The location where the file is created can be specified by the client software in the client record area of the job control structure. The message could be sent through any message passing system on the network.

Detaching from the queue

When the server application is going to shut down, the server should detach from the queue. The sample code in Fig. 8-2 also demonstrates detaching from the queue. First, as in the attach, the

server must obtain the queue's bindery object ID. Using this value, a call is made to DetachQueueServerFromQueue. Once the server is detached, it should kill the Windows timer being used to wake up and check the queue.

QMS clients

Any piece of software that submits jobs to a queue is a QMS client. To submit the jobs to the queue properly so that a value-added server can process them is the most important function of a QMS client software piece.

Submitting jobs

To submit jobs to queues, a QMS client must prepare a job control structure and submit a request to the queue. In the sample code, this is performed by the FillInQueueJobAndMakeRequest function. The code for this function is found in Fig. 8-5. To submit a request to the queue, the application needs to get the queue's bindery object ID by making the GetBinderyObjectID call and passing in the name and type of the call.

The job control structure requires the client to fill in the target server ID, the execution time, the job type, the job control flags, the job description string, and the appropriate information in the client record area.

The serverObjectID we obtained from the GetConnectionInformation table is in low-high word order and must be swapped to be placed in the structure in high-low word order. The object ID for a remote server can be obtained by getting a connection list from the server and making the GetConnectionInformation call for each entry until one with the right bindery object type is found. Another way to locate the server is to scan the bindery for objects of the server type the application has registered. When the object is found, a call can be made to get the connection numbers for that bindery object, then the GetConnectionInformation call can be made. If the client wants any

Sample code for filling in the job control structure and creating a queue job.

Figure 8-5

```
void FillInQueueJobAndMakeRequest (void)
{
    /*-- Here we need to get the queue ID of the queue which
         is in the global variable szQName.  Then we need to
         fill in the JobStruct structure with the required
         parameters.  Once this is done, we can submit the
         queue job by calling CreateQueueJobAndFile.  --*/

    ccode = GetBinderyObjectID (szQName, OT_JOB_QUEUE, &qID);

    /*-- Fill in the structure fields needed. --*/
    job.targetServerIDNumber = LongSwap(jobServerObjID);
    *(DWORD *)&job.targetExecutionTime[0] = 0xFFFFFFFF;
    *(WORD *)&job.targetExecutionTime[4] = 0xFFFF;

    /*-- Let's fill in the type as EMPLOYEE_JOB_TYPE, 99.
         This is just a random number that we will have our
         application recognize. --*/
    job.jobType = EMPLOYEE_JOB_TYPE;
    job.jobControlFlags = 0;
    lstrcpy (job.textJobDescription, "Employee Info Request");
    memset (job.clientRecordArea, 0, 152);

    CreateQueueJobAndFile (qID, &job, &dosFileHandle);
}
```

available server to process the queue job, it should set the server object ID field in the job control structure to 0xFFFFFFFF (−1).

The job execution time can be used to delay the processing of the job until a later time. An example of when this might be useful is for backup jobs serviced by backup servers. These jobs usually are run at night. A backup service that implements a QMS request interface allows the user to schedule a job and go home rather than waiting until the appropriate time. If the client software wants the job to be serviced as soon as possible, all six bytes of this field should be set to 0xFF.

The job type field in the job control structure specifies the type of job. When the queue server checks the queue for jobs, it specifies the job type that must correspond to this value. If this value is placed in the structure swapped, then the server code is not required to swap it. If this value is placed directly in the structure, as is done in the sample code, then the server code must use it in swapped format.

The job control flags indicate the state of the job. These flags indicate if the job is on hold by the system or on hold by the user. Other bits indicate if the job should autostart or has been restarted by the server and whether it is open and being processed.

The job description string is simply a text string set by the client to describe the job. This field can be set to a zero length string if no description is desired.

The client record area is a small data buffer that can be used to specify processing parameters for the queue server such as the path to the source file to process or client mapping information.

Once the job control structure is initialized, the sample in Fig. 8-5 calls CreateQueueJobAndFile function. This function creates an entry in the queue and opens the queue file. The handle to the queue file is returned to the application and can be used to write the information necessary for the job. A print or fax server would write the binary data to be sent to the printer or the fax in the queue file. A backup server might specify files and directories to be backed up in the queue file. The contents of the queue file are highly specific to the application. The sample application uses the AddRequestToFile and WriteFileAndSubmit functions (Fig. 8-6) to write the necessary information into the queue file.

Once the information has been written to the queue file, the WriteFileAndSubmit function calls CloseFileAndStartQueueJob to close the queue file and to leave it ready to be processed by a server.

Getting results

Once the queue job has been processed, the client application needs to know the results. If the server is providing a service that consists of moving data to another location such as a printer, a fax, or a tape backup system, then notification of job completion or error is a sufficient result for the user. If the data is to be returned to the user, the options outlined in the "Returning the information" section of this chapter should be used.

Adding to the queue file and submitting it for processing.   Figure 8-6

```
void WriteToFileAndSubmit (void)
{
    WORD wBytes;
    int  writeErr;

    /*-- Write it to the file. --*/
    wBytes = lstrlen (szRequest);
    writeErr = _lwrite (dosFileHandle, szRequest, wBytes);
    if (writeErr == -1)
        wsprintf (errMsg, "Couldn't write to file.");

    /*-- Now we are ready to send the request on its way. --*/
    CloseFileAndStartQueueJob (qID, job.jobNumber,
        dosFileHandle);
}

void AddRequestToFile (void)
{
    wsprintf (szRequest, "%d", request);
    lstrcat (szRequest, ">");
    lstrcat (szRequest, dbFileName);
    lstrcat (szRequest, ">");
}
```

The sample application sends the DISPLAY_LIST_MSG to the main message loop when the job is complete. This message case then displays the information retrieved by the job server. The sample code for handling this message can be found in Fig. 8-7.

QMS is an excellent method for creating scheduled value-added client-server applications on the network. The best uses of QMS consist of moving data from one location to another in a background rather than a real-time environment. QMS services can greatly simplify the work done by a developer to distribute processing on the network, leaving him or her free to increase the value and features of the service being provided.

Figure 8-7   *The code for processing a response from the job server.*

```
case DISPLAY_LIST_MSG:
    GetClientRect(hwnd, (LPRECT) &rect);
    hwndList = CreateWindow ("listbox", NULL,
            WS_CHILD | WS_VISIBLE | LBS_STANDARD,
            CW_USEDEFAULT,
            CW_USEDEFAULT,
            (rect.right-rect.left),
            (rect.bottom-rect.top),
            hwnd, IDC_LIST, hInstance, NULL) ;

    for (i=0; i<maxNames; i++)
        SendMessage (hwndList, LB_ADDSTRING, (WORD)0,
                (LONG)&displayBuf[i*50]) ;
    break;
```

Introduction to print
server services

THIS chapter is intended to introduce you to the print server and its functionality. A general understanding of the SPX communications is helpful. The communication protocols IPX and SPX are discussed in chapters 11 through 14.

Print servers

What is a print server? A *print server* is a software program in the form of an NLM (NetWare Loadable Module), a VAP (Value Added Process), or an EXE (Executable) that allows a file server or dedicated workstation to be capable of offering information about a printer. The program that provides these services is called PSERVER.NLM, PSERVER.VAP, or PSERVER.EXE. The NLM version can run on NetWare 3.*x* file servers, and the VAP version can be run on NetWare 2.*x* file servers. The PSERVER.EXE can be run at a workstation that is dedicated to being a print server. We will refer to this program as PSERVER for simplicity.

Loading a print server

PSERVER allows workstations to access and manipulate information about the print server, print queue jobs, and the printer itself. PSERVER is loaded on a file server at the console by typing LOAD PSERVER <Print Server Name> for a file server running a 3.*x* version of the operating system. If the file server is running NetWare 2.*x*, then the PSERVER.VAP should have been copied into the SYS:SYSTEM directory during the installation of NetWare. When you boot the file server, it will search this directory and prompt you to load the VAPs that it found in that directory. You would type Y to load the PSERVER.VAP. The print server name is the name of the print server that you previously have attached using PCONSOLE or the APIs.

Remote printing

Another program that is available with NetWare is RPRINTER.EXE. This is a TSR (Terminate and Stay Resident) program that allows you

to have a printer connected to a workstation rather than a file server (hence the name RPRINTER stands for *remote printer*). One reason that RPRINTER.EXE might be used is so that a printer can be set up in a location other than at the file server. This way if the file server wasn't located in a convenient spot for getting printouts, then you could use RPRINTER and have your printer attached to a workstation that is more strategically located. Another reason to use RPRINTER is to reduce the traffic on the file server.

⇨ Writing your own PCONSOLE utility

A lot of the functionality that is provided in the PCONSOLE utility can be found in the Print Server Services of the NetWare C Interface for DOS and/or Windows. The DOS version consists of a set of libraries containing API (Applications Programming Interfaces) functions. The libraries are named (x)NIT.LIB where (x) refers to the model of the library (i.e., (S)mall, (M)edium, (L)arge, (C)ompact). Under the Windows environment, the same functionality is provided by a set of DLLs (Dynamic Link Libraries) and a set of LIBs (Libraries).

Because the DLLs are divided into service groups, the ones needed for the Print Server Services are NWIPXSPX.DLL, which provides the IPX/SPX functionality that is needed to access the print server, and NWPSERV.DLL, which contains all of the print server functions. Many times an application might want to combine the services provided by the Print Services and Queue Services with the Print Server Services and, therefore, also might need the NWNETAPI.DLL. While there might be some overlap in the functionality of the Print Services and the Print Server Services, there also are many differences. I'll try to list the similarities and differences in the following sections.

 # Print Services

The Print Services provide an application running on a workstation with a means of capturing data and redirecting it from a local LPT device to a file server's printer or to a file on the network. There are a few functions that will let an application get information about a printer such as its status, whether the printer is stopped or offline, and what type of form the printer is expecting. This information can be obtained by making a call to the API function, GetPrinterStatus, and passing the printer number as the first parameter. The printer number can be determined by making a function call to GetDefaultCaptureFlags that will return the capture flags for the default LPT device.

One of the fields returned is the printer number. The queueID, as we will refer to it, is the bindery object ID of the print queue. This is a 32-bit number that uniquely identifies an object within the bindery. The queueID of the queue that is servicing a printer can be obtained by calling GetPrinterQueue with the printer number as the first parameter. Even though these services provide some general information about a printer and its queue, the print services are more concerned with capturing of data. Now for the Print Server Services.

 # Print Server Services

The Print Server Services provide an application with the tools necessary to control the printer and print server as well as get information about the printer and print server. A list of the functions available through the Print Server Services and their ordinal values are listed in Table 9-1.

The print server services use the SPX protocol to communicate with the print server. For an application to access information about the print server, it first must attach and login to the print server. There are two function calls that do not require the application to login to the print server—PSGetPrintServerInfo and PSAttachToPrintServer—but these APIs return only limited information about the print server.

The Print Server Services and their ordinal values   Table 9-1

Function name	Ordinal value
PSAbortPrintJob	@4
PSAddNotifyObject	@5
PSAddQueueToPrinter	@6
PSAttachPrintServerToFileServer	@7
PSAttachToPrintServer	@8
PSCancelDownRequest	@9
PSChangeNotifyInterval	@10
PSChangeQueuePriority	@11
PSChangeServiceMode	@12
PSDeleteNotifyObject	@13
PSDeleteQueueFromPrinter	@14
PSDetachFromPrintServer	@15
PSDetachPrtServerFromFileServer	@16
PSDownPrintServer	@17
PSEjectForm	@18
PSGetAttachedServers	@19
PSGetNextRemotePrinter	@20
PSGetNotifyObject	@21
PSGetPrintersServicingQueue	@22
PSGetPrinterStatus	@23
PSGetPrintJobStatus	@24
PSGetPrintServerInfo	@25
PSGetQueuesServiced	@26
PSLoginToPrintServer	@27
PSMarkTopOfForm	@28
PSRequestRemotePrinter	@29
PSRewindPrintJob	@30
PSSetMountedForm	@31

Table 9-1	Continued
PSSetRemoteMode	@32
PSStartPrinter	@33
PSStopPrinter	@34

Novell, Inc.

For any detailed information, the application needs to make calls to both the attach and login functions mentioned earlier.

 # Print Server Services & Sequenced Packet Exchange (SPX)

The PSAttachToPrintServer function initializes SPX by calling SPXInitialize. This ensures that SPX is installed on that workstation. It gets the net address of the print server, then creates a connection with the print server by calling SPXEstablishConnection. After the initialization is completed, an SPX connection ID is returned to the application. This SPX connection ID is needed in every print server function call thereafter. For more information on the SPX connection ID, refer to chapter 13, "Sequenced packet exchange." As you can see in Fig. 9-1, we have established an SPX connection with the print server. All of the print server APIs are based on this connection. If the connection cannot be completed, an error will be returned by the PSAttachToPrintServer function.

Table 9-2 lists some common return codes associated with the print server APIs. Once you have established the SPX connection with the print server and have logged into it, you are ready to manipulate (if you are a bindery equivalent to an OPERATOR) or monitor (if you have USER equivalent rights) the print server and its attached printers.

Figure 9-1

Establish an SPX
connection with
the print server

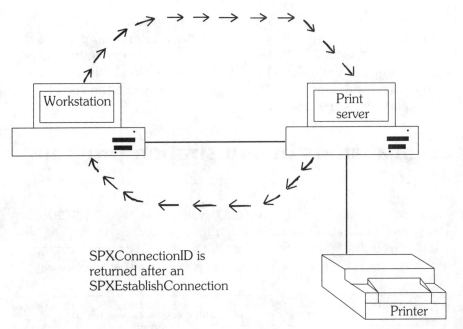

SPXConnectionID is
returned after an
SPXEstablishConnection

Attaching to a print server.

The common print server services return codes

Table 9-2

0x0000	SUCCESSFUL
0x0113	PSE_ACCESS_DENIED
0x00ED	SPX_CONNECTION_TERMINATED
0x0302	PSE_NO_SUCH_PRINTER
0x0307	PSE_NOT_CONNECTED
0x030A	PSE_NOT_ATTACHED_TO_SERVER
0x030E	PSE_NO_RIGHTS

Novell, Inc.

→ Setting up a print server, printers, & print queues

This next section describes the steps necessary to install PSERVER on your file server as well as how to set up the printers and print queues from within PCONSOLE. It uses DOS as the environment because there is no equivalent utility to PCONSOLE for Windows. After we step through this process, we can discuss how to use the APIs to accomplish the same results.

→ Logical steps demonstrating program logic

✳ **Step 1**   Run PCONSOLE from your workstation: type PCONSOLE and press Enter. Select Change Current File Server, and select the file server that you want to add a print server to. For this discussion, we'll use the name THE_SERVER to represent that file server. See Fig. 9-2

Figure 9-2

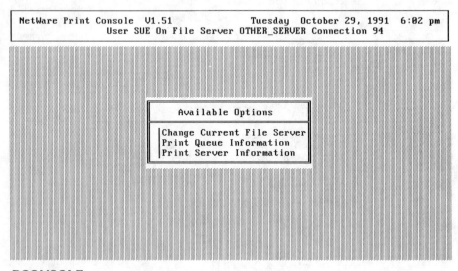

```
NetWare Print Console  V1.51              Tuesday  October 29, 1991  6:02 pm
             User SUE On File Server OTHER_SERVER Connection 94
```

```
                        Available Options
                 Change Current File Server
                 Print Queue Information
                 Print Server Information
```

PCONSOLE. Novell, Inc.

✳ **Step 2**   Select `Print Server Information`. A list of print servers, or an empty list if no print servers have been added, will be displayed. To add a new print server to this list press Ins, type in the name of the print server that you want to add, and press Enter. In this example, we will use the name "EXAMPLE_SERVER." Select EXAMPLE_SERVER (Fig. 9-3).

Figure 9-3

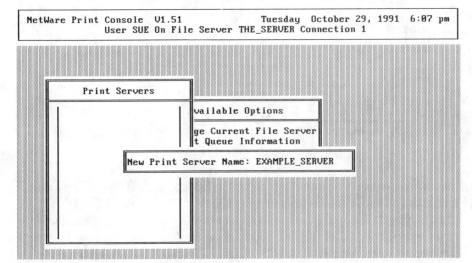

```
NetWare Print Console  V1.51              Tuesday  October 29, 1991  6:07 pm
                  User SUE On File Server THE_SERVER Connection 1
```

```
         Print Servers
                                    vailable Options
                                  ge Current File Server
                                  t Queue Information
                    New Print Server Name: EXAMPLE_SERVER
```

Print Server Information. Novell, Inc.

✳ **Step 3**   Select `Print Server Configuration`. Select `File Servers To Be Serviced`. This displays the file servers that the selected print server will service. Because we have just added a new print server, there won't be any file servers listed except for the file server that we created the print server on. To add a file server to this list, press Ins. A list of available file servers will be displayed. Select the file server that you want the EXAMPLE_SERVER to service (i.e., which file server has print queues that you want your newly created print server to service). See Fig. 9-4.

✳ **Step 4**   Press Esc to back up to the Print Server Configuration Menu, and select `Printer Configuration`. A list of configured printers appears. If none are installed and you want to add one, select a "Not Installed" printer. A Printer *X* (where *X* is the printer number) configuration menu will appear. Type in the name of the printer queue or a name that is

Figure 9-4

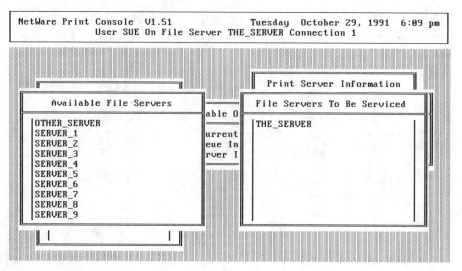

```
NetWare Print Console  V1.51              Tuesday  October 29, 1991  6:09 pm
                 User SUE On File Server THE_SERVER Connection 1
```

The file server that the print server is to service. Novell, Inc.

meaningful to you (for instance, HPLaser, Epson, or OTC). We'll use the
name Example_Queue for this example. Select `Type`. A list of defined
printer types will appear. Select the appropriate type. You can change
other information on this menu if you need to. After you have set up your
printer, press Esc and save your changes. Your new print queue name
"Example_Queue" now will appear as a configured printer. See Fig. 9-5.

Figure 9-5

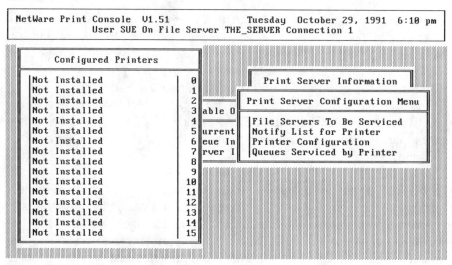

```
NetWare Print Console  V1.51              Tuesday  October 29, 1991  6:10 pm
                 User SUE On File Server THE_SERVER Connection 1
```

Printer Configuration. Novell, Inc.

❋ **Step 5**   Press Esc to back up to Available Options, and select `Print Queue Information`. A list of print queues will appear. If a new print queue is needed, press Ins, type the name of a queue, and press Enter. We'll use the name Example_Queue. See Fig. 9-6.

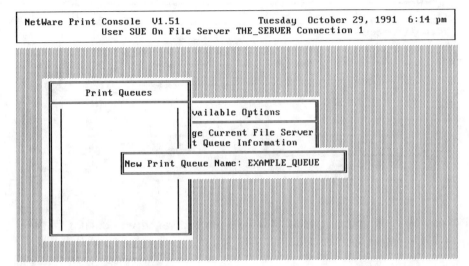

Figure 9-6

Adding a new print queue. <small>Novell, Inc.</small>

❋ **Step 6**   Select the newly created queue (Example_Queue), then select `Queue Servers` and press Ins to get a list of queue server candidates. Next, select the EXAMPLE_SERVER print server that you set up in step 2.

❋ **Step 7**   Press Esc back up to Available Options, and select `Print Server Information`. Select the print server, EXAMPLE_SERVER, which you set up in step 2. Select `Print Server Configuration`.

❋ **Step 8**   Select `Queues Serviced By Printer`. Example_Queue should appear in the Defined Printer list. Select `Example_Queue`. A menu with the `File Server`, `Queue`, and `Priority` is displayed. Press Ins to get a list of the available queues. Select the queue that you created previously—Example_Queue. A Priority box appears. You can change your priority now or, if you decide to change it later, you can do so then. After typing the priority, you want press Enter to add this queue to your list of queues to be serviced. See Fig. 9-7.

Figure 9-7

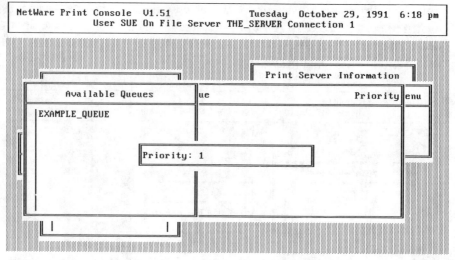

```
NetWare Print Console  V1.51          Tuesday  October 29, 1991  6:18 pm
              User SUE On File Server THE_SERVER Connection 1
```

```
                                      ┌─ Print Server Information ─┐
    ┌──────────────────────┐ ┌────────────────────────────────────┤
    │   Available Queues    │ │ue                        Priority│enu
    │ EXAMPLE_QUEUE         │ │                                   │
    │                      │ └──────────────────────────────────┘
    │              ┌────────────────────────────┐
    │              │ Priority: 1                │
    │              └────────────────────────────┘
    │
    └──────────────────────┘
```

Q Priority. Novell, Inc.

❋ **Step 9**   If you are planning have a print server service queues that are on file servers other than the one that the print server was added to, then continue with the remaining steps in this section. Otherwise, go to step 21.

❋ **Step 10**   Press Esc back up to Available Options, and select `Change Current File Server` (Fig. 9-8). Select the file server that has the print queue that you want EXAMPLE_SERVER to service.

❋ **Step 11**   Select `Print Server Information`. Because the print server EXAMPLE_SERVER was just added, it shouldn't be in the list of print servers for the selected file server. Let's let the file server selected be named OTHER_SERVER for convenience. Press Ins, type EXAMPLE_SERVER, and press Enter. See Fig. 9-9.

❋ **Step 12**   Select EXAMPLE_SERVER. Select `Print Server Configuration`. Select `File Servers To Be Serviced`. Press Ins, and SELECT the file server that you added the print server to (THE_SERVER).

❋ **Step 13**   Press Esc to back up to the Print Server Configuration menu. Select `Printer Configuration`. No printers should be configured, so press Enter on a "Not Installed" printer. Type the name of the print

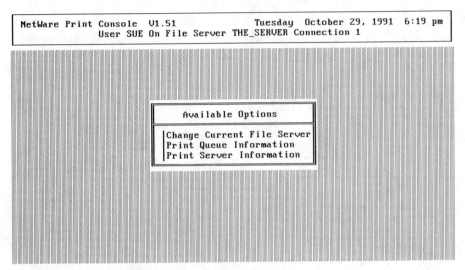

Change current file server. Novell, Inc.

Figure 9-8

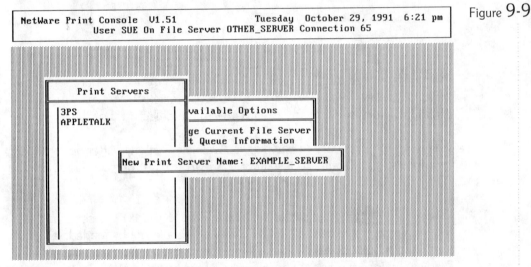

Adding a new print server to the available list. Novell, Inc.

Figure 9-9

queue on the OTHER_SERVER that you want EXAMPLE_SERVER to service. We'll use Other_Queue for this example. Repeat step 4 for Other_Queue.

✻ **Step 14**   Now, if you look under the Print Server Configuration menu and select Queues Serviced By Printer, Other_Queue should appear in the list. See Fig. 9-10.

Figure 9-10

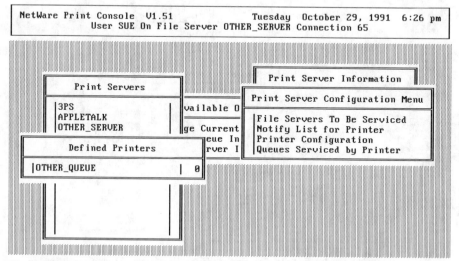

Defined Printers. Novell, Inc.

✻ **Step 15**   Press Esc to back up to the Print Server Configuration menu. Select Queues Serviced By Printer, select Other_Queue. Press Ins. Next, select Other_Queue again. Select Priority.

✻ **Step 16**   Press Esc to back up to Available Options. After doing the previous steps, it's time to install the PSERVER.NLM on your file server. The following paragraph explains how.

✻ **Step 17**   At the file server's console, type MONITOR to see what NLMs already have been loaded. PSERVER should not be loaded. If it is, that means that you already have a print server loaded on that file server. You can unload the one that is already loaded by typing UNLOAD PSERVER and pressing Enter. This will remove the print server that currently is loaded. After this, you will type LOAD SYS:PSERVER EXAMPLE_SERVER and press Enter. This will load the print server NLM and tell it that the name of the Print Server is EXAMPLE_SERVER.

✳ **Step 18**   After you have loaded PSERVER, switch to the console display by pressing Alt–Esc until you find that window. Now, type the following command using the generic form: SPOOL *<Printer Number>* TO QUEUE *<Queue Name>*.

```
SPOOL 0 TO QUEUE Example_Queue
```

This sets up your print server and file server so that it recognizes the name Example_Queue when used by the APIs.

✳ **Step 19**   Now, go back to your workstation. Select Print Server Information, then select EXAMPLE_SERVER. Next, select Print Server Status/Control followed by Queues Serviced By Printer. See Fig. 9-11. Finally, select Example_Queue.

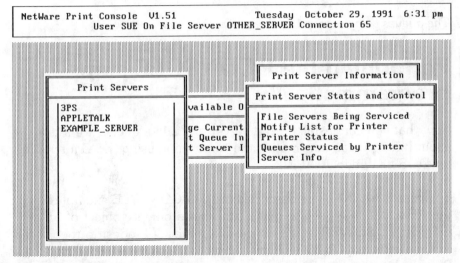

Figure 9-11

Print Server Status and Control. Novell, Inc.

✳ **Step 20**   You can see that there are two queues being serviced by the one printer Example_Queue. The queues are Example_Queue and Other_Queue. See Fig. 9-12.

✳ **Step 21**   You can follow steps 18 and 19 to load the print server on your file server. At this point, you should have successfully installed a print server, added a queue, configured a printer, and loaded PSERVER on your file server.

Figure 9-12

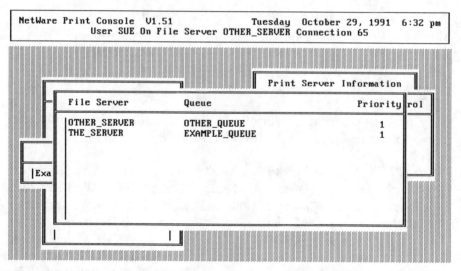

```
NetWare Print Console   V1.51              Tuesday  October 29, 1991  6:32 pm
                  User SUE On File Server OTHER_SERVER Connection 65


                                        Print Server Information

   File Server          Queue                        Priority rol

   OTHER_SERVER         OTHER_QUEUE                       1
   THE_SERVER           EXAMPLE_QUEUE                     1



Exa
```

The queues being serviced by one printer. Novell, Inc.

 # Performing the PCONSOLE steps programmatically

Now that you can install a print server and add a queue, we'll talk about how you can accomplish the same thing using the C Interface for DOS or Windows APIs.

To accomplish the steps described in the PCONSOLE example using the APIs, you first need to make sure that a bindery object of type OT_PRINT_SERVER exists on the file server. If it doesn't, then a call to CreateBinderyObject will have to be made to create the Print Server object:

```
CreateBinderyObject ("EXAMPLE_PSERVER", OT_PRINT_SERVER,
                     BF_STATIC, 0x31);
```

Next, you need to attach to the print server to get an SPX connection ID. This is accomplished with a call to PSAttachToPrintServer. One thing to keep in mind is that you must be attached to the file server that the print server is attached to and make sure that our preferred NCP connection ID is set. To do this, you attach and login to the file

154

server if you aren't already connected, then set our preferred NCP connection ID to the server that is running the print server. See the example code in Fig. 9-13.

Sample code for attaching to the file server and the print server.   Figure 9-13

```
/*--  Attach to file server and then login to it --*/
ccode = AttachToFileServer ("FILE_SERVER", &serverConnectionID);

/*-- Note:  the serverConnectionID above is NOT the same as the one that is
            returned from PSAttachToPrintServer call below. --*/
LoginToFileServer ("PSOPERATOR", OT_USER, "password");

/*-- Get the connection id of the file server that has the
     print server on it --*/
GetConnectionID ("FILE_SERVER", &psServerConnectionID);

/*-- Save the connection id that we are using currently --*/
oldServerConnectionID = GetPreferredConnectionID ();
SetPreferredConnectionID (psServerConnectionID);
PSAttachToPrintServer ("EXAMPLE_PSERVER", &spxConnectionID);
```

Now, log in to the print server using the PSLoginToPrintServer function call:

```
PSLoginToPrintServer (spxConnectionID, &accessLevel);
```

You will want to add a file server to the list of file servers that will be serviced by the print server. To do this, you should use the function call PSAttachPrintServerToFileServer. To get a list of the print queues as in step 5, a call to ScanBinderyObject until no more objects exist can give this information. To get a list of the print queues like in step 8, a series of calls to PSGetQueuesServiced will return this information. See the example code in Fig. 9-14.

In the next chapter, we will look at an example of how to use the print server functions in an application that scans the printer and gives the status of the jobs in the queue, how much of the job is finished, if the printer is off-line, and other useful statistics.

155

Figure 9-14   *Sample code for getting a list of print queues.*

```
WORD spxConnectionID;        //  Got this from PSAttachToPrintServer
BYTE printerNumber = 0;      //  Start with 0
WORD sequence=0;             //  Start with 0, will be incremented
                             //  automatically.
char fileServer[48];         //  Queue returned is on this file server
char queueName[48];          //  Name of queue being serviced
BYTE priority;               //  The priority of the queue 1-8

do
    {
    ccode = PSGetQueuesServiced (spxConnectionID,
            printerNumber, &sequence, fileServer, queueName,
            &priority);
    /*-- Display the fileServer, queueName, and priority --*/
    } while (!ccode);
```

Details on the Print Server APIs under Windows

CHAPTER 10

THIS chapter discusses how to use the Print Server APIs in a programming environment. We will clip code fragments from a larger program while describing what we are doing. The completed program is provided in the appendix and on the enclosed disk.

This program focuses on getting information from the print server and displaying it in an easy to read window. There are numerous ways to enhance the program for more information, features, and functionality. However, this program does show how to use many of the APIs in the Print Server Services and some Print Services functions.

Communicating with print servers

The general idea of the program is to establish a connection with the print server and retrieve statistics from it. Once this has been done, the information is displayed on the screen. Sounds simple enough right? First, let's look at the declarations and definitions used at the top of the program.

Include files

The include files in Fig. 10-1 are needed for the functions used in this program. The include files that are part of the C Interface-Windows SDK are NWBINDRY.H, NITQ.H, NPT.H, and NWPRINT.H. The TEMP.H file is one that defines a slightly different structure for the job structure used in many of the print server functions. It has been changed slightly for this program so that it will be easy to get the information from the structure. We will examine this structure more closely a little later. The next include file is PS.H, which is one that was created for this program. It contains definitions for the windows routines and windows that are created with this program.

The include files for the print server application.

Figure 10-1

```
#include <windows.h>
#include <stdio.h>
#include <stdlib.h>
#include <string.h>
#include <direct.h>
#include <sys\types.h>
#include <nwbindry.h>
#include <nitq.h>
#include <npt.h>
#include <nwprint.h>
#include <temp.h>
#include "ps.h"
```

⇨ Definitions

Next, in Fig. 10-2, we have definitions that are used throughout this example program.

Global application definitions.

Figure 10-2

```
#ifndef TRUE
        #define  TRUE  1
#endif
#ifndef FALSE
        #define  FALSE 0
#endif

#define  ESCAPE_KEY            0x1B
#define  GET_STATUS_TIMER      1
#define  TWO_SECONDS           2000
#define  MAX_JOBS              20
#define  MAX_JOBANDNAME        30
#define  MAXPATH               120
#define  MAX_MESSAGES          100
```

The definitions in Fig. 10-3 are the message values used to send messages to and to get messages from the message loop. Each value corresponds to a specific task within the program. The program is initialized when we receive the INITIALIZE_PS_MSG. We get the status of the print server when we receive the second message and display various information when the DISPLAY messages are received.

Figure 10-3   *Message definitions.*

```
#define INITIALIZE_PS_MSG         ( WM_USER + 1  )
#define GET_STATUS_MSG            ( WM_USER + 2  )
#define DISPLAY_STATUS_MSG        ( WM_USER + 4  )
#define DISPLAY_JOB_ACTIVE_MSG    ( WM_USER + 5  )
#define DISPLAY_PRINTERNAME_MSG   ( WM_USER + 6  )
#define DISPLAY_TROUBLE_MSG       ( WM_USER + 7  )
#define DISPLAY_ACTIVE_MSG        ( WM_USER + 8  )
#define DISPLAY_QUEUENAME_MSG     ( WM_USER + 9  )
#define DISPLAY_JOBNAME_MSG       ( WM_USER + 10 )
#define DISPLAY_JOBNUMBER_MSG     ( WM_USER + 11 )
#define DISPLAY_COPY_MSG          ( WM_USER + 12 )
#define DISPLAY_PERCENT_MSG       ( WM_USER + 13 )
#define CLEANUP_MSG               ( WM_USER + 14 )
#define LIST_JOB_NAMES_MSG        ( WM_USER + 15 )
#define NOTIFY_MSG                ( WM_USER + 16 )
```

⇨ Global variables

After the definitions, we declare variables that are used in Windows specific functions. These variables are shown in Fig. 10-4.

Figure 10-4   *Variable declarations for inter-window communication.*

```
MSG      msg ;
HWND     parentInstance;
HWND     hButton;
HWND     hParent;
HWND     hwndList, hwndText;
char     buf[25];
```

There are many variables that are used in the creation and painting of the parent windows and their children. These variables are found in Fig. 10-5.

We need variables to be used in displaying the text in the button window. This is the window with the status of the current print job:

```
int nWidth, nHeight;
int nMaxLines, nLineSpace, nCenterX, nCenterY;
```

We also have a number of global variables that the JOBSTAT program needs. These are variables related to the APIs.

```
int ch;
BYTE text;
.

.
char notifyMsg[50];
WORD oldJobNumber, jobNumber;
```

Windows variables declared.   Figure 10-5

```
HDC             hdc;        // Handle to the device context
PAINTSTRUCT     ps;         // Paint structure
TEXTMETRIC      tm;         // TextMetric structure
RECT            clientRect, windowRect, statRect;
int             clientHorzPix, clientVertPix;
int             jobWndWidth, jobWndHeight, statWndWidth;
int             jobX, jobY, statX, statY, xSeparator, leftover;
short int       charHeight;
int             rectX1, rectY1, rectX2, rectY2;
int             xx, yy;
int             textX, textY;
int             len;
char            errorMsg[50];
BOOL            bChangeColor;
DWORD           lColor;
```

⇨ The WinMain function

Once we have our global variables and definitions completed, we
finally get to the WinMain function! The WinMain function is for
Windows what the main function is for a DOS program. It is the first
function in the application to be called by the Windows operating
environment. Windows provides information to the application
through the WinMain function. This information includes the
HANDLE to the current instance running and the HANDLE to the
previous instance, if there is one, as well as a pointer to the
command line. The declaration and beginning of our WinMain can be
found in Fig. 10-6.

The WinMain is where we set up all the window definitions and
information necessary to run our program. We want to get some
information from the user such as the print server's name, the file
server's name, and which printer (number) the user wants to monitor.
To do this, we use some of the standard C functions along with some

Figure 10-6   *WinMain and message queue variable declarations.*

```
int PASCAL WinMain (HANDLE hInstance, HANDLE hPrevInstance, LPSTR lpszCmdLine,
         int nCmdShow)
{
         static char szAppName [] = "JOBSTAT" ;
         WNDCLASS  wndclass ;
         BOOL      bQueueCreated;
         int       sizeOfQueue;
```

Windows-specific functions to read the environment, then parse out
the information needed. The code for doing this is found in Fig. 10-7.

We then initialize our old job number and current job number to be
zero. This is done so that we can later check against each other:

```
         oldJobNumber = jobNumber = 0;
```

Figure 10-7   *Getting the environment information.*

```
lstrcpy (environment, lpszCmdLine);
PSNamePtr =  strtok (environment, ";");
serverNamePtr = strtok (NULL, ";");
pPtr =  strtok (NULL, ";");
lstrcpy (PSName, PSNamePtr);
lstrcpy (serverName, serverNamePtr);
p = (BYTE)atoi (pPtr);
```

We increase the size of the message queue because the default size is
8. We do this because we will be posting a lot of messages. This is a
good practice for all Windows applications. Increasing the size of the
message queue must be done in the loop shown in Fig. 10-8. When
The SetMessageQueue function is called, it deletes the message
queue, then tries to create a new one of the new size. A Windows
application can't run without a message queue, so the largest one
possible is created.

As with other Windows programs, in the WinMain, we register the
class, then create the window. We accomplish this through specifying
the information in the window class structure and making a call to
RegisterClass. Code demonstrating how this is done can be viewed in
Fig. 10-9. After the class is registered, we can create our main
window with our menu. Then, we create and display the main
window. This code is demonstrated in Fig. 10-10.

Increasing the size of the message queue.

Figure 10-8

```
sizeOfQueue = MAX_MESSAGES;
while( ( sizeOfQueue > 0 ) && ( !bQueueCreated ) )
        {
        bQueueCreated = SetMessageQueue( sizeOfQueue );
        sizeOfQueue—;
        }
if( sizeOfQueue == 0 )
        return( NULL );
```

Registering application windows.

Figure 10-9

```
parentInstance = hInstance;
if (!hPrevInstance)
    {
    wndclass.style          = CS_HREDRAW | CS_VREDRAW;
    wndclass.lpfnWndProc    = WndProc;
    wndclass.cbClsExtra     = 0;
    wndclass.cbWndExtra     = 0;
    wndclass.hInstance      = hInstance;
    wndclass.hIcon          = LoadIcon (NULL, IDI_APPLICATION);
    wndclass.hCursor        = LoadCursor (NULL, IDC_ARROW);
    wndclass.hbrBackground  = COLOR_WINDOW + 1;
    wndclass.lpszMenuName   = szAppName;
    wndclass.lpszClassName  = szAppName;

    if (!RegisterClass (&wndclass))
        return FALSE ;
    }

hParent = CreateWindow (
    szAppName,              // window class name
    "Job Status",           // window caption
    WS_OVERLAPPEDWINDOW |
    WS_CLIPCHILDREN,        // window style
    CW_USEDEFAULT ,         // initial x position
    CW_USEDEFAULT ,         // initial y position
    CW_USEDEFAULT ,         // initial x size
    CW_USEDEFAULT ,         // initial y size
    NULL,                   // parent window handle
    NULL,                   // window menu handle
    hInstance,              // program instance handle
    NULL);                  // create parameters
```

⇨ The WndProc function

When we register the window class, we specify which function will process our messages. That is the WndProc procedure. The WndProc procedure takes care of any selected menu items. It also provides a

Figure 10-10   *Displaying the application window.*

```
ShowWindow (hParent, nCmdShow) ;
 UpdateWindow (hParent) ;

while (GetMessage (&msg, NULL, 0, 0))
       {
       TranslateMessage (&msg);
       DispatchMessage (&msg);
       }

 return (msg.wParam);
}
```

place for us to trap any user-defined messages such as the ones
defined at the top of this program. WndProc decides what functions
to call based on the message that it gets. Let's take a closer look at
the code in Fig. 10-11.

Figure 10-11   *WndProc and the message switch statement.*

```
Long FAR PASCAL WndProc (HWND hParent, unsigned iMessage,
    WORD wParam, LONG lParam)
{
    static FARPROC    lpfnAboutDlgProc;
    static FARPROC    lpfnNotifyDlgProc;
    static int        width, height;
    char              buffer[85];

    switch (iMessage)
            {
            case WM_CREATE :
                hdc = GetDC (hParent);
                SelectObject (hdc,
                GetStockObject (SYSTEM_FIXED_FONT));
                GetTextMetrics (hdc, &tm);
                ReleaseDC (hParent, hdc);
```

Because the WM_CREATE is the first message the Windows
procedure receives, it is a good place to put any type of initialization
routines. In our example, we get the text metrics and create two
windows. We then post an INITIALIZE_PS_MSG to the parent
window. Next, we are getting the window dimensions of our parent.
This is so that we know how big to make our child windows. Take a
look at the code in Fig. 10-12.

Creating child windows.   Figure 10-12

```
GetParentDimensions (hParent);

    hwndList = CreateWindow (
            "listbox",
            "Jobs In Queue",
            WS_CHILDWINDOW | WS_VISIBLE | LBS_STANDARD |
            WS_CAPTION | LBS_WANTKEYBOARDINPUT,
            jobX,            // X coordinate for listbox
            jobY,            // Y coordinate for listbox
            jobWndWidth,     // Width of listbox child window
            jobWndHeight,    // Height of listbox child window
            hParent,         // Handle of the parent window
            IDC_LISTBOX,     // ID of the listbox in jobstat.h
            GetWindowWord (hParent, GWW_HINSTANCE),
            NULL);

    hwndText = CreateWindow (
            "static",
            NULL,
            WS_CHILDWINDOW | WS_VISIBLE | SS_CENTER |
            WS_CAPTION,
            statX,           // X coordinate for status box
            jobY,            // Y coordinate for status box
            statWndWidth,    // Width of static child window
            jobWndHeight,    // Height of static child window
            hParent,         // Handle of the parent window
    IDC_STATUSBOX, // ID of the listbox in jobstat.h
    GetWindowWord (hParent, GWW_HINSTANCE),
    NULL);

SetWindowText (hwndText, "Status");
GetStatusBoxCenter ();
PostMessage (hParent, INITIALIZE_PS_MSG, wParam, lParam);
return (0);
  .
  .
  .
```

We trap for a WM_TIMER message every TWO_SECONDS so that
we can update our status of the print job. When we trap it, we then
post another message to tell the program to get the status again. By
using a timer, we can avoid getting into an infinite loop. Because
Windows is nonpreemptive, we cannot use a do (forever) loop. It will
hang your machine:

```
case WM_TIMER :
    PostMessage (hParent, GET_STATUS_MSG, NULL, (DWORD) NULL);
    break;
```

In the initialize message, we find out what the connection ID of the server that our user is interested in is. Then, we store the original connectionID in oldConnID so that we can restore it when the user is finished. Next, we change our preferred connection ID so that we will be getting information from the correct file server:

```
case INITIALIZE_PS_MSG :
        ccode = GetConnectionID (serverName, &newConnID);
        oldConnID = GetPreferredConnectionID ();
        SetPreferredConnectionID (newConnID);
```

Now, we need to attach to the print server by making the call in Fig. 10-13.

Figure 10-13   *Attaching to the print server.*

```
ccode = PSAttachToPrintServer (PSName, &SPXConnection);
if (ccode)
    {
    MessageBox (hParent,
            (LPSTR)"Cannot Attach To Print Server",
            (LPSTR)"ERROR", MB_OK);
    PostQuitMessage (0);
    }
```

If we successfully attach to the print server, we then try to login to it. This will allow us to get more than just minimal information from the print server. It returns the user's access in pAccess. If there is an error, we display the error message or code, then we quit the application. How to do this is illustrated in the code in Fig. 10-14. If we are successful, we post a message to get the print server's status. The code in Fig. 10-15 shows the remainder of the WndProc function and what actions are taken according to which message is received.

⇨ NotifyProc

If this program is being run and someone has selected the option to notify users when their print jobs have finished, a message will be sent to their workstation telling them that their print job has completed. The function to handle this message is the NotifyProc. This function is shown in Fig. 10-16.

Error handling when attaching to the print server.

Figure 10-14

```
ccode = PSLoginToPrintServer (SPXConnection, &pAccess);
if (ccode)
     {
     if (ccode == 0x400)
               {
               MessageBox (hParent, (LPSTR)
                    "Cannot Access Print Server",
                    (LPSTR)"ERROR", MB_OK);
               }
     else
               {
               sprintf (errorMsg,
               "LoginToPrintServer returned %4X", ccode );
               MessageBox (hParent, errorMsg, (LPSTR)"ERROR", MB_OK);
               }

     PostQuitMessage (0);
     }
```

WndProc and message handling.

Figure 10-15

```
     PostMessage (hParent, GET_STATUS_MSG, wParam, lParam);
               break;

case GET_STATUS_MSG :
     WndGetPrtJobStatus (hParent);
     break;

case DISPLAY_STATUS_MSG :
     DisplayStatus ((char *) lParam, (int) wParam);
     break;

case DISPLAY_JOB_ACTIVE_MSG :
     DisplayStatus ((char *) lParam, (int) wParam);
     break;

          .
          .
          .

case DISPLAY_JOBNUMBER_MSG :
     DisplayStatus ((char *) lParam, (int) wParam);
     break;

case LIST_JOB_NAMES_MSG :
     ListJobNames (hParent, (int) wParam, (WORD) newConnID);
     break;

case NOTIFY_MSG :
     SendNotifyMessage ();
     break;
```

Figure 10-15   *Continued.*

```
case CLEANUP_MSG:
    ccode = PSDetachFromPrintServer (SPXConnection);
    if (ccode)
            {
            sprintf(errorMsg,"Error in DetachFromPrintServer %04X", cco
            MessageBox (hParent, errorMsg, (LPSTR)"ERROR", MB_OK);
            }
    SetPreferredConnectionID (oldConnID);
    PostQuitMessage (0);
    break;

case WM_CHAR :
    {
    char keystroke;

    keystroke = (char)wParam;
    switch (keystroke)
            {
            case ESCAPE_KEY:    // Quit if ESC key was pressed
                PostMessage (hParent, CLEANUP_MSG, NULL,
                            (DWORD) NULL);
                break;
            }
    break;
    }

case WM_COMMAND :
    switch( wParam )
            {
            case IDM_ABOUT :
                lpfnAboutDlgProc = MakeProcInstance (AboutProc,
                                parentInstance);
                DialogBox (parentInstance, "AboutBox",
                        hParent, lpfnAboutDlgProc);
                FreeProcInstance (lpfnAboutDlgProc);
                SendMessage (hwndList, LB_ADDSTRING, NULL,
                            (LONG)(LPSTR)"abc.txt");
                break;
            case IDM_NOTIFY :
                lpfnNotifyDlgProc = MakeProcInstance (NotifyProc,
                                parentInstance);
                DialogBox (parentInstance, "NotifyBox", hParent,
                        lpfnNotifyDlgProc);
                FreeProcInstance (lpfnNotifyDlgProc);
                break;

            case IDM_EXIT :
                PostQuitMessage (0);
                break;

            }
    break;
```

```
    case WM_DESTROY:
        KillTimer (hParent, GET_STATUS_TIMER);
        PostQuitMessage (0);
        break;
    }
    return (DefWindowProc (hParent, iMessage, wParam, lParam));
}
```

Print job completion notification.

Figure 10-16

```
BOOL FAR PASCAL NotifyProc (HWND hDlg, unsigned iMessage, WORD wParam,
    LONG lParam)
{
    HWND listBox;
    char tmpPath[120];

    switch (iMessage)
        {
        case WM_COMMAND:
            switch (wParam)
                {
                case IDB_NOTIFYNO :
                    bWantToBeNotified = FALSE;
                    EndDialog (hDlg, FALSE);
                    break;

                case IDB_NOTIFYYES :
                    bWantToBeNotified = TRUE;
                    MessageBox (hParent, (LPSTR)"You will be notified!",
                            (LPSTR)"Notify Me?", MB_OK);
                    EndDialog (hDlg, FALSE);
                    break;

                default:
                    return FALSE;
                }
            break;

        default:
            return FALSE;
        }

    return TRUE ;
}
```

The GetParentDimensions function is used to retrieve the latest dimensions of the parent's client window. This way, when a WM_SIZE message is received, we can resize everything according to the new dimensions. We also have to know how tall the tallest letter will be. The code in Fig. 10-17 shows the GetParentDimensions call.

169

Figure 10-17   *Determining the dimensions of the parent window.*

```
void GetParentDimensions (HWND hParent)
{
    hdc = GetDC (hParent);
    GetTextMetrics (hdc, &tm );
    ReleaseDC (hParent, hdc);
    charHeight = tm.tmHeight;

    GetWindowRect (hParent, &windowRect);
    GetClientRect (hParent, &clientRect);

    clientHorzPix = clientRect.right - clientRect.left;
    clientVertPix = clientRect.bottom - clientRect.top;
    jobWndWidth = clientHorzPix / 4;
    jobWndHeight = clientVertPix * 3 / 4;    // 3/4 height of client area
    xSeparator = clientHorzPix / 3;
    jobX = (xSeparator - jobWndWidth) / 2;
    jobY = (clientVertPix - jobWndHeight) / 2 + clientRect.top;
    leftover = clientHorzPix - xSeparator;
    statWndWidth = leftover / 4 * 3;
    statX = (leftover - statWndWidth) / 2 + xSeparator;

    SetRect (&statRect, 0, 0, statWndWidth, jobWndHeight);
}
```

After we have the appropriate information, we set up a rectangle for the status window so that, when updating is needed, we can repaint this area:

```
void GetStatusBoxCenter (void)
{
    Get the center of the new rectangle
    xx = statWndWidth / 2;
    yy = jobWndHeight / 2;
}
```

The function RedrawListBox redraws the listbox to the correct size if the window has been resized:

```
void RedrawListBox (HWND hWnd)
{
    MoveWindow (hWnd, jobX, jobY, jobWndWidth, jobWndHeight,
TRUE);
}
```

➡ The WndGetPrtJobStatus function

The WndGetPrtJobStatus function does most of the work for the JOBSTAT program. We get the print job status with the first call and display the completion code. If everything goes well, we get the printer's status and post "display" messages to the parent window. The code for the WndGetPrtJobStatus function is in Fig. 10-18.

Determining the status of the print job.   Figure 10-18

```
void WndGetPrtJobStatus (HWND hParent)
{
    WORD        ccode;

    ccode = PSGetPrintJobStatus (SPXConnection, p, fileServer, queueName,
            &jobNumber, description, &copiesNeeded, &jobSize, &activeCopy,
            &bytesIntoCopy, &formNeeded, &text);

    if (ccode)
        {
        switch (ccode)
            {
            case 0x400:
                MessageBox (hParent, (LPSTR)"Print Server DOES NOT exist",
                        (LPSTR)ERROR, MB_OK);
                PostMessage (hParent, CLEANUP_MSG, NULL, (DWORD) NULL);
                break;

            case 0x309:
                sprintf (jobActiveMsg, "NO JOB ACTIVE");
                PostMessage (hParent, DISPLAY_JOB_ACTIVE_MSG,
                        (WORD) (yy - charHeight), (DWORD)
                        (LPSTR)jobActiveMsg);
                SendMessage (hwndList, LB_RESETCONTENT, NULL,
                        (DWORD) NULL);
                SetTimer (hParent, GET_STATUS_TIMER, TWO_SECONDS,
                        NULL);
                break;

            default:
                sprintf (errorMsg, "Error getting status %04X", ccode );
                MessageBox (hParent, errorMsg, (LPSTR)ERROR, MB_OK);
                PostMessage (hParent, CLEANUP_MSG, NULL, (DWORD) NULL);
                break;
            }
        }
    else
        {
```

Figure 10-18   *Continued.*

```
ccode = PSGetPrinterStatus (SPXConnection, p, &status, &trouble,
        &active, &serviceMode, &mountedForm, formName, name);

if (ccode)
    {
    sprintf (buffer, "Get Status returned %x", ccode);
    MessageBox (hParent, buffer, (LPSTR)"ERROR", MB_OK);
    }
else
    {
    PostMessage (hParent, DISPLAY_PRINTERNAME_MSG,
                (WORD) (yy - charHeight * 4), (DWORD) (LPSTR) name);

    switch (status)
        {
        case PSTAT_WAITING_FOR_JOB:
            sprintf( statusMsg, "WAITING FOR JOB");
            PostMessage (hParent, DISPLAY_STATUS_MSG,
                        (WORD) (yy - charHeight * 3),
                        (DWORD) (LPSTR) statusMsg);
            break;
        .
        .
        .

        case PSTAT_PRIVATE:
            sprintf( statusMsg, "PRIVATE");
            PostMessage (hParent, DISPLAY_STATUS_MSG,
                        (WORD) (yy - charHeight * 3),
                        (DWORD) (LPSTR) statusMsg);
            break;
        }

    if (trouble == 1)
        {
        sprintf( troubleMsg, "O F F   L I N E");
        bChangeColor = TRUE;
        lColor = RED;
        PostMessage (hParent, DISPLAY_TROUBLE_MSG,
                    (WORD) (yy - charHeight * 2),
                    (DWORD) (LPSTR) troubleMsg);
    }
            else
                if (trouble == 2)
                    {
                    sprintf( troubleMsg, "O U T   O F   P A P E R");
                    bChangeColor = TRUE;
                    lColor = RED;
                    PostMessage (hParent, DISPLAY_TROUBLE_MSG,
                                (WORD) (yy - charHeight * 2),
                                (DWORD) (LPSTR) troubleMsg);
                    }
```

```
        else
            {
            sprintf( troubleMsg, "NO TROUBLE");
            PostMessage (hParent, DISPLAY_TROUBLE_MSG,
                        (WORD) (yy - charHeight * 2),
                        (DWORD) (LPSTR) troubleMsg);
            }

    if (active)
        {
        sprintf( activeMsg, "ACTIVE JOB");
        PostMessage (hParent, DISPLAY_ACTIVE_MSG,
                    (WORD) (yy - charHeight), (DWORD) (LPSTR)
                    activeMsg);
        }
    else
        {
        sprintf( activeMsg, "NO JOB ACTIVE");
        PostMessage (hParent, DISPLAY_ACTIVE_MSG,
                    (WORD) (yy - charHeight), (DWORD) (LPSTR)
                    activeMsg);
        }
    }

sprintf( qNameMsg, "QUEUE: %s/%s", fileServer, queueName );
PostMessage (hParent, DISPLAY_QUEUENAME_MSG, (WORD) yy,
            (DWORD) (LPSTR) qNameMsg);
.
.
.
```

Determine what percentage of the print job has completed by
dividing the total number of bytes for the job into the number of
bytes completed. Next, as in Fig. 10-19, display this information.

Post a message to get the status all over again. This way, if anything
has changed in the status, the window will be updated accordingly:

```
        PostMessage (hParent, GET_STATUS_MSG, NULL, (DWORD)NULL);
        }   // End of if statement with switch inside of it
    }
```

The DisplayStatus function is used as a generic printing routine.
When it is called, the vertical position is passed to it in the yPos
parameter. This way we can display the status information
generically. This function is found in Fig. 10-20.

Figure 10-19

Calculating the current print job completion and sending a message for display.

```
percentCompleted = (int)(((float)bytesIntoCopy/(float)jobSize) * 100.0);
sprintf( percentMsg, "%d%% Completed", percentCompleted );
SendMessage (hParent, DISPLAY_PERCENT_MSG,
                (WORD) (yy + charHeight * 5),  (DWORD) (LPSTR) percentMsg);

if ((oldJobNumber != jobNumber) && bWantToBeNotified)
    PostMessage (hParent, NOTIFY_MSG, NULL, (DWORD) NULL);

oldJobNumber = jobNumber;
```

Figure 10-20

Displaying the current job status.

```
void DisplayStatus (char *buffer, int yPos)
{
    InvalidateRect (hParent, NULL, TRUE);
    hdc = GetDC (hwndText);
    SetTextAlign (hdc, TA_CENTER);
    TextOut (hdc, xx, yPos, buffer, lstrlen (buffer));
    ReleaseDC (hwndText, hdc);
}
```

⇨ ListJobNames

The ListJobNames function is used to list all of the print jobs that currently are in the queue. We get the printer queue ID, then we get the jobs in the queue by calling GetQueueJobList. We then reset the listbox and add the queue jobs to the listbox. The code for this call is in Fig. 10-21.

⇨ SendNotifyMessage

The SendNotifyMessage function sends a message to the person whose print job has just completed. First, you must get the connection ID of the server from which he or she is printing. In this example, found in Fig. 10-22, we assume that the user is attached to the file server one time.

Listing the print jobs in the queue.   Figure 10-21

```
void ListJobNames (HWND hWnd, int printerNumber, WORD newConnID)
{
    XTRA_PRINT_INFO    job;
    DWORD              queueID;
    DWORD              jobsInQueue, jobList[MAX_JOBS];
    char               nameBuffer[MAX_JOBANDNAME];
    int                i, jobsToList;
    WORD               ccode;
    char               volume[16], dir[255];

    SetPreferredConnectionID (newConnID);
    ccode = GetPrinterQueue ((BYTE) printerNumber, &queueID);
    ccode = GetQueueJobList (queueID, &jobsInQueue,
            jobList, MAX_JOBS);
    jobsToList = min (MAX_JOBS, jobsInQueue);
    SendMessage (hwndList, LB_RESETCONTENT, NULL, (DWORD) NULL);

    for (i=0; i<jobsToList; i++)
        {
        ReadQueueJobEntry (queueID, jobList[i], (JobStruct far *)&job);
        sprintf (nameBuffer, "%s", job.textJobDescription);
        lstrcat (nameBuffer, "    ");
        lstrcat (nameBuffer, job.bannerNameField);
        if (i != 0)
            {
            SendMessage (hwndList, LB_ADDSTRING, NULL,
                    (DWORD) (LPSTR) nameBuffer);
            }
        else
            {
            ParsePath (job.directoryPath, usersServer, volume, dir);
            lstrcpy (oldBannerName, job.bannerNameField);
            lstrcpy (oldFileName, job.textJobDescription);
            SendMessage (hwndList, LB_ADDSTRING, NULL,
                    (DWORD) (LPSTR) nameBuffer);
            }

        }
}
```

This is just the beginning of the information that the Print Server
Services APIs can provide to an application that wants to take
advantage of that information. An application can add jobs to the
queue and change the status of queue servers if necessary.

Figure 10-22   *Notifying on completion of the print job.*

```c
void SendNotifyMessage ()
{
    char  notifyMsg[50];
    int   ccode;
    WORD  newConnID, oldConnID;
    WORD  usersConnection, numConnections;

    ccode = GetConnectionID (usersServer, &newConnID);
    oldConnID = GetPreferredConnectionID ();
    SetPreferredConnectionID (newConnID);

    lstrcpy (notifyMsg, "PRINT JOB ");
    lstrcat (notifyMsg, oldFileName);
    lstrcat (notifyMsg, " HAS FINISHED");

    ccode = GetObjectConnectionNumbers (oldBannerName, (WORD) OT_USER,
            (DWORD far *) &numConnections, (DWORD far *) &usersConnection,
            (DWORD) 1);

    ccode = SendConsoleBroadcast (notifyMsg, (DWORD) 1,
            (DWORD far *) &usersConnection);
    SetPreferredConnectionID (oldConnID);
}
```

Internetwork Packet Exchange overview

CHAPTER 11

I nternetwork *Packet Exchange* (IPX) is a high-speed
communications protocol designed by Novell and is the basis
of all communication in the native NetWare environment, whether
between servers and workstations, servers and servers, or
workstations and workstations. This protocol is a datagram or
connectionless communications protocol. IPX can be used for
creating applications that are client-server oriented or peer-to-peer
oriented. Applications that are client-server oriented would have a
server providing a service and awaiting requests. Applications that
are peer-to-peer in nature would allow equal bidirectional access
with either side initiating communication. NetWare 3.11 is an
example of a client-server orientation. NetWare Lite is an example
of a peer-to-peer application.

⇨ Programming with IPX

When programming with IPX, several decisions need to be made,
including whether or not to be peer based or server based, the most
efficient method of passing data back and forth, what format the data
will be in, whether the application will be synchronous or
asynchronous in nature, and whether the application will do batch
processing or real time processing.

⇨ Distribution models

When deciding whether the application should be peer based or
server based, the basic purpose of the application should be
evaluated. If the application is to be used bidirectionally by more than
one client a peer-to-peer model might be best. If the application is
providing a service that needs centralized control of one or more
resources, a client-server model would be more workable. For
example, a read/write database to be shared by many individuals is
more easily kept up to date if it is in a centralized location and all the
users share the data with locking controlling who is able to change
what and when. However, a read-only database could be split out
across several machines and accessed simultaneously by all users
without a potential for data corruption.

❋ **The peer-to-peer model**   The peer-to-peer model performs processing independent of the NetWare server and allows the user to control and define all aspects of the distribution. This model allows machines to communicate directly, resulting in an increase of speed.

The peer-to-peer model allows the developer more freedom and control in the design. However, the developer has increased responsibility in designing and maintaining the processing at a lower level, thus increasing the complexity of the programming involved.

❋ **The client-server model**   The client-server model uses a well-known location as a holding area to enable distribution by the application. This model is less interactive, with communication between the resources used by the client controlled through the server and not accessed directly by the client.

 # Choosing your protocol

After the distribution model is chosen, the protocol to be used should be chosen. Novell provides IPX, SPX, NetBIOS, Named Pipes, and RPC for applications to use in distributing processing on the network. IPX is connectionless and does not guarantee delivery of packets. When this protocol is used, the programmer has the freedom to implement whatever method is most efficient for the application to maintain communications between the workstations. SPX (Sequenced Packet Exchange) provides guaranteed delivery and session maintenance for the developer, but packetization and formatting still is the programmer's responsibility. NetBIOS provides similar services to SPX, as does Named Pipes. These two interfaces also allow a programmer to write applications that also will run on non-NetWare networks. RPC provides developers with an added level of service by packetizing the information requested while still allowing programmers to decide what operations will be performed remotely and what operations should be performed locally. This interface is less complex to manage than the protocols that require programmers to packet their own data and allows more freedom than the standard NetWare interface functions that perform all packetization locally and request information directly from the NetWare file servers.

Choosing the format of the data will be discussed in the section that describes IPX packets and their structure and in the section that describes SPX packets and their structure.

Choosing your processing mode

Choosing to implement an application as batch processing or as real-time processing will depend upon the kinds of resources provided. For example, file servers and database servers must be real time because the clients are using the information in real time. A print server or fax server, however, can be implemented as batch processing because the users don't need to wait for the job to complete.

Whether an application will be synchronous or asynchronous also can be determined by how it is to be used. If the information or service requested from the application is necessary before the user can proceed, then the application can be a combination of asynchronous on the network and synchronous for the user or fully synchronous for the user and on the network. If the service provided by the application can occur in the background while the user continues to do other work, the application can be fully asynchronous both on the network and to the user.

Networking standards

The Open Systems Interconnection (OSI) Model was designed by the International Standards Organization (ISO) and has seven layers that describe network functionality. These layers are illustrated in Fig. 11-1.

Physical layer

The Physical layer is the layer that details the physical configuration of the network. For example, what kind of cabling and connectors are used on the network.

Figure 11-1

OSI Layer	Function
Application	Application Interface
Presentation	Format/Translation of Data
Session	Virtual Connection Maintenance
Transport	Sequencing/Guaranteed Delivery
Network	Packet Addressing and Routing
Data Link	Transmission Techniques
Physical	Physical Data Transmission

OSI layers and functional description.

Data Link layer

The Data Link layer covers the transmission techniques used for communication on the network, for example, what kind of protocol is used to pass data from one network node to another. Token passing and collision detection are examples of data transmission techniques.

Network layer

The Network layer of the model is responsible for packet addressing and routing. Packet addressing is the method used to determine where a packet has come from on the network and where it is going to. Packet routing determines how a packet gets where it is going.

 # Transport layer

The Transport layer is responsible for sequencing and guaranteed delivery of the packets. *Sequencing* is when the packets are sent and received in a certain order. *Guaranteed delivery* means that the packets have arrived at the destination and been acknowledged or the application determines the destination isn't able to respond and therefore not able to process data.

 # Session layer

The Session layer maintains the session or virtual connection between nodes on the network. Maintenance of the session includes keeping track of what address the other partner in the session is using and sending periodic tickle packets to that address to keep current on the status of the other node. For example, a tickle packet is sent to the other node in a session and no response is received. Then, the next time communication is tried on that session, no packet must be sent because the session manager already knows something has happened to the other node.

 # Presentation layer

The Presentation layer of the model deals with how the data is formatted or how it needs to be translated. For example, data encryption and decryption logically occurs at this layer.

 # Application layer

The final layer, the Application layer, in the OSI model is the application programming interface presented to the application for general network access. The layers at which the various NetWare services operate are detailed in Fig. 11-2.

Figure 11-2

OSI LAYER   **NETWARE EQUIVALENTS**

OSI LAYER	NETWARE EQUIVALENTS	
Application	NW C Interface	
Presentation		
Session	SPX	NCP
Transport		
Network	IPX	
Data Link	LAN drivers and Protocols	
Physical		

OSI layers and NetWare equivalents.

⇨ NetWare systems & the OSI model

IPX operates at the Network layer of this model. Routing information also is contained at this level. A connectionless protocol makes no guarantee as to the reception of the data. The data will be directed to the proper workstation, but the sender will not be given any information as to whether the data arrived safely. Other Novell protocols compare to the OSI model as seen in Fig. 11-2.

Because Service Advertising Protocol (SAP) and Routing Information Protocol (RIP) use IPX broadcast datagrams to pass information between NetWare servers and routers, they also fit on the Network layer and perform addressing and routing functions.

 # Data enveloping

A packet generally is divided into sections that represent the software layers or protocols that it has passed through. The data an application wants to send is the first section. As this data is handed down to the next software layer, information pertinent to that layer is added to it. This continues until the packet is placed on the physical network by the LAN card. This adding of information is called enveloping. For example, if an application requests an open file from the file server, it is enveloped with an NCP header, then an IPX header, and finally an Ethernet header (on an Ethernet network). This is illustrated in Fig. 11-3.

Figure 11-3

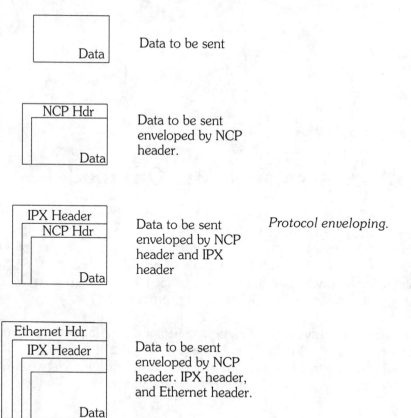

The Event Control Block (ECB)

All IPX packets and actions are called events and are controlled by an Event Control Block (ECB). An Event Control Block contains the necessary information for IPX to send or receive a packet as well as how to schedule asynchronous events. The ECB has the structure shown in Fig. 11-4.

Figure 11-4

| Link |
| ESR Address |
| In Use |
| Completion Code |
| Socket |
| IPX Workspace |
| Driver Workspace |
| Immediate Address |

IPX ECB.

Count   Fragmernt Descriptor List

Address 1   —> to IPX Header

Size

Address 2   —> to IPX Packet Data

Size

.
.
.

⇨ Link field

The Link field is used internally by IPX to create a linked list of ECBs. If the ECB is not in use by IPX, this field can be used by the application. The size of this field is 4 bytes.

⇨ Event Service Routine address

The ESR Address is the segment:offset far address of the Event Service Routine (ESR) that IPX will call when the IPX event completes. If this field is set to 0x00, control returns immediately to the interrupted process after an IPX event completes. This field is 4 bytes wide.

⇨ IPX events

There are three types of IPX events: sending packets, listening for packets, and timer-scheduled events. IPX calls ESRs on the completion of the IPX event associated with the ECB. ESRs are called with interrupts disabled. An ESR is similar to an interrupt service routine (ISR) and should be short operations. On entry to the ESR, the application should set the DS register to its data segment. If the process will be enabling interrupts, then the application should change stacks to the prevent the possibility of stack overflow or should queue the incoming events to be processed by the main Windows control procedure for the application. Using PostMessage to place a message in the application's message queue is the preferred method for ESR processing under Windows. This allows the main Windows message loop to process the ECB and repost it if necessary.

Parts of IPX are re-entrant and can be called from an ESR for some operations. These operations include IPXSendPacket, IPXListenForPacket, and IPXScheduleIPXEvent, but not IPXGetLocalTarget.

When an ESR is called by IPX, the address of the ECB for which the event has completed is contained in ES:SI.

⇨ In Use flag

The In Use flag indicates that the ECB is in use or not in use by IPX. A nonzero value for this flag indicates in use. No fields should be modified by the application while the ECB is in use by IPX. This is a one-byte field.

⇨ Completion code

The completion code indicates the status of the event upon completion. This field is valid only after the in use flag has been set to zero. A value of zero for the completion code indicates the IPX event completed successfully. A nonzero value is an error code indicating failure of the IPX event. This is a one-byte field. Table 11-1 contains a list of possible IPX completion codes in Windows and their meaning.

The completion codes under IPX and SPX   Table 11-1

Completion code	Meaning	Circumstances
0xFF	SPX_SOCKET_NOT_OPENED SOCKET_NOT_OPEN	Socket not opened before ECB submitted
	TRANSMIT_FAILURE	Packet could not be sent
	ECB_NOT_IN_USE	On ECBs being canceled
0xFE	PACKET_UNDELIVERABLE	Packet could not be delivered, the address is incorrect or the destination can no longer be found
0xFD	SPX_MALFORMED_PACKET	Packet does not have at least 1 fragment or first fragment (header) less than 42 bytes long
	SPX_PACKET_OVERFLOW	Packet received is larger than the total of all the fragments defined by the ECB. Packet being sent is larger than max packet size
	PACKET_OVERFLOW	Same as above for IPX
0xFC	SPX_LISTEN_CANCELLED	Cancelled SPX Listen
	ECB_CANCELLED	Cancelled ECB successfully

Table 11-1   **Continued**

Completion code	Meaning	Circumstances
0xFA	NO_PATH_TO_DESTINATION_FOUND	Packet destination has no local target
0xF9	CANCEL_FAILURE	ECB could not be cancelled
0xF6	IPXSPX_PREV_INIT	IPX/SPX was previously initialized for the currently running instance. To multiply initialize, see below
0xF5	OVER_MAX_LIMIT	Packet size greater than specified on initialization
0xF4	WINLOCK_FAILED	DLL management memory could not be locked
0xF3	NO_FREE_ECB	All low memory ECBs in use
0xF2	NO_DOS_MEMORY	Not enough DOS memory to allocate the number of ECBs requested
0xF1	IPXSPX_NOT_INIT	IPX/SPX not initialized for the specified IPX task ID
0xF0	NO_MGMT_MEMORY	Not enough memory for DLL to complete request
0xEF	SPX_CONNECTION_TABLE_FULL	Socket table full
0xEE	SPX_INVALID_CONNECTION	Connection specified not valid
0xED	SPX_TERMINATED_POORLY	Connection aborted from other end
0xEC	SPX_NO_ANSWER_FROM_TARGET	Partner no longer answering
	SPX_CONNECTION_FAILED	Connection dead on other end or killed by watchdog
	SPX_CONNECTION_TERMINATED	Connection terminated by other end

Novell, Inc.

⇨ Socket

The Socket is the source socket to use for the connection. The socket
is a demultiplexing mechanism. The socket is a word in high-low order.
The high-low order is necessary, because this is the socket number
that IPX places in the packet header. The entire packet header is in

high-low word order. The socket number could be compared to an apartment number in an addressing scheme. The network number is similar to the street—the node address to the building number. The socket functions much like an apartment number by further resolving the process to which the packet should be directed in the node the way a letter is directed to an apartment in a building.

 IPX Workspace

The IPX Workspace is space reserved for IPX to use while processing the event associated with the ECB. This field is 4 bytes in size.

Driver Workspace

The Driver Workspace is space reserved for the LAN driver to use during packet processing. This field is 12 bytes in size.

Immediate Address

The Immediate Address is the node address of the local router. This field must be filled before a packet can be sent. The application can get the immediate address by using either the IPXGetLocalTarget procedure or by receiving a packet with IPXListenForPacket. When a packet is sent to another node, the first place that it must go is to a routing node that has information concerning the route to the destination. This router must be on the local net with the node sending the packet. The immediate address is the node's six-digit LAN card address. This field is 6 bytes wide.

Fragment Descriptor List

The Fragment Descriptor List consists of the Count, Address, and Size of each fragment to be used as part of an IPX packet. This list is used by IPX to construct the packet. The count field is a word in size, the address field is 4 bytes in length and is in segment:offset format, and the size field is a word in size. All packets must have at least one fragment. The first fragment must always point the beginning of the

IPX header and be at least 30 bytes in length. How many fragments make up a packet is defined by the user. A packet guaranteed to cross all NetWare routers can be no larger than 576 bytes in total length, with 30 bytes for the header and 546 bytes remaining for data. If packets are to be sent only on the local net and will not be crossing routers, the size is determined by the LAN driver unless the packet size parameter is set in the NET.CFG. To set this parameter, `IPX Packet Size Limit=<packet size>` must be on a line in the NET.CFG when IPX.COM is loaded.

⇨ IPX Header

The IPX Packet consists of two defined areas: the IPX Header and the Data. The IPX header is in high-low word format because the protocol originally was designed on machines where the word format is high-low. The IPX header consists of 30 bytes arranged in 6 fields: the checksum, the length, the transport control, the packet type, the destination address, and the source address. The IPX Header is illustrated in Fig. 11-5.

Figure 11-5

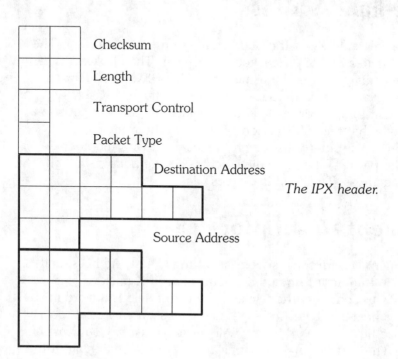

The IPX header.

 # Packet checksum

The checksum makes up the first 2 bytes of the header. Prior to NetWare v3.11, this field was not used to checksum the packet but to maintain conformity to the IDP (Internet Datagram Protocol) packet. When it is not being used to checksum the packet, it is set to 0xFFFF by IPX. Starting with IPXODI.COM v2.0, this field is used for checksumming the packets for the NCP packet burst protocol. For an application to use checksumming, three assembly calls will need to be called. These are illustrated in Figs. 11-6 through 11-8.

Sample code for IPX send with checksum.

Figure 11-6

```
mov     bx, 0020h
les     si, offset myECB
call    _IPXLocation
```

Sample code for IPX generate checksum.

Figure 11-7

```
mov     bx, 0021h
les     si, offset myECB
call    _IPXLocation
```

Sample code for IPX verify checksum.

Figure 11-8

```
mov     bx, 0022h
les     si, offset myECB
call    _IPXLocation
```

Packet length

The packet length field is two bytes long and is the total length of the packet including the header.

Transport control

The transport control is set to 0x00 by IPX and is the number of hops the packet has taken. A *hop* is every time a network router is

crossed. When this value reaches 16, the packet is discarded and no longer forwarded to other nets.

⇨ Packet type

The packet type is the XEROX defined type. For IPX, this value is 4. This field should be set to 4 by the application when sending packets.

⇨ Destination address

The destination address is 12 bytes long and is the internetwork address of the destination workstation plus the socket to demultiplex on. This address is the Network, Node, and Socket of the process to be communicated with. This address must be set by the application when sending packets. The network number is assigned by a network administrator and is the logical address of the physical length of cable connecting the workstation with the nearest router. A destination network of 0x00000000 means the local network.

The node address of a workstation is either burned into the card being used as in Ethernet and Token Ring or is toggled on the card as in Arcnet. A node address of 0xFFFFFFFFFFFF means the packet is a broadcast packet. A broadcast packet does not cross a router. To broadcast to a network other than the local network, the network number must be set to the network for which the broadcast is intended.

The socket number is defined by the application and used to demultiplex communications. Sockets below 0x4000 are reserved for Novell internal use. Sockets from 0x4001 to 0x5000 are dynamically allocated. Sockets above 0x8000 are assigned by Novell to companies writing applications needing their own socket numbers.

⇨ Source address

The source address is 12 bytes long and is the internetwork address of the workstation the application is running on.

 IPX data

The data in an IPX packet is limited to 546 bytes for packets crossing routers or to the media packet size from IPXGetMaxPacketSize minus the 30-byte header for local packets. The data area structure and protocol are defined by the application. IPX uses the fragment descriptor list to locate the data to be placed in the packet. If the data is in one contiguous block of memory following the header, only one fragment would be necessary. However, allowing the multiple fragments permits the user to build a packet using non-contiguous locations in memory.

The format of the packet and the protocol the application uses will depend on the actions that need to be taken or the requests that can be made. If an application allows only read access of a data base, then any request will only need to specify a record to read. There are many ways to specify this record, so many types of requests could be designed. Each one could be identified by a number in the first byte of data in the IPX packet. The information following would be the data needed to perform the request and could be organized like the structure used in the application. The response packets could all have the same structure. They could be the fields of the record as defined in the database. In a distributed application with many requests and responses, the format of the packets can all include function numbers. The response number can use the same function number as the request. This would be an acknowledgment that the request had been received and was the type of the response being returned.

IPX & Windows

To use IPX under Windows, you need the NWIPXSPX.DLL, a current IPX.COM or IPXODI.COM, and VIPX.386 v1.10. These drivers have been written to allow Windows applications to use IPX and to allow DOS-based applications to run from the DOS prompt in Windows. Beginning with NetWare v4.0, only IPXODI.COM will be shipped with NetWare servers.

 # NWIPXSPX.DLL

The original NetWare IPX libraries written for DOS were not sufficient for programming under Windows unmodified. Real mode programming techniques had been used, such as writing to the code segment. Also, IPX lives in real mode, and the libraries would call IPX directly with a far call passing global memory ECBs and fragment pointers.

This isn't possible in the same manner under Windows. Windows recommends that Dynamic Link Libraries (DLLs) be written for shared code, so the IPX libraries were rewritten to follow protected mode programming requirements and to use the DOS Protected Mode Interface (DPMI), and VIPX.

VIPX, as discussed earlier, virtualizes IPX requests from Windows in enhanced mode and translates the memory to global DOS memory so that the request can be processed by IPX. VIPX allows applications to use protected memory and translates the ECBs and packets to global memory on an as-needed basis. For listens, the packets are allocated when the driver receives a packet. This is called *late packet allocation*. This global ECB has VIPX's ESR address. When the ESR is called, VIPX will free the global ECB after copying the data to the original ECB. For sends, the global ECB is allocated immediately. The global ECB is freed in the same manner as for listens when the ESR is called.

The DLL implemented for IPX, SPX, SAP, and Diagnostics under windows is NWIPXSPX.DLL. The original SDK from Novell contained three DLLs: NWIPXSPX.DLL, NWSAP.DLL, and NWDIAG.DLL. These three libraries then were combined into NWIPXSPX.DLL. In Enhanced Mode Windows, this library interfaces with VIPX (Fig. 11-9).

 # Memory considerations for using IPX in Enhanced Mode

All requests are passed to VIPX from the application and VIPX calls the application's ESR on completion of an event. All memory

Figure 11-9

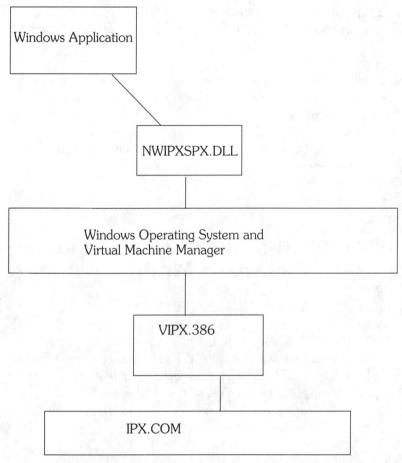

Communication from NWIPXSPX.DLL to VIPX.386 and IPX.

submitted to NWIPXSPX.DLL must have certain characteristics to be available to VIPX or NWIPXSPX upon event completion. First, it needs to be allocated with GMEM_FIXED and GMEM.DDESHARE as the flags. Second, the memory must be locked with a GlobalLock. Third, the memory must be locked with GlobalPageLock.

Under Windows, two levels of memory management exist: the kernel memory manager that manages memory for Windows applications and the system VM and the low-level memory manager that manages memory for all VMs. When an application issues a GlobalPageLock, the kernel memory manager is aware of the necessity of locking the

page in memory for asynchronous access. VIPX in turn locks the memory at a lower level. This lock is directed to the low level memory manager.

To enable applications to move memory as low as possible on the global heap when it must be locked for long periods of time, the GlobalWire call is available in Windows v3.0. GlobalWire can be used in place of GlobalLock. The GlobalWire call moves the allocated memory to the lowest contiguous block of the proper size in the heap and locks it. This then should be followed by the GlobalPageLock. GlobalWire is not available in Windows v3.1. If the ECBs are not dynamically allocated, they must reside in a fixed data segment.

 # Memory considerations for using IPX in Standard Mode

Locking memory in this manner is important for Standard Mode Windows as well. However, VIPX.386 doesn't run in Standard Mode, so the NWIPXSPX.DLL manages all interfacing with IPX. Three parameters were added to the Windows IPX/SPX interface for this purpose: IPXTaskID, maxECBs, and maxPacketSize. All three are used for initialization, and only IPXTaskID is used for all the remaining calls. Two additional calls are provided in the Windows interface: IPXGetMaxPacketSize and IPXSPXDeinit.

Under Standard and Real Modes, processing occurs only in the Windows applications or the DOS prompts, never both simultaneously. When a user switches to a DOS application, the Windows applications are no longer in memory. For this reason, NWIPXSPX.DLL uses TBMI2 to buffer IPX packets and to translate ECBs and fragments into global memory for access by IPX.

 # Communication between NWIPXSPX & TBMI2

Translation of ECBs between protected memory and global memory consists of preallocation of a specified number of ECBs and

corresponding fragments from TBMI2, then copying the Windows applications buffers into this memory from TBMI2. TBMI2 in turn will hold any buffers that are not for the currently active application until the appropriate application is active once more. To allocate the appropriate number of ECBs and corresponding fragments and maintain these as private for an application, the IPXInitialize and SPXInitialize calls have the IPXTaskID, maxECBs, and maxPacketSize parameters.

✳ **IPXTaskID**   IPXTaskID is a unique ID number allocated by the NWIPXSPX.DLL to each application that initializes. If the application is initializing for a singular pool that can be used over and over, the IPXTaskID should be initialized to 0x00000000 before calling IPXInitialize (Fig. 11-10). If the application is a DLL and needs to allocate a pool of ECBs to be shared by several applications, IPXTaskID should be initialized to 0xFFFFFFFF before calling IPXInitialize (Fig. 11-11). This will cause an IPXTaskID to be returned that is unique to that DLL and still allow applications using that DLL to use IPX independently. If an application or DLL needs to allocate a small number of ECBs dynamically, IPXTaskID should be initialized to 0xFFFFFFFE (Fig. 11-12). This will allow the same application or DLL to do multiple initializations.

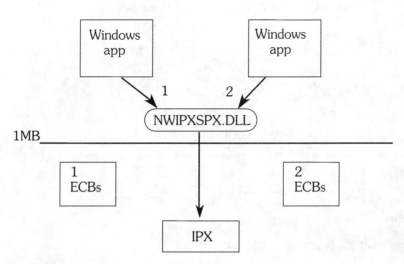

0x00000000

Figure 11-10

Initializing once as an application.

Figure 11-11

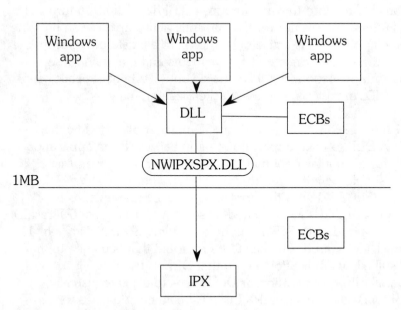

Initializing once as a DLL.

Figure 11-12

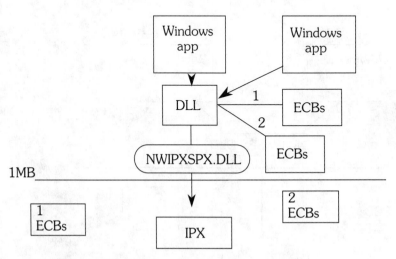

Initializing multiple times as an application or DLL.

For each IPXTaskID allocated from NWIPXSPX.DLL, a call to IPXSPXDeinit must be made to release the resources allocated to that application. If the application has another method of allocating global memory and wants to use NWIPXSPX.DLL only to communicate to IPX, IPXTaskID should be set to 0x70000000 on all calls to NWIPXSPX.DLL. This will indicate to the DLL that all addresses are in segment:offset format rather than selector:offset and should be passed directly to IPX.

✳ **Maximum ECBs**   The maxECBs parameter indicates on initialization how many ECBs should be allocated from TBMI2. The number should be the maximum number of ECBs that the application will submit to IPX concurrently. NWIPXSPX.DLL will return an error if it is not able to allocate the number of ECBs requested.

✳ **maxPacketSize**   The maxPacketSize parameter tells NWIPXSPX.DLL the largest packet size that will be used. NWIPXSPX.DLL then verifies that this packet size can be supported by the network topology being used by the workstation. It is recommended that the application use IPXGetMaxPacketSize and use the smaller of the two values—their own or the one returned from IPXGetMaxPacketSize to be assured of successful initialization. The ECBs allocated by NWIPXSPX.DLL from TBMI2 are managed in a linked list with a pointer to the corresponding protected mode ECB. When an IPX request is made through NWIPXSPX.DLL, the DLL runs through the linked list and finds a free low memory ECB to use for the translation of the request. When there are no longer any free ECBs, the function will return the NO_FREE_ECBS error. When an ECB is canceled, the DLL scans through the list to find the appropriate ECB and cancel the corresponding low memory ECB. Also, when an ECB that has been scheduled for an IPX event is rescheduled, the DLL finds that ECB and reschedules the right low memory ECB.

When IPX calls are made that require memory but do not use an ECB, NWIPXSPX.DLL allocates the necessary low memory dynamically and frees it before returning to the calling application. This is the case with such calls as SPXGetConnectionStatus, IPXGetInternetworkAddress, and IPXGetLocalTarget. All other IPX calls are register based and don't require any low memory.

Loading TBMI2 & TaskID

When using NWIPXSPX.DLL in Standard Mode, TBMI.COM or
TBMI2.COM must be loaded before Windows is executed. Using the
correct version of TBMI or TBMI2 for the version of Windows that
you are using is very important (Fig. 11-13). When using
NWIPXSPX.DLL and TBMI2 in Standard Mode Windows v3.0, it is
imperative that TaskID be loaded in *every* DOS prompt opened,
regardless of whether or not the DOS applications use IPX.

Figure 11-13

Workstation Software	TBMI.COM	TBMI2.COM
DOS 5.0 (only)		X
Windows 3.0 /any DOS	X	X
Windows 3.1		X

Compatibility of TBMI and Windows.

Event service routines

ESRs under Windows also must be managed carefully. In Enhanced
Mode, the ESR is called by VIPX (Fig. 11-14). The ESR itself must
either be in a fixed segment and exported in the DEF file or the
application must do a MakeProcInstance on the function and place
that address in the ESR address. This will assure that the ESR is in
memory once the event completes. In Standard Mode, the ESR is
called by NWIPXSPX.DLL (Fig. 11-15) and the same restrictions
apply as in Enhanced Mode. An ESR is called asynchronously and
with interrupts disabled. If interrupts are to be enabled by the
application, the ESR must be re-entrant. In Windows, PostMessage is
recommended for sending a message to the application queue to
indicate that an ECB has completed.

Figure 11-14

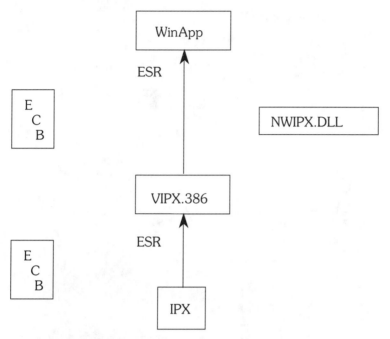

Event completion in Enhanced mode.

A caution must be extended because a bug exists in PostMessage that
enables interrupts. To use the PostMessage call and to be sure that
the application is safe for re-entrancy, two procedures are
recommended. First, that a flag be used to indicate that the ESR is
being re-entered. Second, if the ESR is re-entered, the ECB should be
queued and the ESR should return. After a message is posted to the
application, the ESR should issue a `cli` (Clear Interrupt) and check
the completed ECB queue. If ECBs have been queued, then the
PostMessage routine should be called for each of them until the
completed ECB queue is empty.

➡ Polling the inUseFlag under Windows

If the application chooses to poll the ECB inUseFlag, control must be
released to the Windows system to continue processing of messages.
To do this, the IPXWinYield code in Fig. 11-16 demonstrates how to
wait for an ECB to complete. A tight `while(inUseFlag);` loop

Figure 11-15

Standard Mode Windows

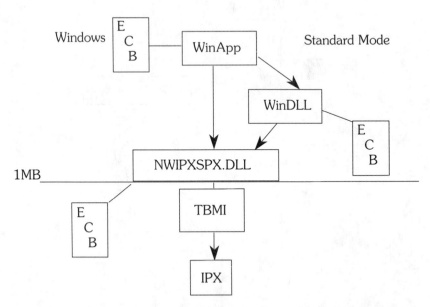

Communications through NWIPXSPX.DLL in Standard mode.

Figure 11-16   *Yielding control to Windows while polling the inUseFlag.*

```
void FAR PASCAL IPXWinYield()
{
    MSG msg;
    msg.message = WM_NULL;
    yielding = TRUE;
    while(PeekMessage ((LPMSG)&msg, NULL, 0, 0, PM_NOREMOVE))
    {
        if (msg.message == WM_QUIT)
                break;
        GetMessage((LPMSG)&msg, NULL, 0, 0);
        TranslateMessage((LPMSG)&msg);
        DispatchMessage((LPMSG)&msg);
    }
    yielding = FALSE;
}
```

must be avoided. Such a loop will never relinquish control in the nonpreemptive world of Windows. A `while(inUseFlag)` `IPXRelinquishControl();` doesn't relinquish control to Windows either, only to the LAN card in certain circumstances.

Another method of polling the ECB is to use a Windows timer. To do this, the application should write a function to be called by the Windows timer that checks the inUseFlags on the outstanding ECBs. A message can be sent to the application if the ECB has completed, otherwise the routine should return. If the application wants to suspend user input until an IPX event completes, then a flag can be set to indicate a state of suspension and messages from the keyboard and mouse treated accordingly. This flag also is used in the yield example for the same purpose, the flag is BOOL yielding.

Service Advertising Protocol (SAP)

When writing IPX applications, programmers also should understand the functioning of Service Advertising Protocol (SAP) and Routing Information Protocol (RIP). Service Advertising Protocol is the method by which servers advertise their services and are located on the network. Developers can call Novell and reserve a service type for their server. This type then is advertised on the network along with the server's internetwork address. A NetWare router or file server listens for broadcasts on socket 0x0452 (high-low order) to know what servers are advertising. A service advertising broadcast must be sent from the server at 60-second intervals. The broadcasts are picked up by NetWare routers and stored in the bindery and in the server table. For this information to be propagated on the network, each file server will advertise itself and seven other servers in each server broadcast packet. Any application listening on socket 0x0452 must use packets large enough to receive the largest service broadcast packets coming from servers. When a server is shutting down, a special shutdown broadcast packet is sent.

 # Finding services

For applications to find a service they require, two methods have been provided in addition to listening on socket 0x0452. These methods are scanning the bindery and making a SAP request. Scanning the bindery is a relatively simple function that requires the

service type, which is the same as the bindery object type or the service name. This will be discussed in greater detail in the chapter on NetWare security. Making SAP requests is simply a matter of sending IPX packets.

Get Nearest Service queries

Two kinds of SAP requests exist, the Get Nearest Service query and the Get General Service query. In the Get Nearest Service query, all NetWare routers respond with the server name of the type requested that is nearest them in terms of hops and transport time. It is assumed that the first server that responds to this query also is the closest server.

For example, a client on network FADE2300 sends a packet requesting information as to the whereabouts of a server of type 180. In Fig. 11-17, making a SAP request for the Get Nearest Service query is illustrated. The NetWare file server knows of two file servers of type 180: one on network ECBFADE and one on network FADE2300. The client making the request is on network FADE2300, so the file server returns the address of the server on network FADE2300.

Get General Service queries

A Get General Service query by the same workstation for all servers of type 180 would generate a response from the file server listing both servers and their respective addresses. With these methods, an application is able to resolve the location of a server on the network.

Router information protocol

Router information protocol (RIP) works in a similar fashion to SAP but on a lower level. This protocol is not used by applications but by NetWare routers to inform other NetWare routers about which networks exist. NetWare routers use a dynamic routing algorithm to route packets on the network. This algorithm requires that each

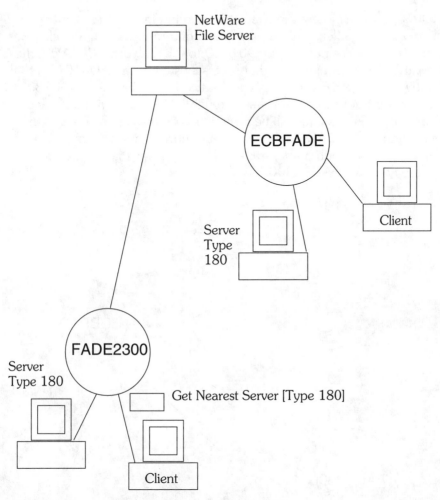

Figure 11-17

The Get Nearest Server query.

router knows about all accessible destination network numbers and all the routers one hop away that can route packets toward those networks.

The decision as to which router a packet is directed is based on the transport time to that router and how many packets are currently queued up to be sent on to that node. A network considered slow will be used only for routing packets if it is the only route available to the network. If the networks 0101FADE, ECBFADE, FADE2300, and

FAD01010 are all interconnected as shown in Fig. 11-18, then any server will have at least two routes to any other network. If a packet was to be sent from the network FAD01010 to the network ECBFADE, the NetWare routers would know that routes existed from FAD01010 directly to ECBFADE with a distance of two hops, through FADE2300 with a distance of three hops, and through 0101FADE with a distance of four hops. The packet will be routed directly through a server with a connection to ECBFADE unless there are more packets waiting to be sent to that node with a total transport time greater than that of going indirectly through FADE2300.

Figure 11-18

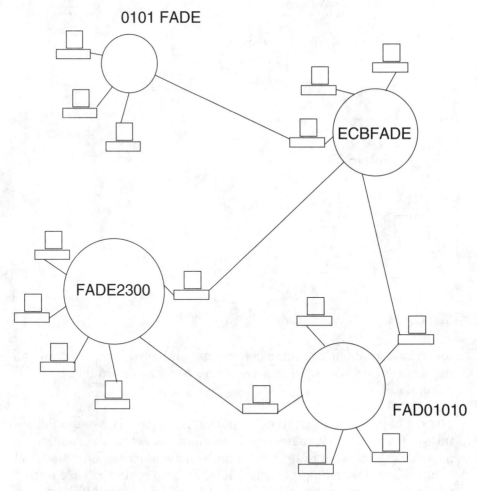

A NetWare routing example.

IPX programs are able to communicate on the local network without using the services of NetWare routers for routing or advertising. The next chapter details a sample IPX program that runs on a local network and allows communications between workstations. This program could be modified to run on an internet simply by adding code to make a Get General Service query or to scan the bindery of an attached file server.

12

IPX programming & distributed applications

CHAPTER 12

I NTERNETWORK Packet Exchange (IPX) is the basis of most communications on NetWare LANs. Many decisions lead to developing applications based on IPX. Typically, IPX is chosen over other protocols for its high performance. When an application initially is designed, decisions are made based on the needs of the service being provided. If the service is request-reply by nature, some sort of guaranteed delivery mechanism often is required. Taking advantage of the high throughput achievable on IPX, many developers opt to write their own simple, application specific guaranteed delivery protocol. Other factors to be decided during the design phase of an application include those found in Fig. 12-1.

Figure 12-1   *Considerations in the design of a distributed application.*

```
1. Where will the application be distributed?
2. Is the service client-server or peer-to-peer in nature?
3. To how many nodes will the process be distributed?
4. How do you maintain high performance in the distibuted application?
5. What communications protocol should be used?
6. What mechanism will guarantee the reliability of the communications?
7. How will clients find and access the service? Will nodes be referenced
   through physical addresses or names?
8. Will the application be asynchronous or synchronous in nature?
```

Application architecture

In considering these factors, the specific pieces of the application are designed including the distribution architecture, where and how to distribute the application, the time spent in network transit and in real processing, the packet or communications formats, managing data access, how to find your service, and the request processing algorithms.

Distribution architecture: client-server vs. peer-to-peer

If a service is interactive and the location needs to be centralized, as in database access, then the service is inherently client-server in nature. In these circumstances, the processing algorithms will need to

be aware of the interaction occurring on a remote basis. A timely response to the requests coming in is necessary. To achieve this end, the processes local to the service provider will need to be optimized to provide the service.

However, if the process is passive or is strictly to share data among a few nodes, the service provider will be able to run as a background process. This is one good application of a peer-to-peer architecture. Then, the service provider is able to process information and send it off to the other nodes on the network in a manner that does not take resources from the foreground processing. Other applications of a peer-to-peer architecture include the dissemination of data to multiple locations on the network and real-time communication. EMAIL and workgroup communications programs fit these descriptions. The IPX application example in this chapter will illustrate a chat program for real-time communication between members of workgroups. The SPX application example will illustrate an interactive example.

Distribution & processing location

Once the distribution architecture and service have been decided upon, where and how the service is to be distributed needs to be resolved. For the service, will it be necessary for all processing to occur on a single node? For example, can the application be divided up and placed on separate nodes with each node providing a portion of the processing? Some applications have several granular processes, and these can be distributed across the network to machines that better suit the needs of the process.

For example, building an application consists of compiling and linking. Each of these actions could occur at different locations. If a portion of the application is highly computational, it can be performed on a node with high-end processing abilities. This will reduce the need for all users to have high-performance machines. Other easily and commonly distributed processes include access to resources and sharing of data. Some applications obviously are distributed to the workstation where the user will send his or her electronic mail from or where the user sits and communicates with other workers. Other services, such as application building, can be

done in real-time at an individual's workstation or can be distributed to other locations allowing the user to perform other tasks while the application is building.

Distribution granularity & performance

When deciding which pieces to distribute and which pieces should remain local, a balance should exist between cost of resources, ease of access, and performance. When architecting an application, a small portion or a large majority can be distributed based on this balance. How many nodes the service provider will use to provide the service and how many nodes can access the service simultaneously will be limited by the usefulness of spreading the processing around versus the amount of time that communication between those nodes will take. If only one user is going to use or edit a file at the same time, then distributing the processing would be more frustrating and time consuming than is useful. For this reason, most word processing applications run locally and allow distribution of only the printing process of the application and storage of the data file, not indirect access to the file. However, multiple access to the same file, as in order-entry databases, involves a single location for the file with a service providing access to the information contained within the file.

Another consideration in separating the individual processes of the application is whether the distribution of a certain part of the application will require multiple packets for each request or the application will need to communicate the information to a device. If the information already would be communicated to a device such as printing a file, sending that print job to a remote printer over the network should compare favorably to using a local printer. Distributed resources are a lower cost solution for businesses and reduce the frustration that happens when you have to go to the location of the resource in order to share it rather than accessing it indirectly from your workstation. File access is another example of something that doesn't degrade significantly when distributed on a network, especially when compared to accessing a file from floppy.

Performance of a distributed application is dependent on several things, including packet size, the amount of distribution, and the

location of the information. How the application is architected will determine where performance can be optimized and where performance will be second priority to access to the service provided. Some methods of improving performance include:

❶ Having multiple replicas of global data bases that are kept synchronized.

❷ Locating the information or service being managed on the same node as the service manager/provider.

❸ Using fewer packets can mean less network time or bigger delays.

⇨ Formatting the communications

An application has many choices as to the protocol chosen for communicating information. Three methods for communicating with services are discussed in this book: IPX, SPX, and QMS. IPX and SPX are actual communications protocols and QMS (Queue Management System) is a higher-level protocol for using, managing, and servicing queues. Use of these methods is determined by what level of guarantee and control the application chooses to have. QMS is easier to program to, but the application then relies on the file server to be available with queues. QMS is discussed more fully in chapters 7 and 8. IPX and SPX don't require a file server to be operating but do require more complex architecture to be controlled by the application.

IPX is a datagram-level protocol that allows applications to send messages without getting a response or waiting to be sure the message got to a specified location. IPX also allows applications to do broadcasts to all nodes simultaneously. This protocol is very useful in an application sending lots of broadcasts of information that often is changing and that does not need to be saved as in stock market trades. IPX also is the base for other protocols to build on. For example, SPX is built on IPX. SPX is discussed in chapters 13 and 14.

Because IPX as a protocol does not inherently require acknowledgments or responses, a lot of data can be sent very quickly. If the packets sent aren't purely informational broadcasts for whoever might be listening, then an application using IPX is required to

establish some protocol to ask for resends or verify that data has arrived at the appropriate location.

 # Communications reliability

Whether the service is client-server or peer-to-peer by nature, some sort of mechanism can be used to assure that the requests and replies are arriving at the destination. One way to accomplish this is through periodic retransmission of the packets, as is done in the Service Advertising Protocol or in the Routing Information Protocol. This method does have a tendency to increase the network traffic but allows for constant updates of dynamic data. A second method of assuring the timely arrival of packets is to create a guaranteed delivery mechanism. An application can rely on existing protocols or can design its own protocol. SPX makes use of a sequence number, an acknowledge number, and an allocation number to guarantee the delivery of packets in the proper sequence. For more information on these fields, see the discussion of the SPX header in chapter 13.

 # Service access

Access to the service must be defined in terms of how to find the service, how to communicate with the service, and how much access the service will allow and to whom. Access to the service involves definition of packet formats, connection processing, request processing, and security. The location and detection of the clients or the service on the network can be network address-based or name-based. The network addresses are easier to program with as all the calls require addresses. However, the names are easier for users to remember and use. The names can be resolved programmatically to addresses, it just takes more time.

 # Processing network requests & responses

The processing of network requests and responses can be done synchronously or asynchronously. Network traffic occurs

asynchronously. An application can be architected to complete or allow other processing while it is waiting for information from the network. This will allow other applications to run. If, however, the application must have the information to complete its processing, then it can be architected in a synchronous fashion. This would require the application to block user access until the network action has completed.

A sample IPX application design

In the sample in this chapter, the individual decisions made in designing and implementing a peer-to-peer distributed network application are discussed as we walk through the application. In the course of this discussion, we will bring out the information relevant to the decisions highlighted in Fig. 12-1.

The sharing of resources and information as well as the location of independent processing power at each node are inherent advantages to a network. Services typically offered on the network include print services, file services, data base access, fax services, modem services, and communications to other computing environments. Now that a desktop no longer needs to be isolated, the total cost of these services can be reduced by sharing the resources. Often in the course of a business day, a worker in the middle of a task will need some information to complete the task. Instead of picking up the phone, he or she could switch to a chat application, contact the person with the information and have it on the screen immediately. The example application was chosen to illustrate an application that gives the user just such an ability.

Definition of the sample application

The IPX application provides a facility to communicate between two nodes on the network or to "chat." This allows you to focus on the protocol and service implementation of a peer-to-peer application. The steps taken in the design and implementation of the sample include defining the services provided, designing the packet formats,

determining the request processing methods, designing for performance on the network, and suggested enhancements. As a peer-to-peer application, the example demonstrates how to write an application using IPX under Windows.

To run the application, the user must choose `Listen` to wait for a connection or `Call` to create a connection. Once the connection is established, the user needs to type only until the conversation is complete. At that point, one of the users chooses the `Hang Up` item from the menu and the connection is terminated. The `Send` option is available for later enhancements.

⇨ Defining the services

This application allows the user to choose another node on the network to communicate with. After choosing the node, the application makes a virtual connection with it to verify that it is available for communication. Once this virtual connection is established, the users at each end of the connection can type messages. These messages are displayed on both the sender's and the receiver's screens. When one end or the other of the conversation is done, the user chooses the `Hang Up` option to break the virtual connection. If the user doesn't exit the application, then connection requests can be received at any time.

⇨ Distribution & service access

The distribution in this application essentially is between two points: the caller and the listener. To simplify the example, network addresses are input. Name resolution could be added as an enhancement. To implement naming, the application would need to define a packet for advertising the name of the user or would need to use SAP and a packet for generating identification packets from all the nodes listening.

NetBIOS uses names and broadcasts a "name claim" packet to verify that no one else is using the name specified. If no response comes on the "name claim" packet, the application can use the name

advertised. To make naming useful, the application also would need to be enhanced to send the ID packet. All nodes listening would respond to this packet. The response of the name along with the source address from the IPX header would tell the application where each user is located. The application could place all the names in a list box for the user to choose from. Another method of name to address resolution relies on a file server being present. The application could scan the file server's connection table and display the names for each of the users logged in.

This application supports four actions: listen, call, send message, and receive message. Each of these actions generates a packet. With this information defined, the packet formats can be designed.

Packet formats

The packet format for this application is very simple. It consists of an IPX header, a request code, and a data buffer. The structure type used for the packet is in the file IPXCHAT.H and can be seen in Fig. 12-2. For processing simplicity, the request code is the same as the Windows message ID for the action being requested. The data buffer is filled with each character that is typed.

The Chat program packet structure.

Figure 12-2

```
typedef struct
{
    int     requestCode;
    char    str[5];
} CHAT_PACKET;
```

Communications reliability

Many smaller networks have a high reliability at the physical level of the network. This reliability degrades as network traffic increases. This application uses only IPX and does no guaranteed delivery on top of that. The simplest way to achieve guaranteed delivery would be to convert the application to SPX. Additionally, the application

could make use of a sequence and an acknowledge number to guarantee delivery in a very simple fashion. The packet structure could be modified to have a length preceded array of acknowledge numbers. After sending a defined number of packets (the protocol window size), the transmitter would wait to get a packet back that verified the receipt of those packets. All the packets sent would need to remain queued for possible retransmission until the acknowledgment was received.

Let's turn now to the implementation of this application and examine how to use the individual IPX calls.

A sample IPX application implementation

The implementation of the application consists of the code in the procedures. The discussion of each procedure highlights the information that is necessary for good programming techniques in IPX.

WinMain

WinMain is the main procedure for all Windows programs. It is responsible for the initialization of the application and for the acquisition and dispatch of messages from the message queue. The default message queue size is eight. The first step of the WinMain is to increase the size of the message queue. The SetMessageQueue call destroys the current queue first, then attempts to create a new queue of the specified size. If the call fails for all sizes, the application must exit because it has no message queue.

InitApplication & InitInstance

The InitApplication function also is standard in Windows applications. It is responsible for registering the application's Window class for the application main window. This function works in conjunction with the

InitInstance function, which sets up the main window and paints it on the screen. If your application can be launched multiple times, the InitInstance function is where to locate any task specific information that will need to be set up each time an instance is launched.

 MainWndProc

The MainWndProc is the function specified in the window class from the InitApplication function to process messages for the main window. Messages come through this function to trigger actions. This application essentially is a message switch statement that calls all the appropriate functions for each message that the application has chosen to treat.

In our IPX application, we act on 10 messages. These messages are WM_COMMAND, WM_LISTENESR, WM_CHAR, WM_LBUTTONDOWN, WM_MOUSEMOVE, WM_LBUTTONUP, WM_KEYDOWN, WM_KEYUP, WM_PAINT, and WM_DESTROY. With the exception of WM_LISTENESR, these are all system messages from Windows. The WM_LISTENESR message is generated by the listen ESR when a packet is received. We will discuss this later in more detail. Figure 12-3 contains the custom action taken on a WM_CHAR message. This action consists of getting the necessary information to output the character to the screen and to send a packet to the remote end of the conversation containing the character just entered.

 MenuHandler

The IPX Chat example calls the MenuHandler function on every WM_COMMAND message. The WM_COMMAND message is generated when an item is chosen from one of the menus. The MenuHandler function switches on the IDM_ message definitions from the IPXCHAT.H that are listed in Fig. 12-4. This application provides four types of functions. The IDM_REC_MESSAGE is generated by the Listen command on the menu. This command must be issued by one of the users prior to the other user issuing the Call command so that the application is ready for communications to begin.

Figure 12-3   *The action taken on WM_CHAR message.*

```
case WM_CHAR:
    stringToSend[2] = (char)wParam;
    hDC = GetDC(hWnd);
    if (charWidth == 0)
    {
        GetTextMetrics(hDC, (TEXTMETRIC FAR *)&tm);
        charWidth = tm.tmMaxCharWidth;
        charHeight = tm.tmHeight;
    }
    SetTextAlign(hDC, TA_UPDATECP);
    MoveTo(hDC, localX, localY);
    TextOut(hDC, 0, 0, &stringToSend[2], 1);
    localX+=charWidth;
    if (localChars >= 44)
    {
        localY+=charHeight;
        localX=10;
    }
    SendPacket();
    break;
```

Figure 12-4   *Menu command message definitions.*

```
#define IDM_ABOUT              1100
#define IDM_EXIT               1101
#define IDM_SEND_MESSAGE       1102
#define IDM_REC_MESSAGE        1103
#define IDM_CALL_MESSAGE       1104
#define IDM_HANG_UP_MESSAGE    1105
```

⇨ IDM_CALL_MESSAGE

The Call command generates the IDM_CALL_MESSAGE. This message will pop up a dialog box that asks for the address to call. The address should be entered in the following format:

    <network number>:<node number>;<socket number>

The socket number is always 0x5555 for this sample. Once the address has been input, the application initializes IPX, then sends the packet. Figure 12-5 shows the code for initializing IPX.

The first step in initialization is to query IPX for the maximum packet size. The maximum packet size can vary from a size configured in NET.CFG to the maximum size permitted by the media. If the

Initialization of IPX.   Figure 12-5

```
BOOL FAR PASCAL Init()
{
    int rcode;

    psize = IPXGetMaxPacketSize();
        if (ipxinit)
            return TRUE;
        if (!(rcode = IPXInitialize(
                &IPXTaskID,
                (WORD)MAX_LISTEN_ECBS+MAX_SEND_ECBS,
                (WORD)psize)))
            ipxinit = TRUE;
        OpenSocket();
        GetNetworkAddress();
        GetLocalTarget();
        return TRUE;
}
```

application supports internetworked LANs, it is possible for the
media size to vary between the LANs. The maximum packet size
always guaranteed to cross a router is 576 bytes. As the sample
supports only a local net, the code for the internetworked LANs
would vary slightly in the initialize statement where `psize` would be
replaced by `((psize > 576) ? 576 : psize)`.

The IPXInitialize function call expects three parameters. The first
parameter is the IPXTaskID. The values used to initialize IPXTaskID
are discussed in chapter 11. The IPXTaskID is ignored by
NWIPXSPX.DLL for enhanced mode. If, however, you want your
application to run in standard or real mode, you will need to use a
variable for this parameter and pass it in on all subsequent calls to
IPX. The second parameter is the maximum number of ECBs. The
sample application uses global data ECB buffers. Each of the types of
ECBs (sends or listens) has a define for the maximum number. The
total of these maximum values is passed to IPXInitialize as the
maximum number of ECBs. The last parameter is the packet size.
This should be passed to the function either as psize or as the tertiary
operation shown at the end of the last paragraph.

The second step in initializing IPX is to open the socket that is going
to be used for communication. The socket doesn't need to be opened
if only sends are going to be done on it. The socket does need to be

open if the application is going to listen on it or is going to use IPXScheduleIPXEvent.

The third step in IPX initialization is for the application to get the address for the machine that it is running on. This is done with a call to IPXGetInternetworkAddress. This call will return the 10 bytes of network and node numbers.

The final step in initializing IPX is to call IPXGetLocalTarget. IPXGetLocalTarget will return the node address to be used as the immediateAddress in the ECB. The immediate address is the node address of the nearest router that knows how to send packets to the network specified in the destination parameter. The transport time returned from the IPXGetLocalTargetCall can be used as a timeout interval for an application to retry if it hasn't had a response from the destination.

Once IPX is initialized, the sample application sends a connection request packet. The connection request packet contains IDM_CALL_MESSAGE as the request code. Any data following the request code will be ignored in this packet. To send a packet in IPX, several fields in the ECB and IPX header must be initialized. In the ECB, these fields are the ESRAddress (if necessary), the socket, the immediateAddress, the fragmentCount, and enough fragmentDescriptors to equal the fragmentCount. In the header, the destination address needs to be set and the data ready in the data fragments.

Two simple asynchronous methods exist to verify when the ECB event has completed. One method is to use an ESR. This method is used by the listens in the sample application and are discussed in more detail in the paragraphs on the listen message. The other method, used by IDM_CALL_MSG, is to use a Windows timer. Only 16 Windows timers are available, so this resource should be used sparingly. To use a Windows timer, the application needs to have a timer function that will be called every time the timer interval (in milliseconds) runs out. The timer function in IPXChat checks the ECB inUseFlag. If it is zero, KillTimer is called to cancel the timer and then a message box is used to notify the user if the ECB finished successfully or not.

⇨ IDM_REC_MESSAGE

The IDM_REC_MESSAGE case calls the same initialization procedure as IDM_CALL_MESSAGE. Following initialization, the application sets up to receive packets by posting a pool of listen ECBs and packet buffers. A listen ECB has four fields that must be initialized to function properly. The fields are the ESRAddress, the socket, the fragmentCount, and the fragmentDescriptor list.

The ESRAddress for the listen is set to the address of the ReceiveESRHandler. The ReceiveESRHandler is an assembly language front-end to the ReceiveESR that initializes the DS and pushes the address of the ECB on the stack. The codes for the ReceiveESRHandler and the ReceiveESR are in Fig. 12-6. ESRs are called with interrupts disabled and should perform the smallest amount of processing possible. Because Windows allows multiple tasks running simultaneously, a single application does not own the machine. Therefore, ESRs must be re-entrant. An ESR is re-entrant if it avoids changing any global information and instead relies on the foreground processing to perform that task by sending a message to the MainWndProc of the application. Because the ESR is called with interrupts disabled, it should use PostMessage rather than SendMessage. The ESR in Fig. 12-6 uses the wParam variable to pass

The ESR code for the receive.

Figure 12-6

```
cProc _ReceiveESRHandler, <FAR,PUBLIC> <ds, ax>
cBegin _ReceiveESRHandler
    mov     ax, DGROUP
    mov     ds, ax
    push    es
    push    si
    cCall   ReceiveESR
cEnd    _ReceiveESRHandler

void far pascal ReceiveESR(ECB far *ecb)
{
    BOOL rcode;
    CHAT_PACKET FAR *req;

    req = (CHAT_PACKET FAR *)(ecb->fragmentDescriptor[1].address);
    rcode = PostMessage(myWinHandle, WM_LISTENESR,
                        (WORD)req->requestCode, (DWORD)ecb);
    return;
}
```

the request code and the lParam variable to pass the ECB address. The message sent is the WM_LISTENESR message mentioned earlier.

The WM_LISTENESR case calls the ProcessPacket function found in Fig. 12-7. The ProcessPacket function checks the value of the request code. If the packet is an IDM_CALL_MESSAGE request, then the listen ECB is reposted to receive packets as they come in. If the packet is an IDM_HANG_UP_MESSAGE, then the application deinitializes IPX. If the packet is an IDM_REC_MESSAGE, the function goes through the same process as the WM_CHAR message to write the character from the packet to the screen, then reposts the listen ECB.

Figure 12-7   *Processing the receive packets.*

```
BOOL ProcessPacket(ECB FAR *ecb, WORD processFlag, HWND hWnd)
{
    HDC hDC;
    CHAT_PACKET far *data;

    data = (CHAT_PACKET far *)ecb->fragmentDescriptor[1].address;
    if (processFlag == IDM_HANG_UP_MESSAGE)
    {
        if (ipxinit)
        {
            IPXCloseSocket(IPXTaskID,socket);
            IPXSPXDeinit(IPXTaskID);
            ipxinit = FALSE;
        }
        wsprintf(message, "Connection Terminated");
        MessageBox(GetFocus(),message,
                "ListenForPacket", MB_ICONASTERISK | MB_OK);
        return (TRUE);
    }
    else if (processFlag == IDM_CALL_MESSAGE)
    {
        IPXListenForPacket(IPXTaskID, ecb);
        return (TRUE);
    }
    else
    {
        hDC = GetDC(hWnd);
        if (charWidth == 0)
        {
            GetTextMetrics(hDC, (TEXTMETRIC FAR *)&tm);
            charWidth = tm.tmMaxCharWidth;
            charHeight = tm.tmHeight;
        }
        SetTextAlign(hDC, TA_UPDATECP);
        MoveTo(hDC, remoteX, remoteY);
```

```
            TextOut(hDC, 0, 0, (LPCSTR)&(data->str), _fstrlen(data->str));
            remoteX+=charWidth;
            if (remoteChars >= 44)
            {
                remoteY+=charHeight;
                remoteX=10;
            }
            IPXListenForPacket(IPXTaskID, ecb);
            return (TRUE);
        }
    }
```

IDM_HANG_UP_MESSAGE

The IDM_HANG_UP_MESSAGE calls the termination function
Terminate() listed in Fig. 12-8. The first step in a termination is to
cancel all outstanding ECBs. This is followed by closing the sockets and
calling IPXSPXDeinit. Once the sample application is deinitialized, it
could reestablish communications at any time the user chose.

Deinitializing the application.   Figure 12-8

```
BOOL FAR PASCAL Terminate()
{
    int ccode, i;

    packetData[0].requestCode = IDM_HANG_UP_MESSAGE;
    IPXSend.packetType = 4;
    sendECB.ESRAddress = 0x00;
    _fmemcpy(&(sendECB.socketNumber), &(destAddress.socket), 2);
    _fmemcpy(&(IPXSend.destination.network[0]), &destAddress, 12);
    sendECB.fragmentCount = 2;
    sendECB.fragmentDescriptor[0].address = (char far *)&IPXSend;
    sendECB.fragmentDescriptor[0].size = sizeof(IPXHeader);
    sendECB.fragmentDescriptor[1].address = (void far *)&packetData[0];
    sendECB.fragmentDescriptor[1].size = sizeof(CHAT_PACKET);

    IPXSendPacket(IPXTaskID,&sendECB);
    wsprintf(message, "Connection Terminated");
    MessageBox(GetFocus(),message,
            "Terminate", MB_ICONASTERISK | MB_OK);

    for (i=1; i<=MAX_LISTEN_ECBS; i++)
        ccode = IPXCancelEvent(IPXTaskID,&listenECB[i]);

    IPXCloseSocket(IPXTaskID,socket);
    ccode = IPXSPXDeinit(IPXTaskID);
    ipxinit = FALSE;
    return TRUE;
}
```

 # Memory considerations

The sample application uses static ECBs and packet buffers. Any static data used for ECBs or packet buffers must reside in a fixed segment as must any code that will be accessed from the ESR. If the application uses dynamic memory for the ECB and packet buffers, the memory must be allocated using GlobalAlloc with the GMEM_FIXED and GMEM_DDESHARE flags set, locked using GlobalLock, and page locked using GlobalPageLock. ECBs and packet buffers must be accessible at interrupt time, and Windows is not able to page memory in at that point.

You should minimize the number of segments that are fixed to allow Windows to do proper garbage collection on global memory resources. All the code accessed from the ESR can be in its own segment that is the only fixed code segment. The same can hold true with data.

 # Suggested enhancements

This application could be enhanced such that multiple sessions could be active at the same time, input from each conversation could be in its own child window, and a file attachment could be sent with the Send menu option. Electronic chat capabilities allow users to continue their work without picking up a phone and can be a sharing resource.

13

Sequenced Packet Exchange overview

CHAPTER 13

SEQUENCED Packet Exchange (SPX) is a guaranteed delivery
protocol written by Novell. SPX is modeled on the Sequenced
Packet Protocol designed by Xerox. However, SPX does not have a
sliding window or sparse acknowledgments. SPX works on the
session and transport layers of the OSI model as is illustrated in Fig.
13-1.

Figure 13-1

Application	NW C Interface	
Presentation		
Session	SPX	NCP
Transport		
Network	IPX	
Data Link	LAN drivers and Protocols	
Physical		

OSI layers and NetWare equivalents.

⇨ SPX & connections

SPX is a connection-oriented protocol. SPX maintains a virtual
connection between two endpoints (one or more computers) and
guarantees the delivery of packets in the same sequence that they are
sent. This is accomplished through a series of timeouts and retries.
When one end of an SPX connection sends a packet using SPX, the
other end of the connection has a time out period within which to
respond. After the time out period expires, SPX will resend a packet
in an attempt to elicit an acknowledgment is received from the
connection partner. If the total number of retries has been used and
no acknowledgment has been received from the partner, then the
local SPX will abort the session and will clear it from the session
table. The number of retries is set in the SPXEstablishConnection call

or in the SPXListenForConnection call. The time out period between retries is set in the NET.CFG configuration file as the SPX abort timeout. The number of retries multiplied by the timeout value will be the total time that a session will stay alive without an acknowledgment. Each connection has an optional connection watchdog. When the watchdog is enabled on a connection, SPX will send a packet every 30 seconds once the session has been inactive for 10 minutes. This added security guarantees that the connection is in working order when the application attempts to use it once more.

⇨ Event control block

As in IPX, SPX uses an event control block for all communications with the NetWare SPX driver found in IPXODI.COM (Fig. 13-2). The ECB structure for SPX is the same as that in IPX, but the management of the fields differs.

Figure 13-2

Link		
ESR Address		
In Use		
Completion Code		
Socket		
IPX Workspace		
Driver Workspace		
Immediate Address		
Count	Fragment Descriptor List	
Address	1	-> to SPX Packet Header
Size		
Address	2	-> to SPX Packet Data
Size		

The SPX event control block.

229

⇨ Link field

The Link field is used internally by IPX to create a linked list of ECBs. If the ECB is not in use by IPX, this field can be used by the application. The size of this field is 4 bytes.

⇨ Event Service Routine Address

The ESR Address is the segment:offset far address of the Event Service Routine (ESR) that IPX will call when the SPX event completes. If this field is set to 0x00, control returns immediately to the interrupted process after an SPX event completes. This field is 4 bytes wide.

⇨ SPX events

There are several types of SPX events: establishing connections, listening for connections, sending packets, listening for packets, and terminating connections. IPX calls ESRs on the completion of the SPX event associated with the ECB. ESRs are called with interrupts disabled. An ESR is similar to an interrupt service routine (ISR) and should be short operations.

On entry to the ESR, the application should set the DS register to its data segment if it is going to access any data. Under Windows, this will be taken care of automatically by exporting the ESR function. If the process will be enabling interrupts, then the application should change stacks to the prevent the possibility of stack overflow or should queue the incoming events to be processed by the main Windows control procedure for the application. Using PostMessage to place a message in the application's message queue is the preferred method for ESR processing under Windows. This allows the main Windows message loop to process the ECB and repost it if necessary.

Only SPXSendSequencedPacket and SPXListenForSequencedPacket should ever be called directly from ESRs. When an ESR is called by

SPX, the address of the ECB for which the event has completed is contained in ES:SI.

⇨ In Use flag

The In Use flag indicates that the ECB is in use or not in use by SPX. A nonzero value for this flag indicates in use. No fields should be modified by the application while the ECB is in use by SPX. This is a one-byte field.

⇨ Completion code

The completion code indicates the status of the event upon completion. This field is valid only after the In Use flag has been set to zero. A value of zero for the completion code indicates the IPX event completed successfully. A nonzero value is an error code indicating failure of the IPX event. This is a one-byte field. Table 13-1 contains a list of possible IPX completion codes in Windows and their meaning.

The possible ECB completion codes   Table 13-1

Code	Meaning	Circumstances
0xFF	SPX_SOCKET_NOT_OPENED SOCKET_NOT_OPEN	Socket not opened before ECB submitted
	TRANSMIT_FAILURE	Packet could not be sent
	ECB_NOT_IN_USE	On ECBs being canceled
0xFE	PACKET_UNDELIVERABLE	Packet could not be delivered, the address is incorrect or the destination can no longer be found
0xFD	SPX_MALFORMED_PACKET	Packet does not have at least 1 fragment or first fragment (header) less than 42 bytes long
	SPX_PACKET_OVERFLOW	Packet received is larger than the total of all the fragments defined by the ECB. Packet being sent is larger than max packet size

Table 13-1   **Continued**

Code	Meaning	Circumstances
0xFC	SPX_LISTEN_CANCELLED	Cancelled SPX Listen
	ECB_CANCELLED	Cancelled ECB successfully
0xFA	NO_PATH_TO_DESTINATION_FOUND	Packet destination has no local target
0xF9	CANCEL_FAILURE	ECB could not be cancelled
0xF6	IPXSPX_PREV_INIT	IPX/SPX was previously initialized for the currently running instance. To multiply initialize, see below
0xF5	OVER_MAX_LIMIT	Packet size greater than specified on initialization
0xF4	WINLOCK_FAILED	DLL management memory could not be locked
0xF3	NO_FREE_ECB	All low memory ECBs in use
0xF2	NO_DOS_MEMORY	Not enough DOS memory to allocate the number of ECBs requested
0xF1	IPXSPX_NOT_INIT	IPX/SPX not initialized for the specified IPX task ID
0xF0	NO_MGMT_MEMORY	Not enough memory for DLL to complete request
0xEF	SPX_CONNECTION_TABLE_FULL	Socket table full
0xEE	SPX_INVALID_CONNECTION	Connection specified not valid
0xED	SPX_TERMINATED_POORLY	Connection aborted from other end
0xEC	SPX_NO_ANSWER_FROM_TARGET	Partner no longer answering
	SPX_CONNECTION_FAILED	Connection dead on other end or killed by watchdog
	SPX_CONNECTION_TERMINATED	Connection terminated by other end

Novell, Inc.

⇨ Socket

The Socket is the source socket to use for the connection. In SPX, the socket is set only in an ECB being used for SPXEstablishConnection or for SPXListenForConnection. The socket is a demultiplexing mechanism. The socket is a word in high-low order. The high-low order is necessary, because this is the socket number IPX places in the packet header. The entire packet header is in high-low word order. The socket number could be compared to an apartment number in an addressing scheme. The network number is similar to the street, and the node address to the building number. The socket functions much like an apartment number by further resolving the process to which the packet should be directed in the node the way a letter is directed to an apartment in a building.

 IPX Workspace

The IPX Workspace is space reserved for IPX to use while processing the event associated with the ECB. This field is 4 bytes in size.

Driver Workspace

The Driver Workspace is space reserved for the LAN driver to use during packet processing. This field is 12 bytes in size.

Immediate Address

The Immediate Address is the node address of the local router. When using SPX, this field is managed by SPX. The immediate address is the node's six-digit LAN card address. This field is 6 bytes wide.

Fragment Descriptor List

The Fragment Descriptor List consists of the Count, Address, and Size of each fragment to be used as part of an IPX packet. This list is used by IPX to construct the packet. The count field is a word in size, the address field is 4 bytes in length and is in segment:offset format, and the size field is a word long. All packets must have at least one fragment. The first fragment must always point to the SPX header. The size of the first fragment must always be at least 42 bytes to accommodate the larger SPX header.

 # Connection ID

The connection ID from SPXListenForConnection is returned in the first word of the IPXWorkspace in the ECB. This value is the local session ID. It is a hash value for the session table. The SPXEstablishConnection call returns this value as a variable. The local session number received from SPXEstablishConnection is a tentative value. This connection ID is not valid for communications until the ECB posted in the SPXEstablishConnection call completes with no error.

 # SPX header

The SPX header is identical to the IPX header for the first 30 bytes. The next 12 bytes are used to sequence packets and to control the session. These 12 bytes are divided into 7 fields: Connection Control, Datastream Type, Source Connection ID, Destination Connection ID, Sequence Number, Acknowledge Number, and Allocation Number. These fields are illustrated in Fig. 13-3. The Destination Network Address is set by the application only on an SPXEstablishConnection call. After the connection is established, SPX takes care of filling in all the fields in the SPX Header. The SPX packet type is five.

 # Connection Control

Connection Control is one byte and is used for session maintenance. This field is used to indicate if the packet is a system packet (bit 7 set), an acknowledgment (bit 6 set), attention (bit 5 set), or an end of message (bit 4 set). These bit definitions are according to the SPP definition. Bits from 0 to 3 are undefined. An establish, terminate, or acknowledgment packet is a system packet. Acknowledgments in SPX are piggy-backed on the sends. This means that, if a packet is received by one side of the connection and that side is about to send another packet, the acknowledgment bit will be set in the Connection Control field. This makes it possible to reduce traffic on the network by not requiring an individual acknowledgment for each packet.

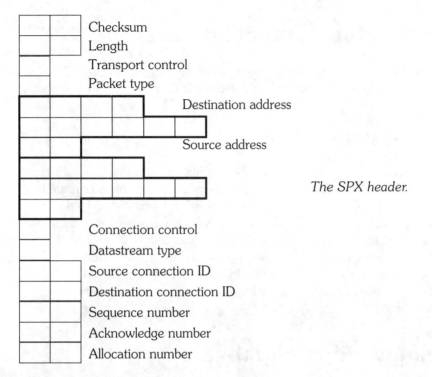

Figure 13-3

Checksum
Length
Transport control
Packet type
Destination address
Source address
Connection control
Datastream type
Source connection ID
Destination connection ID
Sequence number
Acknowledge number
Allocation number

The SPX header.

⇨ Datastream Type

The Datastream Type is a one-byte field used by SPX to flag the end of the session. When a terminate packet is sent, this field is set to 0xFE. In the acknowledgment to the termination packet, this field is set to 0xFF. This field is not cleared by SPX. If the ECB and packet header are going to be reused, then this field must be cleared of 0xFE or another session might be terminated erroneously.

⇨ Source Connection ID

The Source Connection ID is the connection ID in the SPX located on the node specified as the source address in the packet. This connection identification is a hash into the connection table for the local SPX. The connection ID values under dedicated IPX and IPXODI do not appear similar. This is no cause for alarm, it just indicates a different algorithm is used internally in IPX and IPXODI.

Destination Connection ID

The Destination Connection ID is the connection ID in the SPX located on the node specified as the destination address in the packet.

Sequence Number

The Sequence Number is the packet number that is being sent. This number is incremented by one for each packet sent on a connection. SPX guarantees that packets are delivered and processed in the sequence they are sent. To do this, SPX keeps track of the sequence number and will drop any packet that arrives out of sequence. If the other end of the connection doesn't receive an acknowledgment for the packet it sends, it will not send the next original packet. SPX will continue to retry the send for which the acknowledgment is outstanding.

Acknowledge Number

The Acknowledge Number is the sequence number of the remote SPX partner. Currently, SPX has a communication window size of one and is not a sparse acknowledgment protocol.

Allocation Number

The Allocation Number is the number of listens available at the time the packet was sent. When the allocation number equals the acknowledge number, the receive window is closed. SPX will continue to watchdog the connection until more listens are posted and the window is reopened. Under SPX in DOS and Windows, listens for sequenced packet are pooled by socket. Therefore, if several connections are active on the same socket, the allocation number will not represent the number of packets the workstation can receive from any single connection, but from all connections on that socket combined.

Establishing SPX connections

Before posting an SPXEstablishConnection or an SPXListenForConnection to SPX, the application must prepost at least one SPXListenForSequencedPacket. An outstanding listen is borrowed periodically for internal use by SPX. This does not conflict with any packets to be received. The listen that is posted before the connection calls is used for receiving the connection acknowledgment. An application can set the retry count to be used by SPX in the session before giving up on a packet. The default is 20 retries and is used when the retry count is set to 0. This count is set in the SPXEstablishConnection and the SPXListenForConnection calls.

An additional level of session maintenance can be invoked using the watchdog flag. The watchdog is invoked by setting the watchdog flag to any nonzero value. The watchdog periodically will query the partner of an inactive connection to verify the connection is still alive. When the watchdog is invoked, the user must always have a minimum of two outstanding listens at all times.

⇨ SPX processing

ECBs are processed in the queue in whatever order they happen to be. No order should be assumed and all ECBs should describe packets large enough to receive the largest packet that will be sent on the socket.

An SPXListenForConnection does not use a packet. Therefore, the packet fragments of an SPXListenForConnection ECB do not need to be initialized to packet pointers. An SPXListenForConnection is used by SPX to reserve space in the internal connection tables for the connection that is expected. If several connection requests can be received simultaneously, then the application should post several listens for connection to reserve sufficient space in the SPX connection table for the expected number of connections.

237

When an application will be processing a high rate of SPX transmissions, the pool of outstanding listens should be large enough to allow for processing time during which the ECBs still will be in use. The number of ECBs that would allow for this processing lag would be on a connection basis. For example, a pool of 5 ECBs per connection probably would be the lower boundary for efficient communications and a pool of 15 ECBs per connection would be the upper boundary with current packet transmission speeds.

Terminating SPX connections

Two ways exist to tear down an SPX connection. These two methods are SPXTerminateConnection and SPXAbortConnection. To properly terminate a connection when communications are complete, an SPXTerminateConnection should be used. The SPXTerminateConnection is sent to the partner in the SPX connection to inform of the pending termination. This allows the remote partner to clean up its session tables and free up resources. An acknowledgment of the receipt of the terminate packet is sent to the initiator. At that point, the tables on both sides of the connection are cleaned up and the connection has been terminated gracefully.

An SPXAbortConnection should be used only when the communication or the application is in an unrecoverable state. The abort connection does not attempt communication with the remote partner in the connection but only removes the connection from the connection table and frees up local resources.

SPX connection information

The SPXGetConnectionInformation call can provide the application with useful information concerning the connections currently in the local connection table. The CONNECTION_INFO structure is defined in the NXT.H header file as in Fig. 13-4.

The SPX connection info structure. Novell, Inc.

Figure 13-4

```
typedef {
BYTE        connectionState;
BYTE        connectionFlags;
WORD        sourceConnectionID;
WORD        destinationConnectionID;
WORD        sequenceNumber;
WORD        acknowledgeNumber;
WORD        allocationNumber;
WORD        remoteAcknowledgeNumber;
WORD        remoteAllocationNumber;
WORD        connectionSocket;
BYTE        immediateAddress[6];
IPXAddress  destinationAddress;
BYTE        destinationSocket[2];
WORD        retransmissionCount;
WORD        estimatedRoundTripDelay;
WORD        retransmittedPackets;
WORD        suppressedPackets;
} CONNECTION_INFO;
```

⇨ Connection state

The connectionState field indicates whether the connection is listening for a connection, has sent an establish connection packet, is active, or has sent a terminate connection packet.

⇨ Connection flags

The connectionFlags field maintains information as to whether or not the connection is being watchdogged. If the connection is watchdogged, the flags are nonzero.

⇨ Connection IDs

Each connection maintains the source connection ID and the destination connection ID. This information can be queried using NetWare Diagnostics. Using the destination connection ID, a packet also can be sent to the connection partner and connection information retrieved from that endpoint as well.

The sourceConnectionID is the connection ID for the local side of the SPX connection. The destinationConnectionID is the connection ID for the remote side of the SPX connection.

Connection packet numbers

The numbers used in the packet to sequence the SPX packets are maintained for both ends of the connection. This enables SPX to easily acknowledge packets from the connection partner and to know whether the remote endpoint can possibly receive a packet (according to the remote allocation number).

The sequenceNumber field is the local sequence number for the SPX connection. The acknowledgeNumber field is the local acknowledge number for the specified SPX connection. The allocationNumber field is the local allocation number for the specified SPX connection. The remoteAcknowledgeNumber is the acknowledge number on the remote side of the SPX connection. This field's value should be very close to the value of the local sequence number.

The remoteAllocationNumber is the allocation number from the remote partner of the SPX connection. This number corresponds to the number of listens posted minus the local sequence number, which is the total number of listens outstanding on a socket. Because the socket is used as a demultiplexing mechanism, it is recommended that only one connection be established per socket.

Packet transmission information

This set of information is maintained by SPX to be set in the SPX header of all packets that are transmitted, including system packets and acknowledgments.

The connectionSocket field is the local socket being used for the SPX connection. The immediateAddress field is the first router to which any SPX packet is sent for the SPX connection. The destinationAddress field is the network and node address of the remote side of the SPX connection specified. The destinationSocket

field is the socket that the remote SPX partner is using to demultiplex communications for the specified connection.

⇨ Packet statistics

The retransmissionCount is the number of times that SPX has to resend a packet for the connection specified before the destination is considered unreachable. SPX will resend a packet any time it doesn't receive an acknowledgment within the time specified by the retry timeout in the NET.CFG. Three reasons exist for a packet to be resent by SPX. Any one of these reasons is indicated by the lack of an acknowledgment to the original transmission. See Fig. 13-5.

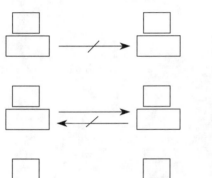

1. A packet doesn't reach the remote workstation.

2. An acknowledgment doesn't reach the local workstation.

3. An acknowledgment isn't received by the local workstation because no listens are outstanding.

Figure 13-5

SPX and transmission retries.

The estimatedRoundTripDelay is the amount of time necessary for a packet to be sent to the remote workstation and an acknowledgment to return. The retransmittedPackets field is the number of packets re-sent because an acknowledgment wasn't received.

The suppressedPackets field is the number of packets SPX has dropped because either the packet arrived out of sequence or the packet was a duplicate. This field along with the retransmittedPackets field can indicate how reliable a network is between the two partners in an SPX connection. If the number of retransmitted packets is equal to the sequence number, the network probably is slow enough that

the timeout count is too small. If it is greater than the sequence number, then the network probably has a lot of packet losses and a lower reliability.

In the next chapter, we will explore an application implement using SPX. The intent with the application is to demonstrate an application that is specifically for performing batch processes in the form of queries or updates on a database of names and addresses.

14

SPX & distributed application architecture

CHAPTER 14

MANY decisions lead to the use of SPX in a peer-to-peer or client-server application. These decisions are specific to the architecture of the application and to the desired results. When an application is designed initially, decisions are made based on the needs of the service being provided. If the service is request-reply by nature, some sort of guaranteed delivery mechanism usually is required. This mechanism can be provided by existing protocols or a protocol unique to the application can be designed. Other considerations for the application include those outlined in the IPX programming chapter and found in Fig. 14-1.

Figure 14-1   *Considerations in the design of a distributed application.*

```
1. Where will the application be distributed?
2. To how many nodes will the process be distributed?
3. Is the service client-server or peer-to-peer in nature?
4. What communications protocol should be used?
5. How will clients access the service?
6. How do you maintain high performance in the distibuted application?
```

⇨ Application architecture

In considering these factors, the specific pieces of the application are designed including the packet formats, the request processing algorithms, the time spent in network transit and in real processing, where to distribute the application, managing data access, and how to find your service.

⇨ Processing location

When the service to provide has been chosen, the next decision involves the determination of the location of the various aspects of the application. For the service, will it be necessary for all processing to occur on a single node? For example, can the application be divided up and placed on separate nodes with each node providing a portion of the processing?

Some applications have several granular processes, and these can be distributed across the network to machines that better suit the needs of the process. If a portion of the application is highly computational, it can be performed on a node with high-end processing abilities. This will reduce the need for all users to have high-performance machines. Other easily and commonly distributed processes include access to resources and sharing of data. When a set of data should be shared by all and kept up-to-date, it can be located on a single node with multiple users accessing it. In this instance, the service provided is data access. To optimize performance in accessing the data, a centralized cache and record locking for individual users could be implemented. Typically, any process or resource that more than one user would find useful is a candidate for distribution.

 Granularity of distribution

When deciding which pieces to distribute and which pieces should remain local, a balance should exist between cost of resources, ease of access, and performance. When architecting an application, a small portion or a large majority can be distributed based on this balance. How many nodes the service provider will use to provide the service and how many nodes can simultaneously access the service will be limited by the usefulness of spreading the processing around versus the amount of time communication between those nodes will take. If only one user is ever going to use or edit a file, then distributing the processing would be more frustrating and time consuming than is useful. For this reason, most word processing applications run locally and only allow distribution of the printing process of the application and storage of the data file, not indirect access to the file. However, multiple access to the same file, like in order-entry databases, involves a single location for the file with a service providing access to the information contained within the file.

Another consideration in separating the individual processes of the application is whether the distribution of a certain part of the application will require multiple packets for each request or the application would need to communicate the information to a device already. If the information already would be communicated to device such as printing a file, sending that print job to a remote printer over the network should

compare favorably to using a local printer. Additionally, printers are easily shared, and fewer printers then will be required by the end user. File access is another example of something that doesn't degrade significantly when distributed on a network, especially when compared to accessing a file from floppy.

Client-server vs. peer-to-peer

If a service is interactive, like database access, then the service is inherently client-server in nature. In these circumstances, the processing algorithms will need to be aware of the interaction occurring on a remote basis. A timely response to the requests coming in is necessary. To achieve this end, the processes local to the service provider will need to be optimized to provide the service.

If, however, the process is passive, the service provider will be able to provide the service in batch or background method. This is one good application of a peer-to-peer architecture. Then, the service provider will need to process information and send it off to the other nodes on the network in a manner that is nondemanding of foreground processing.

Another good application of peer-to-peer architecture is a workgroup communications package that allows individuals to carry on conversations through their workstations rather than over the phone.

Communication protocol

An application has many choices as to the protocol chosen for communicating information. Three methods for communicating with services will be discussed in this book: IPX, SPX, and QMS. IPX and SPX are actual communications protocols and QMS (Queue Management System) is a higher-level protocol for using, managing, and servicing queues. Use of these protocols will be determined by what level of guarantee and control the application chooses to have. QMS is easier to program to, but the application then relies on the file server to be available with queues. QMS and IPX are discussed more fully in other chapters. IPX and SPX don't require a file server

to be operating, but require more complex architecture to be controlled by the application.

IPX is a datagram-level protocol that allows applications to send messages without getting a response or waiting to be sure the message got to a specified location. IPX also allows applications to do broadcasts to all nodes simultaneously. This protocol is very useful in an application sending lots of broadcasts of information that often is changing and that does not need to be saved or has the basis for other protocols built on it. For example, SPX is built on IPX.

SPX is a connection- or session-based protocol that does sequencing and guaranteed delivery of packets. This protocol does require a connection to be established with other nodes before communication can take place. Whether the service is client-server or peer-to-peer by nature, some sort of guaranteed delivery mechanism can be used to assure that the requests and replies are arriving at the appropriate destination. To accomplish the guaranteed delivery, the application can be built upon existing protocols or a unique protocol can be designed.

Typically, the less dependable the physical network itself is, the more reliable the protocol needs to be. The example for SPX detailed in this chapter is a client-server in nature and provides distributed access to a centralized database.

Service access

Access to the service must be defined in terms of how to find the service, how to communicate with the service, and how much access the service will allow and to whom. Access to the service involves definition of packet formats, connection processing, request processing, and security.

Performance issues

Performance of a distributed application is dependent on several things including packet size, the amount of distribution, and the

location of the information. How the application is architected will determine where the performance can be optimized and where the performance will be overruled by needing access to the service provided. Some methods of improving performance include:

❶ Having multiple replicas of global databases that are kept synchronized.

❷ Locating the information or service being managed on the same node as the service manager/provider.

❸ Using less packets can mean less network time or bigger delays.

A sample SPX application design

In the sample in this chapter, the individual decisions made in designing and implementing a distributed network application are discussed as we walk through the application. In the course of this discussion, we will bring out the information relevant to the topics found in Fig. 14-1.

The sharing of resources and information as well as the location of independent processing power located at each node are inherent advantages to a network. Services typically offered on the network include print services, file services, database access, fax services, modem services, and communications to other computing environments. Now that a desktop no longer needs to be isolated, the total cost of these services can be reduced by sharing the resources. One of the most common uses of a network is to share access to a database. The example application was chosen to illustrate a request/reply client-server architecture for accessing a database on the network.

Definition of the sample application

The database in the example provides employee information to the requester. Only a minimum of information is provided, and the format of the data files is very simple. This allows you to focus the majority of the effort on the protocol and service implementation rather than

the database implementation. The information contained in this database includes employee number, employee name, salary, and address. The steps taken in the design and implementation of the sample include defining the services provided, designing the packet formats, determining the request processing methods, designing for performance on the network, and suggested enhancements.

The server portion of the sample is a Windows application that can be started on a workstation and left to manage the database. The client portion of the application makes requests to the server for employee information.

This application demonstrates the ability to share much of the same definitions and flow control between both the client and the server. The application consists of the functions found in Fig. 14-2. Which functions are used by which side of the client-server relationship is detailed in Table 14-1.

Common procedures for the server and client.

Figure 14-2

```
WinMain
AppInit
WndProc
AboutProc
SetupServer
InitializeSPX
CreateListenECBsAndListen
SetupListenECB
CreateSendECBAndHeader
CreateConnectonECBAndHeader
FindServerProc
AttachRoutine
MakeServerReq
PrepareAndSendServerRequest
ProcessReceivedData
RequestESR
DisplayResponse
ServiceRequest
SendConnectESR
```

Table 14-1 **The sample functions and their purposes**

Procedure	Used by	Description
WinMain	Both	Called by Windows to start application
AppInit	Both	Called by WinMain to initialize application and application data
WndProc	Both	Main processing procedure in the application that processes all messages
AboutProc	Both	Called when About is chosen from the menu
SetupServer	Server	Called when Setup is chosen from the Server menu
InitializeSPX	Both	Initialize SPX for either client or server
CreateListenECBsAndListen	Both	Create the pool of listen ECBs for the application to use and initialize the ESR address
SetupListenECB	Both	Called from CreateListenECBsAndListen
CreateSendECBAndHeader	Both	Sets up send ECB and packet
CreateConnectonECBAndHeader	Both	Sets up connect ECB and packet
FindServerProc	Client	Prompts user for name of server to connect to
AttachRoutine	Client	Called when Attach is chosen chosen from the client menu
MakeServerReq	Client	Prompts user to choose which request to make
PrepareAndSendServerRequest	Client	Sets up packet and sends request
ProcessReceivedData	Client	ESR for client listens
RequestESR	Server	ESR for server listens
DisplayResponse	Client	Formats and displays response data
ServiceRequest	Server	Processes service requests
SendConnectESR	Both	Connection ESR

The application allows the user to choose whether the node is to act as a server or as a client. This is accomplished by choosing functions from the server menu or from the client menu. Both functions should not be executed from the same instance of the application but can be executed from the different instances on the same node. Events are

arranged on the menus in the order in which they should be performed. The server menu is illustrated in Fig. 14-3, and the client menu is illustrated in Fig. 14-4.

Figure 14-3

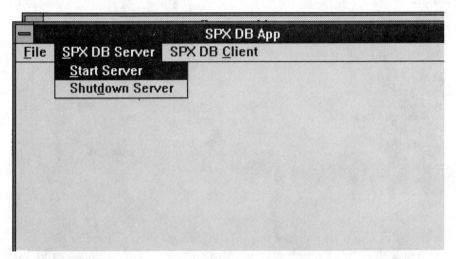

The Server menu.

Figure 14-4

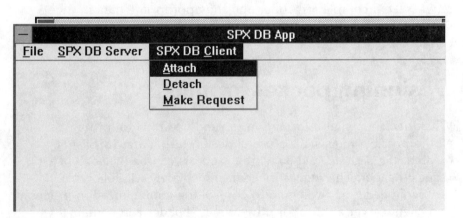

The Client menu.

⇨ Defining the services

The database managed by the server half of this sample consists of employee information. The application is implemented with reading

and writing data to this file. Currently, the application allows only one client to access the database. Additional processing could be added to allow for multiple client access. This will be discussed in the suggested enhancements section. The application provides the requests found in Fig. 14-5.

Figure 14-5   *The requests available to a client sample.*

```
Add Employee
Get Average Salary
Get Employee Number
Get Employee Salary
Get Employee Address
List Employees
Modify Employee Address
Modify Employee Number
Modify Employee Salary
Save Changes
Verify Employment
```

Each of the client requests will require a request ID. The "Get" requests will require a name to be passed to indicate which employee to reference. The responses from the server will need to return the request ID, a completion code, and the appropriate data in the response packet. With this information defined, the packet formats can be designed.

⇨ Designing packet formats

When deciding what information to send and how to format it, listing all the possible requests is a useful design task. After this list is created, the data needed by all the requests can be included in a request header. The request header immediately will follow the protocol header and will help to control the communication process. In a client-server application, the request header can contain information such as the number of requests made, the request ID, an acknowledgment of the data received, a request for additional related information, a referral address, a client ID, a data ID, and any number of other items that provide useful controlling data to the server. In a peer-to-peer application on the other hand, the request header might be more like a process header and include information such as a simple identification of the request and the amount of data

being sent or received. Other useful information for a peer-to-peer process would be an end of message flag and a re-sent flag.

In the case of a large amount of data being contained in the packet, compression might be an issue. If the data is sensitive, encryption of the data could be considered. Checksumming would be an option to check the reliability of the information. These options might generate the need for passing control flags or structures as part of the request header.

For the sample requests, the header is only the first 2 bytes following the SPX header. These two bytes are the request identification number. This field is defined as a word. Immediately following the request ID is the packet data. The request packet structure contains an 80-byte string immediately following the request header. This string is the name for which information is being requested. The definition of the request structure is found in Fig. 14-6. After the name string, the rest of the packet currently is defined as a byte array to reserve space for future expansion of the application.

The Client Request Packet format.

Figure 14-6

```
typedef struct CLIENT_REQUEST
{
    WORD     requestID;
    char     requestName[80];
    BYTE     reserved[452];
} CLIENT_REQUEST;
```

After determining the request header, we turn next to designing a reply header. The reply header might or might not use the same format as the request header. This will be determined by the control information that is held in common between the request and the reply. In this application, the structure of the general server response packet consists of a requestID, a completion code, followed by a 530-byte BYTE array containing the response data. The structure of the general response packet is found in Fig. 14-7.

Following the header designs are the data format design. Data format in packets are dependent on the request or reply being made. The requests have at least one general structure. Similarly, responses have

Figure 14-7   *The Server Reply Packet format.*

```
typedef struct SERVER_RESPONSE
{
    WORD    requestID;
    WORD    completionCode;
    BYTE    responseData[530];
} SERVER_RESPONSE;
```

at least one general structure. Data formats can be designed opaquely on the transport level. The information is differentiated at a different layer of the application than the transport level. The differentiation occurs in the procedure responsible for interpreting, formatting, or processing the response. In the sample application, this differentiation occurs in the display procedure where a switch on the request ID is used to format the different types of information that can be requested. The interpretation of the response data uses different structure definitions to read the information and format it for the screen.

 # Determining the request processing methods

Request processing can be managed on a first come first serve basis or on a priority processing basis. First come first serve is the easiest way to manage and process incoming requests for data. This the standard request/reply algorithm. However, priority processing differs by assigning each request or each client a priority. When multiple packets arrive almost simultaneously, this method allows for a prioritized processing of the packets. These priorities can give precedence to types of requests, types of data processed, or types of clients. Often, processor time is best used in first come first serve processing. This allows the server to process every packet as it comes in and requires less management overhead for the packets.
Processing in a server should be done asynchronously to prevent any time wasted in polling and not allowing other processes to run. Asynchronous processing allows the server to schedule processing or returning a packet at will and not tie up the server host machine for an extended period of time. This is especially important in Windows, which expects processing to be message driven.

The sample SPX application uses the main message loop of the Windows program to control all processing. Modularizing around tasks allows a procedure to be written to perform a specific task. This task then can be executed in any context simply by sending a message to the application that passes the processing to that procedure. The tasks defined in this application are listed in Fig. 14-8.

Modular tasks in the SPX sample application.   Figure 14-8

```
Server Start-up
Client Initialization and Connection
Making Requests
Processing Requests
Shutdown
```

Server start-up and client initialization and connection call the same four calls before completing the process. By single sourcing these modules, less code is generated to complete the application. Making requests and displaying the response are a client function and are handled through switch statements that set up or interpret the packet structures. Shutdown on the client or the server will terminate the SPX connection and clean up.

⇨ Programming for network performance

Performance is a major concern for all Windows applications and all network applications. Performance can be improved through a variety of methods. These methods include appropriate use of ESRs, Windows messaging, sending only the information necessary in a packet, proper packet alignment, and distribution of the appropriate pieces of the application.

Performance improvements are achieved through efficient use of asynchronous event processing, ESRs, and Windows messages. ESRs allow all packets to be processed asynchronously. Windows messages are managed and used by the entire Windows operating system, so they are optimized for the best performance possible.

Under SPX, connections should be established on a different dynamic socket for each connection. This allows all demultiplexing to be performed by SPX on the connection rather than by the application on the socket. SPX is optimized on each platform by Novell for the best performance it can achieve.

ESRs are controlled by the application. ESRs are executed with interrupts disabled and, therefore, should be as short as possible to avoid losing any data that might be communicated through the serial ports or other hardware sources. The optimal use of an ESR in Windows is to post a message to the application to allow processing to occur in the regular processing of the application. This requires the minimal time necessary to be spent in the ESR and allows the application to use the Windows optimized method of processing.

An application reduces time spent on the wire by sending packets only as big as is necessary to communicate the required data. The sample application creates buffers large enough to receive a standard router packet but sets the length for the packet to the actual size of the data. Time spent on the wire also can be reduced by distributing only the processes that can easily be divided and that don't require enormous amounts of data to maintain state.

A good strategy for increasing the performance of a distributed application is to improve or decrease the necessary time spent on the wire to get the information from one location to another. At the same time, performance issues need to be offset by an evaluation of the reliability of the system. For example, if an application sends data very fast but cannot guarantee that the data has reached the receiving end, then it might not meet the needs of the user. Some performance can be sacrificed for reliability, and some reliability can be sacrificed for performance.

To reduce time on the wire and to decrease the latency involved between the data packets sent and their acknowledgments, the most data should be sent in as few packets as possible. This is why a sliding window/sparse acknowledgment or negative acknowledgment protocol is the most efficient and reliable. The efficiency is in the reduction of the number of packets necessary and in requiring retransmissions on only dropped packets. This avoids resends of the

packets sent and received successfully after the packet that was dropped. Another way to reduce network traffic is to use the maximum packet size possible and to possibly negotiate the maximum packet size that the two partners on a connection can handle. Bursting technology involves combining two or more logical packets into one physical packet. Thus, the number of packets necessary to send the information is reduced again.

A sample SPX application implementation

The implementation of the application consists of the code in the procedures. The discussion of each procedure highlights the information that is necessary for good programming techniques in SPX.

WinMain

This is the main procedure called by Windows. This procedure increases the size of the application message queue. The default size of an application message queue is eight messages. Most applications, especially network applications, lose messages unless the message queue size is increased.

After the queue size is increased, the AppInit procedure is called. When this procedure returns, the main application Window is created and shown, then the message loop is begun.

AppInit

The AppInit procedure is responsible for registering the application class. In registering the class, the message control procedure is specified, the icon is loaded, and the cursor is defined.

WndProc

The main control of the SPX database application is the WndProc procedure. The control structure is performed by a "switch" statement that takes action according to the message sent to the procedure by the Windows operating system. Messages are generated by every user action in the system, including every mouse movement. Messages are generated by every menu choice as well. In the SPX application, messages generated by the menu are listed in Fig. 14-9. Other messages generated by the application come from the ESRs and from the other messages. These messages are:

> ➤ CONNECTON_MSG

> ➤ SENDREQ_MSG

> ➤ REQ_MSG

> ➤ TERMINATE_MSG

Figure 14-9   *The messages sent from the Application menu.*

```
IDM_ABOUT    from About on the File menu,
IDM_SETUP    from Setup on the Server menu,
IDM_DOWN     from Down on the Server menu,
IDM_CONN     from Attach from the Client menu,
IDM_REQ      from Make Request from the Client menu,
IDM_EXIT     from Exit on the File menu.
```

AboutProc

The AboutProc procedure is called when an IDM_ABOUT message is generated. This procedure controls the dialog generated by the IDM_ABOUT message. It displays the box and waits for input on any buttons or fields enabled by the dialog definition found in the resource file.

 SetupServer

The Setup Server code displayed in Fig. 14-10 makes calls to functions that perform tasks that also are common to the client. These tasks are made into procedures that can be called in the SetupServer procedure as well as the AttachRoutine procedure. The SetupServer procedure calls the InitializeSPX, CreateListenECBsAndListen, CreateSendECBandHeader, and CreateConnectionECBAndHeader procedures.

Sample code for Setup Server.

Figure 14-10

```
void FAR PASCAL SetupServer (HWND hWnd)
{
    WORD retcode;
    int  serverSocket;

    beServer = SERVER;
    serverSocket = SERVER_SOCKET_SWAPPED;
    InitializeSPX(hWnd);
    retcode = AdvertiseService(SPX_DB_TYPE, "SPX_DB",
            (WORD FAR *)&serverSocket);
    CreateListenECBsAndListen((void far *)RequestESRHandler);
    CreateConnectionECBAndHeader(&connectionECB, &connectionHeader);
    SPXListenForConnection( IPXTaskID, (BYTE)3, (BYTE)0xFF,
                            &connectionECB );
}
```

The CreateListenECBsAndListen procedure sets up the listens necessary for the SetupServer procedure to call SPXListenForConnection. SPXListenForConnection posts an ECB with a packet header to SPX to use to receive an SPX establish connection request after the SPXListenForConnection, AdvertiseService is called. The AdvertiseService call is one of three Service Advertising Protocol (SAP) services calls:

➤ AdvertiseService

➤ QueryServices

➤ ShutdownAdvertising

SAP services allow applications to make their location known to other nodes on the network. Through the use of SAP services, a client application can find a well-behaved service on the network without needing a NetWare file server available. A service can advertise on the network using the AdvertiseService call. The service also should have listens posted on the SAP socket (0x0452) to respond to queries. A client can locate the service using a QueryService call. Either the service itself or a NetWare router will respond to this query. When a service is shutting down, a call to ShutdownAdvertising must be made.

⇨ InitializeSPX

The InitializeSPX function in Fig. 14-11 initializes SPX with the number of ECB and maximum packet size that will be used by the application. This information is necessary for Standard mode programming. It is maintained in the interface for Enhanced mode but ignored by the SPXInitialize call. After the SPXInitialize call, IPXOpenSocket is called. If the socket already is opened, the program ends. Otherwise, this procedure returns to the calling procedure.

Figure 14-11   *Sample code for InitializeSPX.*

```
Void FAR PASCAL InitializeSPX( HWND hWnd )
{
    int     installed;
    BYTE    major, minor;
    WORD    maxConnections, availConnections;
    WORD    maxNumECBs, maxSizeECB;
    char    message[75];

    maxNumECBs = MAX_RECEIVE_ECBS + 3;
    maxSizeECB = 512;

    installed = SPXInitialize( &IPXTaskID,
                maxNumECBs,
                maxSizeECB,
                &major,
                &minor,
                &maxConnections,
                &availConnections );

    if( installed != 0xFF )
    {
        wsprintf( message, "SPX is NOT installed!" );
```

```
                MessageBox( hWnd, message, "Status", MB_OK );
                PostQuitMessage( 0 );
                return;
        }

        memset(&serverAddress, '\0',12);
        memset(&mySAP, '\0',sizeof(SAP));
        if (beServer && !beClient)
            socketNumber = SERVER_SOCKET_SWAPPED;
        else
        {
            socketNumber = 0x00;

            ccode = IPXOpenSocket( IPXTaskID, (WORD FAR *)&socketNumber, NULL );
            if( ccode )
            {
                if( ccode == 0xFF )
                    MessageBox( hWnd, "Socket already open!", "Status", MB_OK );
                else
                {
                    wsprintf( message, "ccode from IPXOpenSocket...  %02X",
                            ccode );
                    MessageBox( hWnd, message, "Status", MB_OK );
                }
                PostQuitMessage( 0 );
            }
        }
}
```

CreateListenECBsAndListen

The function CreateListenECBsAndListen (Fig. 14-12) sets addresses
for the ESR handlers that will be used for processing the listen ECBs
by the application. The necessary pool of listen ECBs for processing is
set up and posted to SPX by calling SetupListenECBs, then by calling
SPXListenForSequencedPacket. SPXListenForSequencedPacket must
be used to set up listens to be used by SPX before the
SPXListenForConnection or the SPXEstablishConnection calls.

SetupListenECBs

In Fig. 14-13, SetupListenECBs fills in the SPX listen ECBs with the
necessary ESRAddress, socketNumber, and fragment descriptor list
before posting them to SPX. This function takes care of initializing

Figure 14-12   *Sample code for CreateListenECBsAndListen.*

```
void FAR PASCAL CreateListenECBsAndListen()
{
    int  count;

    if (initECBCount < MAX_RECEIVE_ECBS)
    {
        for(count=0; count < MAX_RECEIVE_ECBS/2; count++)
        {
            SetupListenECBs( count+initECBCount, ESRHandler );
            SPXListenForSequencedPacket( IPXTaskID,
                (ECB FAR *)&listenECB[count+initECBCount] );
        }
        initECBCount+=count;
    }
}
```

Figure 14-13   *Sample code for SetupListenECBs.*

```
void FAR PASCAL SetupListenECBs( int offset, void FAR *ESRHandler)
{
    listenECB[offset].ESRAddress = (void (far *) () ) ESRHandler;
    listenECB[offset].socketNumber = (WORD)socketNumber ;
    listenECB[offset].fragmentCount = 2 ;
    listenECB[offset].fragmentDescriptor[0].address = &listenHeader[offset];
    listenECB[offset].fragmentDescriptor[0].size = sizeof(SPXHeader) ;
    listenECB[offset].fragmentDescriptor[1].address = &replyInfo[offset];
    listenECB[offset].fragmentDescriptor[1].size = PACKET_DATA;
}
```

this information for the sample application before the ECBs are
posted using SPXListenForSequencedPacket.

⇨ CreateSendECBAndHeader

The CreateSendECBAndHeader procedure (Fig. 14-14) sets up the
sendECB by initializing the ESRAddress, socketNumber, and
Fragment Descriptor List. The second fragment in the fragment list
differs for the client and server. Using the beServer variable, the
application points the second fragment address at a
SERVER_RESPONSE structure for a server and at a
CLIENT_REQUEST structure for a client. The default size for the
send packet second fragment is the SERVER_RESPONSE structure,

Sample code for CreateSendECBAndHeader. Figure 14-14

```
void FAR PASCAL CreateSendECBAndHeader()
{
    sendECB.fragmentDescriptor[0].address = &sendHeader ;
    sendECB.fragmentDescriptor[0].size = sizeof( SPXHeader );
    sendECB.fragmentDescriptor[1].address = returnInfo;
    sendECB.fragmentDescriptor[1].size = sizeof(returnInfo);
    sendECB.fragmentCount = 2;
    sendECB.ESRAddress = (void (far *)() ) 0;
    sendECB.socketNumber = (WORD)SERVER_SOCKET_SWAPPED;
}
```

which will be the largest. This size is adjusted in subsequent procedures for the client.

⇨ CreateConnectionECBAndHeader

Both sides of the client-server application use a connection ECB. The connection ECB needs the SPX header destination address for an SPXEstablishConnection. After a connection is made, SPX will fill in the SPX header for the application. The connection ECB is used for an SPXListenForConnection for the server side of the application and for an SPXEstablishConnection for the client side of the application. This function is called from the SetupServer and the AttachRoutine procedures.

⇨ FindServerProc

The FindServer procedure prompts the user to enter the name of the server to which to attach. Once the application has the name of the server, the QueryServices call (Fig. 14-15) can be made to find the address of the server to use with the SPXEstablishConnection call.

Sample code for making a SAP query. Figure 14-15

```
        .
        .
QueryServices(QUERY_NEAR, SPX_DB_TYPE, PACKET_DATA,
          (SAP FAR *)&myQuery[0]);
        .
        .
```

⇨ AttachRoutine

The AttachRoutine procedure is called when `Attach` is chosen from the Client menu after the FindServer procedure is called. This procedure, found in Fig. 14-16, calls InitializeSPX, CreateListenECBsAndListen, CreateSendECBandHeader, and CreateConnectionECBAndHeader like the SetupServer procedure. Then, the AttachRoutine calls SPXEstablishConnection to attach to the server.

Figure 14-16   *Sample code for creating an SPX connection.*

```
void FAR PASCAL AttachRoutine( HWND hWnd )
{
    beClient = TRUE;

    InitializeSPX( hWnd );
    CreateListenECBsAndListen(ReceiveESRHandler);
    CreateConnectionECBAndHeader(&sendECB, &sendHeader);
    ccode = SPXEstablishConnection( IPXTaskID,
            (BYTE)3,
            (BYTE)0xFF,
            &SPXConnID,
            &sendECB );
}
```

⇨ MakeServerReq

After the client has a connection to the server, choosing `Make Request` from the Client menu will call the MakeServerReq procedure. This procedure creates a dialog box with buttons corresponding to the type of request desired. When the OK button is chosen, the request chosen is made when this procedure calls PrepareAndSendServerRequest. Each request case fills in the requestID which is identical on the client and server (Fig. 14-17).

⇨ PrepareAndSendServerRequest

The PrepareAndSendServerRequest resets the sendECB. This function also is where the packet size is optimized for the request by

Figure 14-17

Sample code for creating a request.

```
       .
       .
       .
case IDC_EMP:
     requestData.requestID = VERIFY_EMPLOY;
     EndDialog(hDlg, FALSE);
     break;
case IDC_EMPNUM:
     requestData.requestID = GET_NUM;
     EndDialog(hDlg, FALSE);
     break;
case IDC_EMPSAL:
     requestData.requestID = GET_SAL;
     EndDialog(hDlg, FALSE);
     break;
case IDC_EMPADDR:
     requestData.requestID = GET_ADDR;
     EndDialog(hDlg, FALSE);
     break;
       .
       .
       .
```

setting the size to the MAX_REQUEST_SIZE rather than the default packet size. Then, the packet is sent. Code for this function call can be found in Fig. 14-18.

Sample code for making a service request.

Figure 14-18

```
void FAR PASCAL PrepareAndSendServerRequest(void)
{
     sendECB.fragmentDescriptor[0].address = &sendHeader ;
     sendECB.fragmentDescriptor[0].size = sizeof( SPXHeader );
     sendECB.fragmentDescriptor[1].address = requestData;
     sendECB.fragmentDescriptor[1].size = PACKET_DATA;
     sendECB.fragmentCount = 2;
     sendECB.ESRAddress = (void (far *)() ) 0;
     sendECB.socketNumber = (WORD)socketNumber;

     SPXSendSequencedPacket( IPXTaskID, SPXConnID, &sendECB );
}
```

⇨ ProcessReceivedData

ProcessReceivedData is a typical ESR for this sample application (Fig. 14-19). The only processing consists of posting a message to the application with the address of the ECB. The ECB then can be processed in the context of the main program loop. This procedure is

Figure 14-19   *Sample code for the ProcessReceivedData ESR.*

```
void FAR PASCAL ProcessReceivedData(ECB far *usedECB)
{
     PostMessage(hWnd, SENDREQ_MSG, NULL, (LONG)usedECB);
}
```

used by the client to indicate when a packet of data is received from the server.

⇨ RequestESR

RequestESR is similar to ProcessReceivedData but is used by the server to process requests for service. If an ESR is to do more processing than just a post message, some tips are in order.

First, Windows is a nonpreemptive environment. Time in the ESR is usually with interrupts disabled, which essentially eliminates the possibility of other applications running during the ESR. This is not how a good Windows application should behave.

Second, time in the ESR also should be limited to avoid losing packets coming in from the network.

Third, because applications are running in protected mode and anything written as a VxD is running at ring 0, interrupts possibly can be enabled when calls are made to IPX/SPX or to the Windows system. To avoid problems, all ESRs should be written to be reentrant. Reentrancy will enable an application to successfully use ESRs in a multiple application environment. A reentrant application does not change global variables without disabling interrupts. Any major stack use is managed through stack changing to avoid overrunning the stack.

PostMessage is the best use of an ESR. A PostMessage call uses minimal stack space. The only background processing done consists of placing a message in the window's message queue. Efficient stack use and efficient CPU use are inherent in an ESR that uses only PostMessage to inform the application that additional processing can be performed on the ECB specified in the message.

⇨ DisplayResponse

DisplayResponse uses the specific packet response definitions to format the information returned from the server. Pointers of different structure types are set up and initialized only for the corresponding requestID. This function is used by the client side of the application. DisplayResponse uses a switch statement to process the different request types. Refer to Fig. 14-20 for more detail.

Sample code for processing received packets.

Figure 14-20

```
      .
      .
switch (responsePacket->requestID)
{
      case VERIFY_EMPLOY:
            if (responsePacket->completionCode)
                  wsprintf(message,
                  "Individual not in employee data base");
            else
                  wsprintf(message,
                  "Individual is employee");
            MessageBox(hWnd, message, "Employee Data", MB_OK);
                  break;
      case GET_NUM:
            response2 = responsePacket;
            wsprintf(message,
            "Employee Number is %s",
            response2->employeeNum);
            break;
      case GET_SAL:
            response3 = responsePacket;
            wsprintf(message,
            "Employee Salary is %s",
            response3->employeeNum);
            break;
      case GET_ADDR:
            response4 = responsePacket;
            length = strlen(response4->employeeAddr);
            wsprintf(message,
            "Employee Address is \n%s\n%s",
            (char far *)(response4->employeeAddr),
            (char far *)(response4->
                  employeeAddr+length+1));
            MessageBox(hWnd, message, "Employee Data",
                  MB_OK);
            break;
      .
      .
```

⇨ ServiceRequest

ServiceRequest is a server procedure that builds and sends the response packet for each client request. The procedure (Fig. 14-21) uses a switch statement to determine which request is being made and to retrieve the appropriate information. The requestID first is copied to the response packet, then the completionCode and, if available, the information requested is placed in the packet. Different procedures have been written to retrieve information from the database file and to write information to the database file.

Figure 14-21 *Sample code for processing service requests.*

```
          .
          .

switch (requestData->requestID)
{
    case VERIFY_EMPLOY:
        empNum = FindName(requestData->employeeName);
        serverResponse.requestID = requestData->requestID;
        if (empNum != 0xFF)
            serverResponse.completionCode = SUCCESS;
        else
            serverResponse.completionCode = NO_SUCH_EMPLOYEE;
        break;
    case GET_NUM:
        empNum = FindName(requestData->employeeName);
        serverResponse.requestID = requestData->requestID;
        if (empNum != 0xFF)
            serverResponse.completionCode = SUCCESS;
        else
        {
          GetEmployeeNumber(empNum,
          (char far *)(serverResponse.responseData));
          serverResponse.completionCode = SUCCESS;
        }
        break;
    case GET_SAL:
        empNum = FindName(requestData->employeeName);
        serverResponse.requestID = requestData->requestID;
        if (empNum != 0xFF)
            serverResponse.completionCode = SUCCESS;
        else
        {
          GetSalary(empNum,
          (char far *)(serverResponse.responseData));
          serverResponse.completionCode = SUCCESS;
        }
        break;
```

```
case GET_ADDR:
     empNum = FindName(requestData->employeeName);
     serverResponse.requestID = requestData->requestID;
     if (empNum != 0xFF)
          serverResponse.completionCode = SUCCESS;
     else
     {
       GetStreetAddr(empNum,
       (char far *)(serverResponse.responseData));
       length = strlen(serverResponse.responseData);
       serverResponse.responseData[length+2] = '\0';
       GetStateAddr(empNum, (char far *)
                    (serverResponse.responseData+ length+1));
       serverResponse.completionCode = SUCCESS;
     }
     break;
default:
     serverResponse.requestID = requestData->requestID;
     serverResponse.completionCode = INVALID_REQUEST;
     break;
```

.
.

 SendConnectESR

The SendConnectESR is called when a connection is attempted by
the client. This ESR will help the application to block other
processing until the connection send is complete.

Suggested enhancements

This application is able to perform several distributed functions.
Other functions to write information to the database have been
provided. The switch statements that perform the packet processing
for the client and server ends of the application, MakeServerReq and
ServiceRequest, can be extended to provide this additional
functionality. The application also can be enhanced to maintain a
client connection table such that the server can support more than
one client.

Additionally, the application could be adjusted to allow multiple servers to be accessing the same file simultaneously.

The information and design process discussed in this chapter will enable an application to be written to take advantage of the power and flexibility of SPX.

15

Managing your network configuration: diagnostics

A NOTHER call on the phone and a user can't figure out why he can't connect to the network. The phone rings, it's your boss and he can't remember which computers needed to have their video boards upgraded this month. Wouldn't it be nice to turn to your computer and, with a few simple choices in your Windows management program, be able to tell your boss which three machines still have monochrome adapters and to tell the first user that the router between his building and the next is down? Using NetWare diagnostics calls, you can create an application that can tell you just that kind of information and more. The calls specified in Fig. 15-1 are just the beginning of what you can do with NetWare Diagnostic Services. These services are all found in NWIPXSPX.DLL. The calls marked with an asterisk are found in only NWIPXSPX.DLL v3.12 or higher.

Figure 15-1   *The NetWare Diagnostic Services.* Novell, Inc.

```
BeginDiagnostics
EndDiagnostics
FindComponentOffset
AbortSendingPackets
GetAllKnownNetworks
GetAllKnownServers
GetBridgeDriverConfiguration
GetBridgeDriverStatus
GetBridgeDriverStatistics
GetBridgeStatistics
GetDiagnosticResponse
GetDiagnosticStatus
GetGNMAInfo*
GetIPXSPXVersion
GetIPXStatistics
GetLocalTables
GetLSLConfiguration*
GetLSLStatistics*
GetMachineDynamicInfo*
GetMachineStaticInfo*
GetMLIDConfiguration*
GetMLIDList*
GetMLIDStatistics*
GetNetCfgPath*
GetNLCacheStats*
GetNLServerCurrentState*
GetNLServerInfo*
GetNLServerStats*
GetOSVersionInfo
GetPrimaryServerNumber
GetProtocolStackConfiguration*
GetProtocolStackList*
GetProtocolStackStatistics*
```

```
GetRemoteSPXSocket
GetServerAddressTable
GetServerNameTable
GetShellAddress
GetShellDriverConfiguration
GetShellDriverStatistics
GetShellStatistics
GetShellVersionInfo
GetSpecificNetworkInfo
GetSpecificServerInfo
GetSPXStatistics
ReturnReceivedPacketCount
SendSPXPacket
StartCountingPkts
StartSendingPktsTimed
```

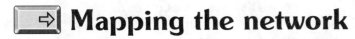

Mapping the network

Using IPX calls, an application can send queries to all the network addresses in a network, whether it is a single LAN or a large enterprise network. After the network map has been created, the application can create SPX connections with the individual nodes and query them for more information. Applications such as NetWare Care and NetMagic take advantage of these calls.

The first step in creating the network map consists of sending a simple IPX diagnostic broadcast, which allows you to create a list of all the nodes on the network. This diagnostic request is referred to as the configuration request packet. The structure of this packet is found in Table 15-1. The packet is broadcast initially on the local network. The responses from each node include information on which socket to use to connect to the node to retrieve more diagnostic information and a component list. Using the socket number and the source network and source node of the packet received, you can build a connection to each node that indicates it has a routing component.

Table 15-1 **The structure of the IPX Get Configuration request**

Offset	Item	Size
0	IPX Header	30 bytes
30	Number Exclusion Addresses	1 byte
31	Exclusion Address List	up to 80 6-byte node addresses

Making a series of inquiries to the routers for all the known networks, the IPX configuration request packet then can be broadcast throughout all the LANs in an internetwork configuration. Once you have a list of all the known networks and all the nodes on each of those nets, you can build a network map on the network and retrieve statistical, configuration, and communication information. An application that creates a map with the ability to retrieve all the information about a node becomes a good tool for remote administration.

Once you have created a list of all the nodes on the network, you can query them to find out what information is available. This information can help you determine if the network is working reliably, if a segment of the network has become unreachable, if an individual workstation configuration is wrong, or if a particular LAN board has failed. The information gleaned from the queries to the network nodes can be used to create an optimal configuration of the network and to improve each workstation or even the way individual software is implemented. You can use diagnostic services to extend the knowledge you have of what is going on in each individual workstation or to improve the monitoring of your own application's performance.

Components on a node

Each network board on the network represents a network node. A network node can be a workstation, a file server, a printer, or some other piece of hardware that can communicate on the network. Each of these nodes has some set of network components installed and running. When the nodes are queried with the IPX configuration request broadcast, they all return a component list of all the components for their node. The component structure returned indicates whether the node in question is a workstation, router, or server. This information then determines which queries can be made to the individual node. The possible components are listed in Table 15-2. For example, you could query any node that had some type of router for AllKnownNetworks. If the component list indicated the node had IPX/SPX loaded, you could query it for IPX or SPX statistical information. The available information can be used for configuration tracking, diagnosing the efficiency of the network, or resource utilization.

The component IDs and what component they identify Table 15-2

Component ID	Component
0	IPX/SPX
1	Router LAN Driver (Bridge Driver)
2	Shell LAN Driver (Shell Driver)
3	Shell
4	VAP Shell
5	Router (Bridge)
6	File Server
7	Non-dedicated IPX/SPX
8	IPX Only (older versions of NetWare)
9	DOS GNMA
10	OS/2 GNMA
11	Personal NetWare Server
12	Personal NetWare Cache

IPX/SPX component

One of the components that can be found at most nodes on the network is the IPX and SPX component. In the case of IPXODI.COM, the SPX support is optional and might not be loaded. Consequently, diagnostic queries beyond the IPX-based Get Configuration query can be supported. The IPX/SPX component information is of great use in the diagnosis of a slow or heavily used network or network segment.

Shell component

The shell component is the NetWare shell or requester running on the network node. It is responsible for the NetWare Core Protocol (NCP) communications to and from that node. This is the piece of software that maintains connections to the server, sends packets to and receives packets from the server, and works in conjunction with the workstation operating system to extend the local services to network access.

GNMA component

The GNMA (Generic NetWare Management Agent) component is a piece of the client software with the NetWare DOS requester. The NetWare DOS requester is new with NetWare v3.12 and provides low utilization of conventional memory with automatic loading in extended memory when available. The GNMA component provides configuration and statistical information on the local workstation and requester.

 # Router (bridge) component

The router, or bridge, component is the software that allows packets to be routed between two network segments. This software is built in to NetWare file servers. With NetWare v2.x, it also was built in to the software used to create bridges. With Personal NetWare v1.0, a routing component can be loaded as a separate piece of software.

LAN driver component

The LAN driver component is present in workstation nodes and file server nodes. This piece of software is responsible for communicating information from the network to IPX in a dedicated IPX environment. In the IPX ODI environment, it consists of two pieces: the LSL and the MLID.

The LSL component is the software responsible for routing communications between the MLIDs (ODI LAN drivers) and the protocol stacks. The LSL also provides the ability to load processing stacks on the node that can perform a variety of functions including packet encryption and protocol translations. The LSL also provides a consistent interface to all PC hardware.

The MLID component is the ODI LAN driver software. The MLID is network board specific and responsible for the protocols necessary for the network board to send and receive packets on the network.

Personal NetWare server component

The Personal NetWare server component is a peer server that can be installed at a workstation to share the resources of that workstation with other nodes on the network. If a workstation has a hard drive, a fax, or a printer, using Personal NetWare servers will allow it to share that resource with members of a workgroup. Personal NetWare servers also provides a low cost method of networking workstations directly without requiring a dedicated file server.

NetWare configuration information

A subset of the NetWare Diagnostic services is those calls that provide you with network configuration information such as all the known networks, all the known servers, all the node addresses on the network, and the components running on the individual nodes. This

277

information and the calls to gather it are the foundation of any application taking advantage of the NetWare Diagnostic Services.

Once a node has responded to the IPX configuration request broadcast, an SPX connection can be established using the BeginDiagnostics call and queries for local information can be sent. The component structure returned in response to the IPX configuration request will indicate which types of software are present at the node. The node could be a workstation, a file server, or a router. The software installed could range from simply IPX to a full-blown file server. Other software that could be running on the node includes any diagnostic extension or a Personal NetWare Server. The workstation diagnostics also will indicate what workstation operating system is running.

Software & hardware information

In addition to finding out what system software is running, the NetWare diagnostics calls also provide information on what versions are running. Using the appropriate calls, you can find out which version of client operating system is running, which IPX version is loaded, which SPX version is loaded, and which shell or requester is running. On a file server, you can discover the file server version and for NetWare 286, what VAP shell version is loaded. If the NetWare DOS requester is loaded, you also can determine what hardware is installed in a DOS workstation. An individual application also could create its own diagnostic responder and respond to queries for software metrics.

GetIPXSPXVersion

The GetIPXSPXVersion call will return the IPX major and minor version numbers and the SPX major and minor version numbers. Even data that seems fairly insignificant can tell you quite a bit about the workstation. If the version is less than 3.10 for IPX, then the workstation is not running Windows with a NetWare client. The minimum version of IPX that supported Windows is version 3.10. The structure returned by the GetIPXSPXVersion call is found in Fig. 15-2.

Figure 15-2

The IPX/SPX version structure. Novell, Inc.

```
typedef struct StructIPXSPXVersion
{
     BYTE      IPXMajorVersion;
     BYTE      IPXMinorVersion;
     BYTE      SPXMajorVersion;
     BYTE      SPXMinorVersion;
} IPXSPXVersion;
```

 # GetShellVersionInfo

GetShellVersionInfo returns a small structure (Fig. 15-3) containing the major and minor versions of the shell along with the revision number. This information can be useful for knowing if a node needs to be updated to a newer version of software or to troubleshoot problems that may be dependent on which version of the shell an application runs with.

Figure 15-3

The shell version structure. Novell, Inc.

```
typedef struct StructShellVersion
{
     BYTE      minor;
     BYTE      major;
     BYTE      rev;
} ShellVersionStruct;
```

GetMachineStaticInfo

The information from GetMachineStaticInfo provides hardware and software information from the workstation. This information (found in Fig. 15-4) can help an administrator verify what hardware and operating system software is installed at a network and even how much memory is available for use. With this ability to query individual workstations, a network administrator could sit in his office and determine whether the hardware needed to be upgraded for a particular software upgrade. This information along with the information returned in GetMachineDynamicInfo will give you all the hardware and software configuration information available for a remote workstation without requiring you to ever leave your office.

Figure 15-4   *The static machine information structure.* Novell, Inc.

```
typedef struct StructMachineStaticInfo
{
    DWORD    StartDate;
    DWORD    StartTime;
    BYTE     OSVerMajor;
    BYTE     OSVerMinor;
    WORD     OSVersionType;
    BYTE     NumberOfSerialPorts;
    BYTE     NumberOfParallelPorts;
    BYTE     FloppyDriveCount;
    WORD     FloppyDriveType;
    BYTE     HardDriveCount;
    BYTE     KeyboardType;
    BYTE     BootVideoType;
    DWORD    DisplayMemory;
    BYTE     MathCoprocessor;
    BYTE     CoprocessorType;
    BYTE     CPUType;
    BYTE     Reserved;
    BYTE     ModelType;
    WORD     SerialAddress[4];
    WORD     ParallelAddress[4];
    BYTE     PointerDevice;
    WORD     SystemMemory;
    BYTE     MemoryTypes;
    BYTE     BIOSType;
    BYTE     BIOSRev[2];
    BYTE     EISA_MCASlots;
    BYTE     EISA_MCAIRQ[16];
    BYTE     EISA_CardName;
    BYTE     BusType;
    BYTE     HardDriveType[4];
    BYTE     MemTypeFlag;
    WORD     TotalXMS;
    WORD     AvailableXMS;
    WORD     TotalEMS;
    WORD     AvailableEMS;
    BYTE     Reserved0[22];
} MachineStaticInfoStruct;
```

⇨ GetMachineDynamicInfo

GetMachineDynamicInfo provides information on the values at a workstation that change or fluctuate. The date and time at the workstation, information on removable drives, and mouse driver information are returned in the structure found in Fig. 15-5.

The dynamic machine information structure. Novell, Inc.   Figure 15-5

```
typedef struct StructNonremoveableDrives
{
    BYTE    DriveNumber;
    DWORD   SectorsPerCluster;
    DWORD   TotalNumberOfClustersPerDrive;
    DWORD   NumberOfAvailableClusters;
    WORD    BytesPerSector;
} NonremoveableDrivesStruct;

typedef struct StructMachineDynamicInfo
{
    DWORD   CurrentDate;
    DWORD   CurrentTime;
    BYTE    MouseDriver;
    BYTE    Reserved[37];
    BYTE    NonremoveableDriveCount;
    NonremoveableDrivesStruct   Drive[31];
} MachineDynamicInfoStruct;
```

 # GetOSVersionInfo

The GetOSVersionInfo call returns the machine ID and operating system version strings for the workstation operating system. The operating system version strings are three strings that take up to 41 bytes. These strings are null terminated and are all in the versionData buffer defined in Fig. 15-6. The three strings are the OS text string, the OS version text string, and the hardware type string.

The workstation OS version information structure. Novell, Inc.   Figure 15-6

```
typedef struct StructOSVersion
{
    BYTE    machineID;
    BYTE    versionData[41];
} OSVersionStruct;
```

GetLocalTables

The GetLocalTables function call returns the structure from Fig. 15-7. The local tables are the list of physical and virtual LAN boards and their corresponding network numbers. An application should

Figure 15-7 *The router local tables structure.* Novell, Inc.

```
typedef struct StructNumber
{
     BYTE   number[4];
} NumberStruct;

typedef struct StructNodeAddress
{
     BYTE   address[6];
     BYTE   reserved[2];
} NodeAddressStruct;

typedef struct StructLocalTables
{
     NumberStruct        localNetworkNumber[16];
     NodeAddressStruct   localNodeAddress[16];
} LocalTablesStruct;
```

make this call to each node with a router (bridge) component. This information provides the addresses of the LANs attached to an individual machine that can be used to make diagnostic connections. Once the connection is established, the GetBridgeDriverConfiguration and GetBridgeDriverStatistics calls can be made to each address.

⇨ GetBridgeDriverConfiguration & GetShellDriverConfiguration

The GetBridgeDriverConfiguration call returns the non-ODI LAN driver configuration information from a NetWare file server or router (bridge). The GetShellDriverConfiguration call returns the non-ODI LAN driver configuration from a workstation. Both calls return the structure in Fig. 15-8 with the appropriate fields set. If a field does not apply to a particular LAN driver, then it is set to −1. This structure contains the network and node address for the LAN board, the mode and configuration it is running in, the LAN board type, the version information, and the maximum data size supported. The maximum data size supported will include the protocol headers. To know the maximum data that can be sent in a packet, the size of all the protocol headers must be subtracted from the maximum data size reported in this call.

The LAN driver configuration structure. Novell, Inc.   Figure 15-8

```
typedef struct StructDriverConf
{
     BYTE      networkAddress[4];
     BYTE      nodeAddress[6];
     BYTE      LANMode;
     BYTE      nodeAddressType;
     WORD      maxDataSize;
     WORD      reserved1;
     BYTE      reserved4;
     WORD      transportTime;
     BYTE      reserved2[11];
     BYTE      majorVersion;
     BYTE      minorVersion;
     BYTE      ethernetFlagBits;
     BYTE      selectedConfiguration;
     BYTE      LANDescription[80];
     WORD      IOAddress1;
     WORD      IODecodeRange1;
     WORD      IOAddress2;
     WORD      IODecodeRange2;
     BYTE      memoryAddress1[3];
     WORD      memoryDecodeRange1;
     BYTE      memoryAddress2[3];
     WORD      memoryDecodeRange2;
     BYTE      interruptIsUsed1;
     BYTE      interruptLine1;
     BYTE      interruptIsUsed2;
     BYTE      interruptLine2;
     BYTE      DMAIsUsed1;
     BYTE      DMALine1;
     BYTE      DMAIsUsed2;
     BYTE      DMALine2;
     BYTE      microChannelFlagBits;
     BYTE      reserved3;
     BYTE      textDescription[80];
} DriverConfigurationStruct;
```

⇨ GetLSLConfiguration

The GetLSLConfiguration function returns the information for the
LSL component on a node. The LSL configuration information
includes the LSL version information and the maximum number of
LAN boards and protocol stacks the LSL is configured to support.
The structure returned by this call is in Fig. 15-9.

Figure 15-9   *The LSL configuration information structure.* Novell, Inc.

```
typedef struct StructLSLConfiguration
{
     BYTE     ConfigMajorVersion;
     BYTE     ConfigMinorVersion;
     DWORD    Reserved;
     DWORD    Reserved0;
     BYTE     LSLMajorVersion;
     BYTE     LSLMinorVersion;
     WORD     MaxBoardsNumber;
     WORD     MaxStacksNumber;
     BYTE     Reserved1[12];
} LSLConfigurationStruct;
```

⇨ GetNetCfgPath

The GetNetCfgPath call returns the path to the NET.CFG file that the
LSL loaded on start-up. This configuration file is used by the NetWare
software on a workstation to determine the configuration set by the
user or administrator. The NET.CFG file is opened by the LSL and all
the other NetWare drivers at the workstation query the LSL for the
location of this file.

⇨ GetMLIDList

The GetMLIDList function will return a list of the ODI LAN drivers on
the node being examined. This list is up to 20 entries in size and each
entry is composed of an ID and a name. This list information can be
used for making subsequent calls to GetMLIDConfiguration. The
definition of the list structure is in Fig. 15-10.

Figure 15-10   *The MLID list structures.* Novell, Inc.

```
typedef struct StructMLIDID
{
     WORD    MLIDId;
     BYTE    Name[18];
} MLIDIDStruct;

typedef struct StructMLIDList
{
     BYTE            NumberOfMLIDs;
     MLIDIDStruct    MLID[20];
} MLIDListStruct;
```

 # GetMLIDConfiguration

The GetMLIDConfiguration call returns the information for the ODI
LAN driver on the node. The information is similar to the non-ODI
LAN driver information but has some information that is specific to
ODI and ODI LAN drivers. This information includes the frame type,
the look ahead size, and the best and worst data sizes. The structure
returned by this function is in Fig. 15-11.

The MLID configuration structure. Novell, Inc.

Figure 15-11

```
typedef struct StructMLIDConfiguration
{
    BYTE      Signature[26];
    BYTE      ConfigTableMajorVersion;
    BYTE      ConfigTableMinorVersion;
    BYTE      NodeAddress[6];
    WORD      ModeFlags;
    WORD      BoardNumber;
    WORD      BoardInstance;
    WORD      MaxPacketSize;
    WORD      BestDataSize;
    WORD      WorstDataSize;
    BYTE      NICLongName[42];
    BYTE      NICShortName[10];
    BYTE      FrameTypeString[42];
    WORD      Reserved;
    WORD      FrameTypeID;
    WORD      TransportTime;
    DWORD     SourceRouteHandler;
    WORD      LookAheadSize;
    WORD      LineSpeed;
    WORD      QueueDepth;
    BYTE      Reserved0[6];
    BYTE      DriverMajorVersion;
    BYTE      DriverMinorVersion;
    BYTE      Flags[2];
    WORD      SendRetries;
    DWORD     ConfigTableLink;
    BYTE      SharingFlags[2];
    WORD      Slot;
    WORD      IOAddress1;
    WORD      IORange1;
    WORD      IOAddress2;
    WORD      IORange2;
    DWORD     MemoryAddress1;
    WORD      MemorySize1;
    DWORD     MemoryAddress2;
    WORD      MemorySize2;
```

Figure 15-11   *Continued.*

```
        BYTE    IntLine1;
        BYTE    IntLine2;
        BYTE    DMALine1;
        BYTE    DMALine2;
        BYTE    OtherData[328];
} MLIDConfigurationStruct;
```

 # GetProtocolStackList

The GetProtocolStackList function will return a list of the protocol
stacks loaded on the node being examined. This list is up to 20
entries in size and each entry is composed of an ID and a name. This
list information can be used for making subsequent calls to
GetProtocolStackConfiguration. The definition of the list structure is
in Fig. 15-12.

Figure 15-12   *The protocol stack list structures.* Novell, Inc.

```
typedef struct StructPStackID
{
    WORD    StackId;
    BYTE    Name[18];
} PStackIDStruct;

typedef struct StructProtocolStackList
{
    BYTE            NumberOfStacks;
    PStackIDStruct  PSID[20];
} ProtocolStackListStruct;
```

GetProtocolStackConfiguration

The GetProtocolStackConfiguration call returns protocol stack name
and version information in the structure in Fig. 15-13. This
information consists of text string names and the stack major and
minor versions.

The protocol stack configuration structure. Novell, Inc.

Figure 15-13

```
typedef struct StructProtocolStackConfig
{
    BYTE    ConfigMajorVersion;
    BYTE    ConfigMinorVersion;
    BYTE    ProtocolLongName[42];
    BYTE    ProtocolShortName[17];
    BYTE    StackMajorVersion;
    BYTE    StackMinorVersion;
    BYTE    Reserved[16];
} ProtocolStackConfigStruct;
```

⇨ GetNLServerInfo

The Personal NetWare server provides extensive configuration and diagnostic information for the administrator as an aid in managing the peer server network. The configuration information can be retrieved using the GetNLServerInfo function call. This call will return the structure from Fig. 15-14. The major version, minor version, and beta versions are for the Personal NetWare server. The server name and workgroup name are those entered at installation of the Personal NetWare server. The remainder of the information deals with the configured and current resources used by the Personal NetWare server.

The Personal NetWare server information structure. Novell, Inc.

Figure 15-14

```
typedef struct StructNLServerInfo
{
    BYTE    MajorVersion;
    BYTE    MinorVersion;
    BYTE    BetaVersion;
    BYTE    ServerName[MAX_SERVER_NAME_LENGTH];
    BYTE    WorkGroupName[WORKGROUP_NAME_LENGTH];
    DWORD   WorkGroupID;
    WORD    RightsMask;
    WORD    CfgDirBuffers;
    BYTE    StartMinutes;
    BYTE    StartHours;
    BYTE    StartSeconds;
    WORD    StartYear;              /* Relative to 1980 */
    BYTE    StartDay;
    BYTE    StartMonth;
    BYTE    OperatingSystem;
    BYTE    DosMajorVersion;
    BYTE    DosMinorVersion;
    WORD    CfgResources;
```

Figure 15-14   *Continued.*

```
            WORD    CurResources;              /* Including CONTROL resource */
            WORD    CfgNetDirs;
            WORD    CurNetDirs;
            WORD    Reserved1;
            BYTE    ServerNetAddr[4];
            BYTE    ServerNodeAddr[6];
            BYTE    ServerSocket[2];
            WORD    Reserved2;
            BYTE    IsShareLoaded;             /* Zero/non-zero */
            BYTE    NetworkAuditing;           /* Zero/non-zero */
            BYTE    AllowRemoteMgt;            /* Zero/non-zero */
            BYTE    ServerLoadType;            /* 0 = No load, 1 = Load Conventional '
            BYTE    NumResponsesWaiting;
            WORD    NumReceiveBuffers;
            WORD    RealSizeReceiveBuffer;
            WORD    Reserved3;
            WORD    SizeIOBuffers;
            WORD    SizeReceiveBuffers;
            WORD    CfgOpenFiles;
            WORD    Reserved4;
            WORD    CfgClientTasks;
            WORD    Reserved5;
            WORD    Reserved6;
            WORD    Reserved7;
            WORD    NumIOBuffers;
            WORD    Reserved8;
            BYTE    NumECBsThatNeedBuffer;
            WORD    CfgConnections;
            WORD    Reserved9;
            WORD    Reserved10;
            WORD    CfgNetPrns;
            BYTE    CurNetPrns;
            WORD    SizePrintBuffers;
            WORD    Reserved11;
            WORD    DOSCriticalSectionCount;
            WORD    DOSOverrideCriticalSection;
            DWORD   Reserved12;
            WORD    DOSSwapDataSize;
            WORD    Reserved13;
            WORD    Reserved14;
            WORD    SwapBytesIfDOSBusy;
            WORD    SwapBytesAlways;
            BYTE    Reserved15;
            BYTE    Reserved16[3];
            DWORD   Reserved17;
            DWORD   Reserved18;
            WORD    ServerTSRSize;
      } NLServerInfoStruct;
```

Statistics

In addition to all the configuration information, the diagnostic services can return statistical information relating to all the nodes and their components. This information can indicate the efficiency and reliability of the network. These statistics include good and bad packet counts, packet routing statistics, and local software processing information such as ECB availability and session listen information.

GetIPXStatistics

The GetIPXStatistics call returns the information found in the structure in Fig. 15-15. This information can provide you with insight on the reliability or level of use of the network segment the node resides on. It also can give you an idea as to whether your application is using enough ECBs. For example, if the getECBFailureCount increments quite a bit during a typical communications sequence, you know that you are using too few ECBs. You could get the statistics before you perform a typical sequence, perform the sequence, then get the statistics again. If, prior to the communications sequence, the getECBFailureCount was zero, then all the failures would likely be attributed to the application being tuned. Otherwise, a change in the ratio of requests to failures would be attributable to the application being tuned. In the case of the IPX statistics, the malformed packet count can also be an indicator of an unreliable network.

GetSPXStatistics

The SPX statistics (Fig. 15-16) from the GetSPXStatistics call are good for monitoring the SPX communications on the network. If the bad packet counts are low, communications and applications are performing smoothly. If, however, these counts are high, either the network is not performing well or the individual applications are not using SPX correctly.

Figure 15-15 *The IPX statistics structure.* Novell, Inc.

```
typedef struct StructIPXStatistics
{
    long   sendPacketCount;
    WORD   malformedPacketCount;
    long   getECBRequestCount;
    long   getECBFailureCount;
    long   AESEventCount;
    WORD   postponedAESEventCount;
    WORD   maxConfiguredSocketsCount;
    WORD   maxOpenSocketsCount;
    WORD   openSocketFailureCount;
    long   listenECBCount;
    WORD   ECBCancelFailureCount;
    WORD   findRouteFailureCount;
} IPXStatisticsStruct;
```

Figure 15-16 *The SPX statistics structure.* Novell, Inc.

```
typedef struct StructSPXStatistics
{
    WORD   maxConnectionsCount;
    WORD   maxUsedConnectionsCount;
    WORD   establishConnectionRequest;
    WORD   establishConnectionFailure;
    WORD   listenConnectionRequestCount;
    WORD   listenConnectionFailureCount;
    long   sendPacketCount;
    long   windowChokeCount;
    WORD   badSendPacketCount;
    WORD   sendFailureCount;
    WORD   abortConnectionCount;
    long   listenPacketCount;
    WORD   badListenPacketCount;
    long   incomingPacketCount;
    WORD   badIncomingPacketCount;
    WORD   suppressedPacketCount;
    WORD   noSessionListenECBCount;
    WORD   watchdogDestroySessionCount;
} SPXStatisticsStruct;
```

GetPrimaryServerNumber

The GetPrimaryServerNumber call returns the primary server number
from the node's shell. The primary server number is the connection
table number of the server from which the login script was executed.
This server typically is the main working server for the individual
logged in.

GetShellAddress

The shell address returned by the GetShellAddress function call is the network, node, and socket of the IPX address that the node uses to communicate with file servers. The network and node numbers are those of the machine, and the socket is a dynamic socket allocated by the shell from IPX. This socket is where all packets are received from the server.

 # GetServerAddressTable & GetServerNameTable

The GetServerAddressTable provides the address table from the shell for the remote diagnostics application. Along with the server name table provided in the GetServerNameTable call, this enables the application to see which servers the node is logged in to along with their network addresses. If you are having trouble with communications between a server and a client, this information would allow you to set a point-to-point test between the two endpoints without creating a network map. The structures for these two calls are listed in Fig. 15-17.

 # GetShellStatistics

GetShellStatistics returns information pertaining to connections to servers, NCP processing, and network traffic. These counts are returned in the structure in Fig. 15-18. The shellRequestsCount indicates how many NCP requests the shell has sent to servers. This value can be used with several of the other counts in the structure—including timeoutsCount, writeErrorCount, invalidReplyHeaderCount, and invalidSequenceNumberCount—to create ratios that can be used to compare the network reliability from day-to-day and configuration-to-configuration. Other counts that help gauge the network throughput or reliability, including the networkGoneCount, errorReceivingCount, and the allocateServerIsDownCount.

Figure 15-17   *The server address table and server name table structures.* Novell, Inc.

```
typedef struct StructAddressTable
{
     BYTE     serverUsed;
     BYTE     orderNumber;
     BYTE     serverNetwork[4];
     BYTE     serverNode[6];
     WORD     serverSocket;
     WORD     receivedTimeOut;
     BYTE     immediateNode[6];
     BYTE     sequenceNumber;
     BYTE     connectionNumber;
     BYTE     connectionOK;
     WORD     maximumTimeOut;
     BYTE     reserved[5];
} AddressTableStruct;

typedef struct StructServerAddressTable
{
     AddressTableStruct     addressTable[8];
} ServerAddressTableStruct;

typedef struct StructNameTable
{
     BYTE     name[48];
} NameTableStruct;

typedef struct StructServerNameTable
{
     NameTableStruct     nameTable[8];
} ServerNameTableStruct;
```

⇨ GetGNMAInfo

The GetGNMAInfo call provides version information on the GNMA (Generic NetWare Management Agent) and on the number of GNMA responders installed at the node (Fig. 15-19). This version information and configuration information indicates what other information is available for an application to query. Each diagnostic responder will have its own information to provide that can be interpreted by an application aware of the packet structures used by the responder.

The shell statistics structure.

Figure 15-18

```
typedef struct StructShellStatistics
{
    long    shellRequestsCount;
    WORD    operatorAbortsCount;
    WORD    operatorRetriesCount;
    WORD    timeoutsCount;
    WORD    writeErrorCount;
    WORD    invalidReplyHeaderCount;
    WORD    invalidSlotCount;
    WORD    invalidSequenceNumberCount;
    WORD    errorReceivingCount;
    WORD    noRouterFoundCount;
    WORD    beingProcessedCount;
    WORD    unknownErrorCount;
    WORD    invalidServerSlotCount;
    WORD    networkGoneCount;
    WORD    reserved1;
    WORD    allocateCannotFindRouteCount;
    WORD    allocateNoSlotsAvailableCount;
    WORD    allocateServerIsDownCount;
} ShellStatisticsStruct;
```

The GNMA information structure.

Figure 15-19

```
typedef struct StructGNMAInfo
{
    BYTE    GNMAMajorVersion;
    BYTE    GNMAMinorVersion;
    WORD    GNMANumberOfResponders;
    ResponderTypeStruct    Type[131];
} GNMAInfoStruct;
```

⇨ GetBridgeStatistics

The GetBridgeStatistics function returns information pertaining to the routing of packets on the network. The structure of the information is in Fig. 15-20. The tooManyHopsCount indicates how many packets were dropped because the hop count hit 16. If this count is high, the network should be monitored to discover the source of the packets. Reconfiguring the network segments can bring all the segments closer together to keep the hop count from being too high. If the noReceiveBuffersCount or the noSpaceForServiceCount are high, then the router's buffers should be increased to allow better throughput on the network.

Figure 15-20   *The bridge statistics structure.* Novell, Inc.

```
typedef struct StructBridgeStatistics
{
     WORD    tooManyHopsCount;
     WORD    unknownNetworkCount;
     WORD    noSpaceForServiceCount;
     WORD    noReceiveBuffersCount;
     WORD    notMyNetwork;
     long    netBIOSPropogateCount;
     long    totalPacketsServiced;
     long    totalPacketsRouted;
} BridgeStatisticsStruct;
```

The netBIOSPropogateCount is how many times a NetBIOS internet broadcast has been received and passed on by the router. The totalPacketsServiced and totalPacketsRouted counts indicate the efficiency of your network configuration. If a server is spending a large portion of the time routing packets rather than servicing them, then some clients on the same network segment as the router might have better performance if they are on a network segment with the server they use predominantly.

 # GetAllKnownNetworks & GetAllKnownServers

Using the information that you receive from the GetAllKnownNetworks call, you are able to continue the process of sending the configuration request packets to each of the networks. Using a combination of this information, you can create a network map indicating which nodes are connected to which networks. The structure returned from the GetAllKnownNetworks call can hold up to 128 network numbers.

In addition to this function, it also is useful to make the GetAllKnownServers call. This function will return information on 10 servers at a time. This call should be made several times indicating the number of servers to be skipped until no new servers are returned. Once the location and existence of the nodes on the network has been ascertained, the map can provide information as to what type of NetWare software is installed at the node. The structures these lists of information are returned in are in Fig. 15-21.

All known networks and servers structures. Novell, Inc.

Figure 15-21

```
typedef struct StructAllKnownNetworks
{
    WORD    numberOfNetworkAddresses;
    NetworkAddressStruct    networkAddress[128];
} AllKnownNetworksStruct;

typedef struct StrSrvrInfo
{
    WORD    serverType;
    BYTE    serverName[48];
} ServerInfoStruct;

typedef struct StructAllKnownServers
{
    WORD    numberOfServers;
    ServerInfoStruct    serverInfo[10];
} AllKnownServersStruct;
```

⇨ GetSpecificNetworkInfo

The structure for the GetSpecificNetworkInfo function call (Fig. 15-22) contains information on how far the network is from the router being queried, how long it takes to route a packet to that network, and how many routes there are to that network. This is followed by a list of routes (RoutingInfoStruct) with the information on how far each route is from the network in question and what the address of the router is.

The specific network information structure. Novell, Inc.

Figure 15-22

```
typedef struct StructRoutingInfo
{
    BYTE    routerForwardingAddress[6];
    BYTE    routerBoardNumber;
    BYTE    reserved[2];
    BYTE    routeHops;
    WORD    routeTime;
} RoutingInfoStruct;

typedef struct StructSpecificNetInfo
{
    BYTE    networkAddress[4];
    BYTE    hopsToNet;
    BYTE    reservedA[7];
    WORD    routeTimeToNet;
    WORD    numberOfKnownRouters;
    RoutingInfoStruct    routingInfo[MAX_ROUTES];
} SpecificNetworkInfoStruct;
```

 # GetSpecificServerInfo

The GetSpecificServerInfo function gets information from router
(bridge) component about a specific known server. This information
(Fig. 15-23) includes the type and name of the server, the address of
the server, the distance the server is from the router, and a list of
routes to the server. This information, along with that from the
GetSpecificNetworkInfo function, is maintained in the server's routing
tables in the same manner that it is returned to the workstation. Each
call to GetSpecificNetworkInfo or to GetSpecificServerInfo returns
one node from the routing table.

Figure 15-23 *The specific server information structure.* Novell, Inc.

```
typedef struct StructRouteSourceInfo
{
    BYTE    routeSourceAddress[6];
    WORD    routeHopsToSource;
    BYTE    reserved[2];
} RouteSourceInfoStruct;

typedef struct StrSpecSrvrInfo
{
    ServerInfoStruct    serverInfo;
    BYTE        serverAddress[12];
    WORD        hopsToServer;
    BYTE        reserved1[2];
    WORD        numberOfRoutes;
    RouteSourceInfoStruct    routeSourceInfo[MAX_ROUTES];
} SpecificServerInfoStruct;
```

 # GetBridgeDriverStatistics & GetShellDriverStatistics

The dedicated IPX LAN driver for the router or the shell will return
statistics on packet transmission and reception. This information is
returned from the GetBridgeDriverStatistics and
GetShellDriverStatistics calls. Additionally, there is space in the
structure for the LAN board to return custom diagnostic information.
The structure in Fig. 15-24 provides the driver and statistics versions

The LAN driver statistics structure. <small>Novell, Inc.</small>

Figure 15-24

```
typedef struct StructDriverStat
{
    BYTE    driverVersion[2];
    BYTE    statisticsVersion[2];
    long    totalTxPacketCount;
    long    totalRxPacketCount;
    WORD    noECBAvailableCount;
    WORD    packetTxTooBigCount;
    WORD    packetTxTooSmallCount;
    WORD    packetRxOverflowCount;
    WORD    packetRxTooBigCount;
    WORD    packetRxTooSmallCount;
    WORD    packetTxMiscErrorCount;
    WORD    packetRxMiscErrorCount;
    WORD    retryTxCount;
    WORD    checksumErrorCount;
    WORD    hardwareRxMismatchCount;
    WORD    numberOfCustomVariables;
    BYTE    variableData[495];
 /*        BYTE    variableData[1]; */
} DriverStatisticsStruct;
```

as the first two fields. How well behaved the IPX and SPX applications running on the node are is demonstrated by the packet counts being too big or too small. The network reliability often can be gauged through examination of the retry count, the checksum error count, and the receiving mismatch count.

GetBridgeDriverStatus

The GetBridgeDriverStatus call returns the status of the LAN boards in the router. For each board, the status could be alive and working, nonexistent, or dead. This is useful information if a node is having trouble communicating to or through a router node.

GetNLCacheStats

The GetNLCacheStats function will return information on the behavior of the cache used by the Personal NetWare server. If the disk access requests for reading and writing are close to the actual disk access for reading and writing, then the cache is not actually helping improve the performance. The reason for bad cache

performance also might possibly be discovered in the statistic packet returned (Fig. 15-25). If the number of disk errors or the number of memory errors is high or the maximum cache size is low, then the node should be investigated further to check the hardware. However, if these values are not out of the ordinary, then the workstation probably is just using the files in a manner that caching doesn't improve.

Figure 15-25   *The Personal NetWare cache statistics structure.* Novell, Inc.

```
typedef struct StructDriverStat
{
    BYTE    driverVersion[2];
    BYTE    statisticsVersion[2];
    long    totalTxPacketCount;
    long    totalRxPacketCount;
    WORD    noECBAvailableCount;
    WORD    packetTxTooBigCount;
    WORD    packetTxTooSmallCount;
    WORD    packetRxOverflowCount;
    WORD    packetRxTooBigCount;
    WORD    packetRxTooSmallCount;
    WORD    packetTxMiscErrorCount;
    WORD    packetRxMiscErrorCount;
    WORD    retryTxCount;
    WORD    checksumErrorCount;
    WORD    hardwareRxMismatchCount;
    WORD    numberOfCustomVariables;
    BYTE    variableData[495];
 /*     BYTE    variableData[1]; */
} DriverStatisticsStruct;
```

⇨ GetNLServerCurrentState

The Personal NetWare server's current state information in Fig. 15-26 is returned by the GetNLServerCurrentState. This information profiles the server in terms of the numbers of connections, currently open files, current client task, free buffers, and semaphores. This information helps an administrator monitor how heavy the use of a particular Personal NetWare server becomes and take steps to minimize the impact of heavy access on the workstation user.

The Personal NetWare current state structure. Novell, Inc.

Figure 15-26

```
typedef struct StructNLServerCurrentState
{
    WORD    CurConnections;
    WORD    CurOpenFiles;
    WORD    CurClientTasks;
    WORD    CurNumFreeBuffers;
    WORD    CurNumSemaphores;
} NLServerCurrentStateStruct;
```

⇨ GetNLServerStats

The GetNLServerStats function call returns the extensive statistics useful in profiling the peer server performance. These statistics are in the structure found in Fig. 15-27. Information is available on how well the server is performing, how much throughput is occurring at the server, and how many errors are occurring. Repeated calls to this function could give an application the ability to graph the performance and fluctuation in server usage.

The Personal NetWare server statistics structure. Novell, Inc.

Figure 15-27

```
typedef struct StructNLServerStats
{
    DWORD    TotalPacketsReceived;
    WORD     BadPackets;
    WORD     PacketsNotProcessedImmediately;
    WORD     LostResponses;
    WORD     PeakConnectionsUsed;
    WORD     PeakOpenFiles;
    WORD     PeakClientTasks;
    WORD     WatchdogPacketsSent;
    WORD     ClientsWatchdogged;
    WORD     ECBRepostsWithNoBuffers;
    WORD     SendPacketWithECBActive;
    WORD     TotalSlistRequests;
    WORD     ServerBusyPackets ;
    WORD     ServerBusyPacketsNoBuffers;
    WORD     UnknownRequests;
    WORD     WriteBehindMisses;
    DWORD    ReadCacheHits;
    DWORD    ReadCacheMisses;
    WORD     ReadsTooLarge;
    WORD     CriticalErrors;
    DWORD    SavedLargeDOSArea;
    DWORD    SavedSmallDOSArea;
    WORD     StarvationCounter;
```

Figure 15-27   *Continued.*

```
        WORD      WriteBehindHits;
        WORD      CacheBlocksInUse;
        DWORD     Reserved;
        DWORD     PacketQueueRuns;
        DWORD     IdleLoopWaitHits;
        DWORD     Int21NotOurs;
        DWORD     TotalInt21Calls;
        DWORD     PasswordFailures;
} NLServerStatsStruct;
```

GetLSLStatistics, GetMLIDStatistics, & GetProtocolStackStatistics

Similar to the GetIPXStatistics, GetBridgeDriverStatistics, and GetShellDriverStatistics calls but for the ODI world, the GetLSLStatistics, GetMLIDStatistics, and GetProtocolStackStatistics return the information found in the structures in Figs. 15-28 through 15-30. This information can provide you with insight on the reliability or level of use of the network segment the node resides on. It also can give you an idea as to whether your application is using enough ECBs. For example, if the getECBFailureCount increments quite a bit during a typical communications sequence, you know that you are using too few ECBs. You could get the statistics before you perform a typical sequence, perform the sequence, then get the statistics again. If, prior to the communications sequence, the getECBFailureCount was zero, then all the failures would likely be attributed to the application being tuned. Otherwise, a change in the ratio of requests to failures would be attributable to the application being tuned. The checksumErrorCount also can be an indicator of an unreliable network.

Testing the network

In addition to the information gathering available in the diagnostic services, network testing is possible. An application running on one workstation can create SPX diagnostic connections to two remote nodes and instruct them to send and receive messages between them.

The LSL Statistics structure. Novell, Inc.

Figure 15-28

```
typedef struct StructLSLStatistics
{
    BYTE    StatMajorVersion;
    BYTE    StatMinorVersion;
    WORD    GenericCounters;
    DWORD   ValidCountersMask;
    DWORD   TotalTxPackets;
    DWORD   GetECBRequests;
    DWORD   GetECBFailures;
    DWORD   AESEventsCount;
    DWORD   PostponedEvents;
    DWORD   CancelAESFailures;
    DWORD   Reserved0;
    DWORD   Reserved1;
    DWORD   TotalRxPackets;
    DWORD   UnclaimedPackets;
    BYTE    OtherData[480];
} LSLStatisticsStruct;
```

The MLID statistics structure. Novell, Inc.

Figure 15-29

```
typedef struct StructMLIDStatistics
{
    BYTE    DriverStatMajorVersion;
    BYTE    DriverStatMinorVersion;
    WORD    NumberGenericCounters;
    DWORD   ValidCountersMask;
    DWORD   TotalTxRequest;
    DWORD   TotalRxRequest;
    DWORD   NoECBAvailableCount;
    DWORD   TooBigTxRequest;
    DWORD   TooSmallTxRequest;
    DWORD   RxOverflowCount;
    DWORD   RxTooBigCount;
    DWORD   RxTooSmallCount;
    DWORD   TxMiscCount;
    DWORD   RxMiscCount;
    DWORD   TxRetryCount;
    DWORD   RxChecksumErrorCount;
    DWORD   RxMismatchCount;
    BYTE    OtherData[468];
} MLIDStatisticsStruct;
```

This is called point-to-point testing. Point-to-point testing will isolate problems on the network with communication between two points. These problems could be caused by router problems, bad network boards, or heavy traffic.

Figure 15-30   *The protocol stacks statistics structure.* Novell, Inc.

```
typedef struct StructProtocolStackStats
{
    BYTE    StatMajorVersion;
    BYTE    StatMinorVersion;
    WORD    GenericCounters;
    DWORD   ValidCountersMask;
    DWORD   TotalTxPackets;
    DWORD   TotalRxPackets;
    DWORD   IgnoredRxPackets;
    BYTE    OtherData[508];
} ProtocolStackStatsStruct;
```

After connecting to the remote nodes, the diagnostic application will send a Start Counting Packets request to the receiving end. Then, a Start Sending Packets request is sent to the transmitting node. This request specifies the number of packets to send to the other node. Once the specified number of packets is sent, data on the results of the sends, including the number of transmission errors is returned to the diagnostic application. The application then is able to send a Return Received Packet Count request to the receiving end of the test. If the number of packets transmitted and the number of packets received varies, then the route between the two end points is suspect. If the two endpoints are on the same local network, then the hardware in one or the other of the nodes or the hardware connecting the nodes is suspect. This test can begin with the two nodes that are having problems communicating and narrowed from each end to isolate the exact location of the problem on the network.

Point-to-point testing also is useful in determining a network's throughput. The instructions to the remote nodes in the test can be sent instructions that force them to send packets at higher and higher rates. The diagnostic application then can determine which rate of sends is the highest rate of reliable network throughput.

Application algorithms

Creating a map of the network is initiated by sending the IPX packet found in Table 15-1. The packet is broadcast initially on the local network. After your map is created, you can start an iterative series

of calls to each of the nodes in your list. You begin by calling
BeginDiagnostics with the socket specified in the response to the
configuration request packet. Once the connection is established,
check the components from the component list. See Fig. 15-31 for a
list of steps to use in creating a network map. Each component has a
set of calls that provide information pertaining to that component.
Several calls are to be used in special situations. The calls and what
they are used to do are discussed next. After that discussion are
algorithms for using the other diagnostics calls.

Steps for gathering information to create a network map.

Figure 15-31

1. Allocate and initialize an IPX Get Configuration Packet and
   initialize the ECB controlling it.
2. Allocate and initialize at least 2 IPX listen packets and their ECBs.
   The data portion of the packet could be a member of an array of the
   type in Fig. 15-32, the ConfigurationResponseStruct. As each packet
   comes in, the second fragment address could be set to the next
   available slot in the array.
3. Set the listen ECB ESRAddress to an ESR that will process the listen
   packets
4. Call IPXInitialize with the appropriate parameters.
5. Open a dynamic socket to receive the configuration responses.
6. Set the source address in the IPX header of the IPX Get Configuration
   packet by passing it in to IPXGetInternetworkAddress.
7. Set the source socket in the send ECB to the dynamic socket opened.
8. Set up the destination address for a broadcast - the network number
   (0000 for the first packet), the node number (0xFFFFFFFF), and the
   socket (0x5604).
9. Post the listen ECBs and packets by calling IPXListenForPacket on
   each one.
10. Send the request using IPXSendPacket.
11. As responses come in, place the information in the appropriate
    location and repost the listen packet.
12. If the component list includes a router (bridge) component, create a
    diagnostic session with the router and issue a GetLocalTables
    function call.
13. Repeat steps 8 through 12 for each network discovered in step 12.

⇨ BeginDiagnostics

Once you have received a response to the IPX Get Configuration
Request, you can create a diagnostic connection to the node that
responded. The SPX diagnostic socket from the response packet
should be copied into a BeginDiagnosticStruct structure along with

the network and node of the source address from the response packet
header. The BeginDiagnostics call will use this information to create
an SPX connection with the other node. The two items that the
BeginDiagnostics call returns are the SPX connection ID for the
newly formed SPX connection and a component list. This component
list is the same as the one received in the IPX Get Configuration
response (Fig. 5-32). It is necessary, however, to use this structure
with the FindComponentOffset call.

Figure 15-32   *Data from the IPX Get Configuration request.* Novell, Inc.

```
typedef struct StructAddr
{
    BYTE    network[4];
    BYTE    node[6];
} AddrStruct;

typedef struct StructConfigurationResponse
{
    AddrStruct    address;
    struct
    {
        BYTE    majorVersion;
        BYTE    minorVersion;
        WORD    SPXDiagnosticSocket;
        BYTE    numberOfComponents;
        BYTE    componentStructure[MAX_IPX_PACKET_SIZE  -
                sizeof(IPXHeader) - sizeof(AddrStruct) - 5];
    } packet;
} ConfigurationResponseStruct;
```

⇨ FindComponentOffset

The FindComponentOffset call returns the component number that
then is passed in to every diagnostic call. Once these two calls have
been made, you will be able to call any of the other diagnostics calls.
The component offset is the offset of the component ID from the
component list returned in the diagnostic packet from the node being
examined. This offset is sent to the node with a request for
information to enable the node to determine which component item
is being queried. This component offset or the component number
should not be confused with the component ID. The component ID
indicates the type of the component.

 EndDiagnostics

When the application is done using the diagnostic services, it must deinitialize by calling the EndDiagnostics call. This call requires the SPX connection ID returned from the BeginDiagnostics call to be passed as a parameter. This call then will terminate the diagnostic SPX connection specified, release all allocated resources, and terminate diagnostics gracefully.

GetDiagnosticResponse

If you create a custom diagnostic extension (diagnostic responder), the GetDiagnosticResponse call can be used to send and receive the custom packets that you have designed. This call will use the same connection established by the BeginDiagnostics call. The first buffer is the request buffer and the second buffer is the reply buffer.

GetDiagnosticStatus

The GetDiagnosticStatus call is used in conjunction with the GetDiagnosticResponse call. You make this call within a loop until the status returns as complete. At completion, the response buffer from GetDiagnosticResponse will contain the response packet from the node being examined.

GetRemoteSPXSocket

If you have a network address for a node that you want to perform a diagnostic call on, you can find out which socket to use to connect to the remote node to be examined. This connection can be used to query the node as well as to send it commands and instructions.

Configuration information

Once you have the address of a node, you can create a diagnostic connection to it by calling BeginDiagnostics and passing in the address. The address is passed as the BeginDiagnosticStruct. The BeginDiagnosticStruct should be set to the address returned in the ConfigurationResponseStruct: the network, the node, and the SPX diagnostic socket.

Once this connection is established, use the FindComponentOffset call to determine whether the node has a particular component and what the offset of the component is. Using the componentNumber returned from this call, any diagnostic call can be made that applies to that component. For example, if the component is the router component, you would issue the GetBridgeStatistics to get statistical information. These steps are listed in Fig. 15-33.

Figure 15-33   *The steps for making configuration and statistical diagnostic queries.*

```
1. Create a list of nodes to query using the steps in Fig. 15-31.
2. Allocate a BeginDiagnosticsStruct.
3. Initialize the BeginDiagnosticStruct to the address from the
   ConfigurationResponseStruct.
4. Set the socket address in the BeginDiagnosticStruct to the SPX
   diagnostic socket from the ConfigurationResponseStruct.
5. Call BeginDiagnostics.
6. Using the componentList returned from BeginDiagnostics and the
   component ID from the list in Table 15-2, call FindComponentOffset.
7. In a switch statement based on the component ID, call the appropriate
   configuration or statistics call using the component number returned
   from FindComponentOffset.
8. Repeat steps 6 and 7 for all the component IDs desired.
9. When finished, call EndDiagnostics using the connection ID from
   BeginDiagnostics.
```

Testing cabling

Testing the cabling is accomplished through the point-to-point testing available in the diagnostic services. Using the information from IPX Get Configuration Request or two known network addresses, an application calls BeginDiagnostics to create a diagnostic connection

to both remote nodes. Once the connections are established, one node is designated as the transmitting node and one node is designated as the receiving node.

After connecting to the remote nodes, the diagnostic application will send a Start Counting Packets request to the receiving node. Then, a Start Sending Packets request is sent to the transmitting node. This request specifies the number of packets to send to the other node. Once the specified number of packets is sent, data on the results of the sends, including the number of transmission errors, is returned to the diagnostic application. The application then is able to send a Return Received Packet Count request to the receiving end of the test. If the number of packets transmitted and the number of packets received varies, then the route between the two end points is suspect. If the two endpoints are on the same local network, then the hardware in one or the other of the nodes or the hardware connecting the nodes is suspect. This test can begin with the two nodes that are having problems communicating and narrowed from each end to isolate the exact location of the problem on the network. The steps for this process are listed in Fig. 15-34.

The steps for performing point-to-point tests on the network.   Figure 15-34

1. Create a list of nodes to query using the steps in Fig. 15-31.
2. Allocate a BeginDiagnosticsStruct.
3. Initialize the BeginDiagnosticStruct to the address from the ConfigurationResponseStruct.
4. Set the socket address in the BeginDiagnosticStruct to the SPX diagnostic socket from the ConfigurationResponseStruct.
5. Call BeginDiagnostics.
6. Complete steps 2-5 for the second node.
7. Using the componentList returned from BeginDiagnostics and the component ID from the list in Table 15-2, call FindComponentOffset.
8. Allocate the StartCountingPacketsStructure and initialize it to the socket on which the transmissions will be made.
9. Call the StartCountingPkts function, passing in the component number from step 7, the connection ID from step 5, and the StartCountingPacketsStructure from step 8.
10. Repeat step 7 for the second node.
11. Allocate and initialize the SendPacketsRequestStruct. Set the immediate address to use, the number of packets to send, how large an interval to use, how many packets per interval, the packet size, and the packet change size.
12. Call StartSendingPktsTimed, passing in the component number from step 10, the connection ID from step 6, and the SendPacketsRequestStruct

Figure 15-34   *Continued.*

```
        from step 11. Also pass in the number of ticks for the node to delay
        before sending any packets.
    13. When the time is up for the packets to be sent, call
        ReturnReceivedPacketCount using the same connection as in step 9.
    14. Repeat steps 7 through 13 for as many tests between these two nodes
        as desired.
    15. Repeat steps 2 through 14 for as many nodes as desired.
```

The point-to-point testing process also can be used to check the network routing configuration. This test can fail due to one endpoint being too many hops from the other endpoint, an unreliable router at some location in the network route, or filtering NLMs installed on servers.

 # Extending NetWare Diagnostic Services

NetWare Diagnostics Services provide a defined well-known method for accessing information available relating to the workstation and network operations. A method for extending the functionality available through these diagnostics also has been defined. This extension is done through the Generic NetWare Management Agent (GNMA). The GNMA provides facilities to register as a diagnostic packet handler, a diagnostic responder, with a specific type. This type is the responder type in the packets coming in from the network. The requests are passed to the appropriate responder according to this type.

 ## Creating a diagnostic responder

Using IPXODI v2.0 or higher, any application can create its own custom diagnostic responder. The application uses just five calls to set up the responder. These calls allow an application to check for GNMA support on the local workstation, register as a diagnostic responder, send acknowledgments, process requests, and deregister as a diagnostic responder.

The responder must create functions that specify request/reply sets. When a request is passed to the diagnostic responder, it will take the action according to the function type in the packet. The steps necessary to set up, process, and shut down as a diagnostic responder are found in Fig. 15-35. The following paragraphs explain each of the steps and the calls necessary at each point.

The steps for diagnostic responder registration, processing, and deregistration.

Figure 15-35

```
1. Determine if GNMA support is present.
2. Call the GNMA Responder Registration Function
3. Process and acknowledge request packets received.
4. Reset when called by GNMA.
5. Call the GNMA Responder Deregistration Function
```

✳ **Detecting GNMA support**   To determine if your application can function properly as a GNMA responder, you need to determine if support for GNMA responders is available on the workstation. To determine this, you will need to use the DOS Protected Mode Interface to emulate in Int 2Fh with the AX register set to 7A2Fh. If the value for the real mode AX is returned as 0000h, then GNMA services are present, BX contains the GNMA support level, and ES:DI points to the GNMA far call handler. Using the far call handler, the application can proceed to make other GNMA calls.

✳ **Registering as a responder**   To receive requests from the network, an application functioning as a diagnostic responder is required to register with the GNMA. When registering as a responder, the application provides a responder structure that is used by GNMA to track registered responders and their responder types. This structure is defined in Table 15-3. To register, you call the GNMA far call handler with BX set to 0000h and ES:SI pointing to an initialized GNMA responder registration structure. On return from the far call, the AX register will be set to 0000h if registration was successful and to 0FFFFh if the responder already was registered.

Table 15-3   **The GNMA responder registration structure**

Offset	Field	Size
0	Responder Link	4 bytes
4	Responder Request Handler	4 bytes
8	Responder Type	2 bytes
10	Responder Version	2 bytes
12	Responder Workspace	4 bytes

✳ **Processing requests**   The responder request handler in the responder registration structure is required to conform to an entry and exit setupdefined by GNMA. See Table 15-4 for the register values on entry to the responder request handler. The request packet structure can be found in Table 15-5. On exit from the responder request handler, the registers should be set according to the values in Table 15-6 and CLD preserved. If the application sets AH to 01h, then it will need to call GNMASendAck when it is ready to acknowledge the request.

Table 15-4   **The registers on entry to the responder request handler**

Register	Value
AL	00h
DS:DI	Points to the request packet
CX	Length of the request packet (without responder type and request fields)
DS:BX	Points to a reply buffer (528 bytes long)
ES:SI	Points to the responder registration structure

The responder request packet structure

Table 15-5

Offset	Field	Size
0	Responder Type	2 bytes
2	Responder Function	2 bytes
4	Request Data	528 bytes maximum

The registers on exit from the responder request handler

Table 15-6

Register	Value
AH	00h = ack now, 01h = will ack with GNMASendAck
AL	00h = success, 0FDh = request invalid, all other values defined by responder
DX:BX	Points to the reply info
CX	Length of reply info

✳ **Acknowledging packets**   Two ways exist to acknowledge packets. The first is synchronously by returning the reply information at the time of exit from the responder request handler. The second way is to acknowledge asynchronously by calling the GNMASendAck function. To call this function, see the register setup in Table 15-7. An application will continue to process and acknowledge packets until it deregisters and exits.

The registers for GNMASendAck

Table 15-7

Register	Value
BX	0003h
DX:SI	Points to the reply info
CX	Length of reply info
AL	00h = success, 0FDh = request invalid, all other values defined by responder

✻ **Deregistering the responder**   When the application shuts down, it will need to deregister with GNMA as a responder. To deregister, theapplication needs to call the GNMADeregisterResponder function with the registers as in Table 15-8. On return from the far call, if the AX register is set to 0000h, the responder successfully deregistered. However, if the AX register is set to 0FFFFh, the responder was not registered.

Table 15-8   **The registers for GNMADeregisterResponder**

Register	Value
BX	0001h
AX	Responder type to deregister

⇨ Accessing a diagnostic responder

Any software that wants to communicate with a custom diagnostic responder needs to send packets of the appropriate type. To do this properly, the application will need to create a diagnostics session with the workstation to be queried by calling BeginDiagnostics. After this connection is created, the application needs to pass the component list returned from the BeginDiagnostics function along with the responder type assigned to their responder to the FindComponentOffset call.

Once this call has returned the component offset, the application can create the data portion of the request packet following the structure in Table 15-9. A call then can be made to GetDiagnosticResponse using the packet created as the request buffer and an empty buffer as the reply buffer. This call will send the packet to the diagnostic partner workstation and wait for a response. The response from the diagnostic responder will be placed in the reply buffer. Any application could take advantage of this technology. The example given deals with a software distribution mechanism.

The GNMA request packet structure   Table 15-9

Offset	Field	Size
0	Component Offset	1 byte
1	Responder Function	1 byte
2	Request Data	528 bytes maximum

 # Software distribution: an example of diagnostic extensions

One application of the diagnostic responder technology is software distribution. To create a remote software distribution product, two pieces would need to be developed: the responder that would be installed at each node on the network that the administrator wishes to be able to update remotely and the management application that would communicate with the responder. The management application would query the responder to determine the directory containing the software to upgrade, send the files to the responder to place in the directory specified, send the responder instructions on which configuration files to change values in, and how to set up for the software to be launched at the appropriate time. The responder obviously would use the calls for registering as a diagnostic responder and would perform the tasks requested by the management application.

Request/reply packet structures would need to be defined for:

➤ Requesting the directory path for the software to upgrade.

➤ Sending the application executable in several packets.

➤ Sending configuration values and file names.

➤ Launching instructions if necessary.

When sending the updated files in several packets, it would be useful to use a control structure at the beginning of each packet that indicated how many packets total would be sent containing the file

313

and the number of the current packet. The files would most safely be read and written in binary.

Many other uses exist for diagnostic services. Whether monitoring the network or upgrading software, the diagnostic services can help network administrators accomplish more from their offices and do so more efficiently.

16

Porting tips for moving applications to the Client SDK

CHAPTER 16

WITH the shipment of NetWare v4.0 came a new SDK. This SDK, the NetWare Client SDK for C v1.0, supports DOS, OS/2, and Windows with the same network interface. This interface also is the interface that Novell uses to develop applications internally. This SDK supports NetWare v2.2, NetWare v3.11, and NetWare v4.0.

⇨ SDK contents

The Client SDK for C supports the core functionality of NetWare systems and Novell's native protocols: IPX and SPX. In addition to the core NetWare support found in the SDK, TLI, NetBIOS, and internationalization support are included in this kit

⇨ API libraries

The SDK consists of five libraries: NWCALLS, NWNET, NWIPXSPX, NWLOCALE, and NWPSRV. The NWCALLS library replaces the NWNETAPI library with the server-oriented NCP-based functionality. The NWNET library is new with the Client SDK and contains the network-oriented services, such as the new NetWare Directory Services. The NWIPXSPX library is the same as that in the C Interface for Windows v1.33, but uses the include file NWIPXSPX.H instead of NXT.H. The NWPSRV library replaces the NWPSERV library and provides updated print server support. The NWLOCALE library also is new with NetWare v4.0 and provides support for the internationalization of applications. The services provided by the NetWare Client SDK for C v1.0 are categorized in Fig. 16-1.

⇨ API documentation

The documentation in the NetWare Client SDK for C consists of five manuals: *NetWare Client API for C Volume I*, *NetWare Client API for C Volume II*, *NetWare Client Internationalization API for C*, *NetWare Client Transport Protocol API for C*, and *NetWare Programmer's Guide for C*. The first four manuals are reference manuals arranged in alphabetical order by the names of the function

The NetWare services in the client SDK for C. Figure 16-1

```
Accounting
AFP
Auditing
Bindery
Communications
Connection
Diagnostics
NetWare Directory
File Server Environment
File System
      Directory
      File
      Name Space
Internationalization
Message
Miscellaneous
Print Server
Print and Capture
QMS
Service Advertising Protocol
Synchronization
TTS
Workstation
```

calls. The fifth manual, the *NetWare Programmer's Guide for C* contains technical discussions of the services in NetWare and selected sample code demonstrating the implementation of those services. The alphabetical references also have an index arranged by API service groups to also aid in finding related calls in addition to the See Also section of each function call.

➡ Programming tips

The NetWare Client SDK provides an increased set of services to the developer. In addition, some differences exist between this API and previous programming interfaces available from Novell. These differences include function call naming conventions, methods for specifying the server to send packets to, different structure names, more space for some parameters, and in some cases new calls. For a list of the function calls for the NetWare C Interface for Windows and the equivalent calls in the NetWare Client SDK for C, see appendix A.

317

Programming differences

Due to the increased services available through the NetWare Client SDK, some applications might need additional stack space. When using NWNET, you should increase your stack space to at least 16K. Finetuning the stack for your application will require that, after you've completed the code, you slowly decrease your stack. If you get a memory protection error and the esp or ebp registers are very high values, then you probably don't have enough stack space. Keep in mind, different code paths will require different amounts of stack space. Some of your functions that use a lot of stack space should be tested in this process.

Naming conventions

The naming conventions for the NetWare Client SDK have changed somewhat as well. All of the function calls in the NWCALLS and NWNET libraries begin with an NW. This prefix will help avoid collisions with function names in other tool kits and will help simplify code maintenance by indicating which calls are from NetWare.

Specifying the server

In the C Interface for Windows, packets were directed to specific servers through the use of the GetPreferredServer and SetPreferredServer calls. When an NCP needed to go to a known server, a programmer typically would call GetPreferredServer and save the connection ID returned, then call SetPreferredServer with the connection ID he/she wanted to use. Once the request was complete, the application would call SetPreferredServer once more using the connection ID returned from GetPreferredServer. In the NetWare Client SDK, all NCP-based function calls require that you explicitly specify the server to send the packet to as one of the parameters of the function call. Specifying the server improves the performance by reducing the number of function calls an application is required to make and gives the developer control over where his packet is getting sent.

Monocasing & internationalization issues

The function calls in the NWCALLS library do no monocasing of any of the parameters including the bindery object names and paths. This is part of the changes necessary for the libraries to be able to handle paths from any language supported by NetWare systems. Be aware, however, that existing file server binderies will be storing object and property names in uppercase. Therefore, it is necessary for applications to do the appropriate monocasing of these types of names just as the NetWare utilities such as SYSCON are required to do so. Function calls that enable the developer to perform monocasing in a locale sensitive fashion are provided as part of the NWLOCALE library in the NetWare Client SDK.

 # Parameter size changes

As the NetWare system's ability to support more users and more requests increases, some parameters have had to grow in size. For example, the connection number returned by the server is no longer a byte, but a double word. The job number in a queue also has increased to a double word to accommodate more outstanding jobs in queues. As you convert your code to use the NetWare Client SDK, pay attention to the size of the parameters or use the abstract types to protect your program as parameters change and improve.

New calls & functionality

With many new services come many new function calls. Additional services in the NetWare Client SDK that were not previous include auditing services, data migration services, and NetWare Directory Services. With the addition of the NetWare Directory Services and a connection heuristic, additional connection services calls also were required. These calls provide support for connecting to the network in the appropriate manner using NetWare Directory Services.

Include files

There are three new general purpose include files used in the
NetWare Client SDK that aren't used in the NetWare C Interface for
Windows. The include files are NWCALLS.H, NWNET.H, and
NWIPXSPX.H. Each of the include files corresponds to the import
and dynamic link libraries of the same name. All include files
implement a duplicate lockout mechanism to prevent symbols from
being multiply defined.

 # Communications services

The communications services calls—including IPX, SPX, SAP and
Diagnostics—had no interface changes between the NetWare C
Interface for Windows and the NetWare Client SDK for C. The
programming model and interfaces remain the same. However, any
application using these services will have one minor change.
Anywhere the NXT.H include file is specified, the reference needs to
be changed to NWIPXSPX.H

The NetWare C Interface for Windows and the NetWare Client SDK
were created to coexist so that the transition from one development
kit to the next can be made in an efficient manner within the
development cycles of each individual developer.

Appendix

NetWare C interface for Windows & NetWare client SDK equivalent call summary

*   Call obselete

** Call replaced by a combination of other calls

Accounting services

AccountingInstalled	NWQueryAccountingInstalled
GetAccountStatus	NWGetAccountStatus
GetCurrentAccountStatus*	
SubmitAccountCharge	NWSubmitAccountCharge
SubmitAccountHold	NWSubmitAccountHold
SubmitAccountNote	NWSubmitAccountNote

AFP services for non-AFP clients

AFPAllocTemporaryDirHandle	NWAFPAllocTemporaryDirHandle
AFPCreateDirectory	NWAFPCreateDirectory
AFPCreateFile	NWAFPCreateFile
AFPDelete	NWAFPDelete
AFPGetEntryIDFromName	NWAFPGetEntryIDFromName
AFPGetEntryIDFromNetWareHandle	NWAFPGetEntryIDFromHandle
AFPGetEntryIDFromPathName	NWAFPGetEntryIDFromPathName
AFPGetFileInformation	NWAFPGetFileInformation
AFPDirectoryEntry	NWAFPDirectoryEntry
AFPOpenFileFork	NWAFPOpenFileFork
AFPRename	NWAFPRename
AFPScanFileInformation	NWAFPScanFileInformation
AFPSetFileInformation	NWAFPSetFileInformation
AFPSupported	NWAFPSupported

Bindery services

AddBinderyObjectToSet	NWAddObjectToSet
ChangeBinderyObjectPassword	NWChangeObjectPassword
ChangeBinderyObjectSecurity	NWChangeObjectSecurity
ChangePropertySecurity	NWChangePropertySecurity

CloseBindery	NWCloseBindery
CreateBinderyObject	NWCreateObject
CreateProperty	NWCreateProperty
DeleteBinderyObject	NWDeleteObject
DeleteBinderyObjectFromSet	NWDeleteObjectFromSet
DeleteProperty	NWDeleteProperty
GetBinderyAccessLevel	NWGetBinderyAccessLevel
GetBinderyObjectID	NWGetObjectID
GetBinderyObjectName	NWGetObjectName
IsBinderyObjectInSet	NWIsObjectInSet
OpenBindery	NWOpenBindery
ReadPropertyValue	NWReadPropertyValue
RenameBinderyObject	NWRenameObject
ScanBinderyObject	NWScanObject
ScanBinderyObjectTrusteePaths	NWScanObjectTrusteePaths
ScanForEquivalence**	
ScanProperty	NWScanProperty
VerifyBinderyObjectPassword	NWVerifyObjectPassword
WritePropertyValue	NWWritePropertyValue

⇨ Broadcast message services

BroadcastToConsole	NWBroadcastToConsole
CheckPipeStatus*	
CloseMessagePipe*	
DisableBroadcasts	NWDisableBroadcasts
EnableBroadcasts	NWEnableBroadcasts
GetBroadcastMessage	NWGetBroadcastMessage
GetBroadcastMode	NWGetBroadcastMode
GetPersonalMessage*	
GetPipeStatus*	
LogNetworkMessage*	
OpenMessagePipe*	
SendBroadcastMessage	NWSendBroadcastMessage
SendPersonalMessage*	
SetBroadcastMode	NWSetBroadcastMode

Communication services

IPXCancelEvent   IPXCancelEvent
IPXCloseSocket   IPXCloseSocket
IPXDisconnectFromTarget   IPXDisconnectFromTarget
IPXGetDataAddress*
IPXGetInternetworkAddress   IPXGetInternetworkAddress
IPXGetIntervalMarker   IPXGetIntervalMarker
IPXGetLocalTarget   IPXGetLocalTarget
IPXGetProcAddress*
IPXInitialize   IPXInitialize
IPXListenForPacket   IPXListenForPacket
IPXOpenSocket   IPXOpenSocket
IPXRelinquishControl   IPXRelinquishControl
IPXScheduleIPXEvent   IPXScheduleIPXEvent
IPXScheduleSpecialEvent   IPXScheduleSpecialEvent
IPXSendPacket   IPXSendPacket
SPXAbortConnection   SPXAbortConnection
SPXEstablishConnection   SPXEstablishConnection
SPXGetConnectionStatus   SPXGetConnectionStatus
SPXInitialize   SPXInitialize
SPXListenForConnection   SPXListenForConnection
SPXListenForSequencedPacket   SPXListenForSequencedPacket
SPXSendSequencedPacket   SPXSendSequencedPacket
SPXTerminateConnection   SPXTerminateConnection

⇨ Connection services

AttachToFileServer   NWAttachToFileServer
AttachToFileServerWithAddress**
DetachFromFileServer   NWDetachFromFileServer
GetConnectionInformation   NWGetConnectionInformation
GetConnectionNumber   NWGetConnectionNumber
GetInternetAddress   NWGetInternetAddress
GetObjectConnectionNumbers   NWGetObjectConnectionNumbers
GetStationAddress   NWGetInternetAddress
LoginToFileServer   NWLoginToFileServer

Logout**
LogoutFromFileServer   NWLogoutFromFileServer

 ## New calls

                                        NWGetConnectionList
                                        NWLogoutWithLoginID

 ## Calls for 4.0 & DOS Requester

                                        NWDSGetConnectionInfo
                                        NWDSSetConnectionInfo
                                        NWFreeConnectionSlot
                                        NWGetConnectionIDFromAddress
                                        NWGetConnectionIDFromName
                                        NWGetConnectionSlot
                                        NWGetDefaultNameContext
                                        NWGetNextConnectionID
                                        NWGetNumConnections
                                        NWGetPreferredDSServer
                                        NWIsDSAuthenticated
                                        NWLockConnectionSlot
                                        NWSetDefaultNameContext
                                        NWSetPreferredDSServer
                                        NWUnLockConnectionSlot

Diagnostic services

BeginDiagnostics   BeginDiagnostics
EndDiagnostics   EndDiagnostics
FindComponentOffset   FindComponentOffset
GetRemoteSPXSocket   GetRemoteSPXSocket
SendSPXPacket   SendSPXPacket
GetDiagnosticResponse   GetDiagnosticResponse
GetDiagnosticStatus   GetDiagnosticStatus
GetIPXSPXVersion   GetIPXSPXVersion
GetIPXStatistics   GetIPXStatistics

GetSPXStatistics
StartCountingPkts
StartSendingPktsTimed
AbortSendingPackets
ReturnReceivedPacketCount
GetBridgeDriverStatus
GetBridgeDriverConfiguration
GetBridgeDriverStatistics
GetShellDriverConfiguration
GetShellDriverStatistics
GetOSVersionInfo
GetShellAddress
GetShellStatistics
GetServerAddressTable
GetServerNameTable
GetPrimaryServerNumber
GetShellVersionInfo
GetBridgeStatistics
GetLocalTables
GetAllKnownNetworks
GetSpecificNetworkInfo
GetAllKnownServers
GetSpecificServerInfo
ReinitializeRouterTables

GetSPXStatistics
StartCountingPkts
StartSendingPktsTimed
AbortSendingPackets
ReturnReceivedPacketCount
GetBridgeDriverStatus
GetBridgeDriverConfiguration
GetBridgeDriverStatistics
GetShellDriverConfiguration
GetShellDriverStatistics
GetOSVersionInfo
GetShellAddress
GetShellStatistics
GetServerAddressTable
GetServerNameTable
GetPrimaryServerNumber
GetShellVersionInfo
GetBridgeStatistics
GetLocalTables
GetAllKnownNetworks
GetSpecificNetworkInfo
GetAllKnownServers
GetSpecificServerInfo
ReinitializeRouterTables

 # File server environment services

CheckConsolePrivileges
CheckNetWareVersion
ClearConnectionNumber
DisableFileServerLogin
DisableTransactionTracking
DownFileServer
EnableFileServerLogin
EnableTransactionTracking
GetBinderyObjectDiskSpaceLeft
GetConnectionsOpenFiles

NWCheckConsolePrivileges
NWCheckNetWareVersion
NWClearConnectionNumber
NWDisableFileServerLogin
NWDisableTTS
NWDownFileServer
NWEnableFileServerLogin
NWEnableTTS
NWGetObjectDiskSpaceLeft
NWScanOpenFilesByConn
NWScanOpenFilesByConn2

GetConnectionsSemaphores	NWScanSemaphoresByConn
GetConnectionsTaskInformation	NWGetTaskInformationByConn
GetConnectionsUsageStats	NWGetConnectionUsageStats
GetConnectionsUsingFile	NWScanConnectionsUsingFile
GetDiskCacheStats	NWGetDiskCacheStats
GetDiskChannelStats	NWGetDiskChannelStats
GetDiskUtilization	NWGetDiskUtilization
GetDriveMappingTable	NWGetFSDriveMapTable
GetFileServerDateAndTime	NWGetFileServerDateAndTime
GetFileServerDescriptionStrings	NWGetFileServerDescription
GetFileServerExtendedInfo	NWGetFileServerExtendedInfo
GetFileServerInformation	NWGetFileServerInformation
GetFileServerLANIOStats	NWGetFileServerLANIOStats
GetFileServerLoginStatus	NWGetFileServerLoginStatus
GetFileServerMiscInformation	NWGetFileServerVersionInfo
GetFileSystemStats	NWGetFileSystemStats
GetLANDriverConfigInfo	NWGetFSLANDriverConfigInfo
GetLogicalRecordInformation	NWScanLogicalLocksByName
GetLogicalRecordsByConnection	NWScanLogicalLocksByConn
GetPathFromDirectoryEntry	NWGetPathFromDirectoryEntry
GetPhysicalDiskStats	NWGetPhysicalDiskStats
GetPhysicalRecordLocksByFile	NWScanPhysicalLocksByFile
GetPhysRecLockByConnectAndFile	NWScanPhysicalLocksByConnFile
GetSemaphoreInformation	NWExamineSemaphore
GetServerInformation	NWGetFileServerInformation
	NWGetFileServerExtendedInfo
SendConsoleBroadcast	NWSendConsoleBroadcast
SetFileServerDateAndTime	NWSetFileServerDateAndTime

 **New calls**

NWClearConnectionNumber
NWGetConnectionStatus
NWGetMaximumConnections

 File system services: directory

AddTrusteeToDirectory	NWAddTrusteeToDirectory
	NWAddTrustee
AllignDriveVectorToPath	NWSetDriveBase
AllocPermanentDirectoryHandle	NWAllocPermanentDirectoryHandle
AllocTemporaryDirectoryHandle	NWAllocTemporaryDirectoryHandle
ClearVolRestrictions	NWRemoveObjectDiskRestrictions
CreateDirectory	NWCreateDirectory
DeallocateDirectoryHandle	NWDeallocateDirectoryHandle
DeleteDirectory	NWDeleteDirectory
DeleteTrustee	NWDeleteTrustee
DeleteTrusteeFromDirectory	NWDeleteTrusteeFromDirectory
GetDirectoryHandle	NWGetDrivePath
GetDirectoryPath	NWGetDirectoryHandlePath
GetDirEntry	NWScanDirectoryInformation
	NWScanDirectoryInformation2
GetDirInfo	NWScanDirectoryInformation
	NWScanDirectoryInformation2
GetDriveInformation	NWGetDriveInformation
GetEffectiveDirectoryRights	NWGetObjectEffectiveRights
GetEffectiveRights	NWGetEffectiveDirectoryRights
	NWGetEffectiveRights
GetObjectDiskRestrictions	NWGetObjDiskRestrictions
	NWGetDirSpaceLimitList
	NWGetDirSpaceInfo
GetPathFromDirectoryEntry	NWGetPathFromDirectoryEntry
GetSearchDriveVector	NWGetSearchDriveVector
GetVolumeInformation	NWGetExtendedVolumeInfo
GetVolumeInfoWithHandle	NWGetVolumeInfoWithHandle
GetVolumeInfoWithNumber	NWGetVolumeInfoWithNumber
GetVolumeName	NWGetVolumeName
GetVolumeNumber	NWGetVolumeNumber
GetVolUsage	NWGetVolumeStats
MapDriveUsingString**	
MapDrive**	
ModifyMaximumRightsMask	NWModifyMaximumRightsMask
MoveEntry	NWMoveDirEntry
RenameDirectory	NWRenameDirectory

	NWRenameDirInNameSpace
RestoreDirectoryHandle	NWRestoreDirectoryHandle
SaveDirectoryHandle	NWSaveDirectoryHandle
ScanDirectoryForTrustees	NWScanDirectoryForTrustees
	NWScanDirectoryForTrustees2
ScanDirectoryInformation	NWScanDirectoryInformation
	NWScanDirectoryInformation2
	NWScanExtendedInfo
ScanDirEntry	NWScanDirEntryInfo
ScanDirRestrictions	NWGetDirSpaceInfo
	NWGetDirSpaceLimitList
ScanEntryForTrustees	NWScanForTrustees
ScanVolForRestrictions	NWScanVolDiskRestrictions
SetDirectoryHandle	NWSetDirectoryHandlePath
SetDirectoryInformation	NWSetDirectoryInformation
SetEntry	NWSetDirEntryInfo
SetDirRestriction	NWSetDirSpaceLimit
SetDrivePath	NWSetDriveBase
SetSearchDriveVector	NWSetSearchDriveVector
SetTrustee	NWAddTrustee
	NWAddTrusteeToDirectory
SetVolRestriction	NWSetObjectVolSpaceLimit

 New calls

NWDeleteDriveBase

 File system services: file

CloseEA	NWCloseEA
CopyEAs**	
EraseFiles	NWEraseFiles
FileServerFileCopy	NWFileServerFileCopy
GetEAInfo	NWFindFirstEA
	NWFindNextEA
GetExtendedFileAttributes	NWGetExtendedFileAttributes
	NWGetExtendedFileAttributes2

OpenEA	NWOpenEA
PurgeErasedFiles	NWPurgeErasedFiles
PurgeSalvagableFile	NWPurgeDeletedFile
ReadEA	NWReadEA
RecoverSalvagableFile	NWRecoverDeletedFile
RestoreErasedFile	NWRestoreErasedFile
ScanEAInfo	NWFindFirstEA
	NWFindNextEA
ScanFileEntry	NWScanFileInformation
	NWScanFileInformation2
ScanFileInformation	NWScanFileInformation
	NWScanFileInformation2
ScanSalvagableFiles	NWScanForDeletedFiles
SetExtendedFileAttributes	NWSetFileAttributes
	NWSetExtendedFileAttributes
	NWSetExtendedFileAttributes2
SetFileInformation	NWSetFileInformation
	NWSetFileInformation2
WriteEA	NWWriteEA

New calls

NWGetEAHandleStruct
NWGetFileConnectionID
NWFileSearchInitialize
NWFileSearchContinue
NWRenameFile

File system services: name space

FillNameSpaceBuffer**
GetDataStreamInfo**

GetNameSpaceInfo	NWGetNSInfo
	NWGetNSEntryInfo

GetNumNameSpaceAndDataStreams**
GetNameSpaceEntry**

 New calls

NWAllocTempNSDirHandle
NWAllocTempNSDirHandle2
NWGetDirectoryBase
NWGetLongName
NWGetNSLoadedList
NWGetNSPath
NWGetOwningNameSpace
NWNSGetMiscInfo
NWNSRename
NWOpenCreateNSEntry
NWOpenDataStream
NWOpenNSEntry
NWReadNSInfo
NWReadExtendedNSInfo
NWScanNSEntryInfo
NWSetLongName
NWSetNSEntryDOSInfo
NWWriteExtendedNSInfo
NWWriteNSInfo

Miscellaneous services

ASCIIZToLenStr*
ConvertNameToFullPath*
ConvertNameToVolumePath*
ConvertToUpperCase*
GetFullPath*
GetMaxSearchOrder*
IntSwap*
IsVersion311*
IsV3Supported*
LenStrCat*
LenStrCmp*
LenStrCpy*
LenToASCIIZStr*

LongSwap*
StripFileServerFromPath   NWStripFileServerFromPath
IsWhiteSpace*
ParsePath   NWParsePath
                                 NWParseNetWarePath

New calls

NWCallsInit
NWConvertPathToDirEntry
NWIsLNSSupportedOnVolume

Print services

CancelLPTCapture   NWCancelCapture
CancelSpecificLPTCapture   NWCancelCapture
EndLPTCapture   NWEndCapture
EndSpecificLPTCapture   NWEndCapture
FlushLPTCapture   NWFlushCapture
FlushSpecificLPTCapture   NWFlushCapture
GetBannerUserName   NWGetBannerUserName
GetDefaultCaptureFlags   NWGetCaptureStatus
GetDefaultLocalPrinter*
GetLPTCaptureStatus   NWGetCaptureStatus
GetPrinterDefaults*
GetPrinterQueue*
GetPrintQueueEntry*
GetPrinterStatus*
GetSpecificCaptureFlags   NWGetCaptureFlags
SetBannerUserName   NWSetBannerUserName
SetCapturePrintJob*
SetCapturePrintQueue   NWStartQueueCapture
SetDefaultCaptureFlags   NWSetCaptureFlags
SetDefaultLocalPrinter*
SetPrinterDefaults*
SetSpecificCaptureFlags   NWSetCaptureFlags
SetSpoolFlags   NWSetCaptureFlags

SpecifyCaptureFile	NWStartFileCapture
StartLPTCapture	NWStartCapture
StartSpecificLPTCapture	NWStartCapture

Queue management services

AbortServicingQueueJobAndFile	NWAbortServicingQueueJob2
AttachQueueServerToQueue	NWAttachQueueServerToQueue
ChangeQueueJobEntry	NWChangeQueueJobEntry2
ChangeQueueJobPosition	NWChangeQueueJobPosition2
ChangeToClientRights	NWChangeToClientRights2
CloseFileAndAbortQueueJob	NWCloseFileAndAbortQueueJob2
CloseFileAndStartQueueJob	NWCloseFileAndStartQueueJob2
CreateQueue	NWCreateQueue
CreateQueueJobAndFile	NWCreateQueueFile2
DestroyQueue	NWDestroyQueue
DetachQueueServerFromQueue	NWDetachQueueServerFromQueue
FinishServicingQueueJobAndFile	NWFinishServicingQueueJob2
GetQueueJobList	NWGetQueueJobList2
GetQueueJobsFileSize	NWGetQueueJobFileSize2
ReadQueueCurrentStatus	NWReadQueueCurrentStatus2
ReadQueueJobEntry	NWReadQueueJobEntry2
ReadQueueServerCurrentStatus	NWReadQueueServerCurrentStatus2
RemoveJobFromQueue	NWRemoveJobFromQueue2
RestoreQueueServerRights	NWRestoreQueueServerRights
ServiceQueueJobAndOpenFile	NWServiceQueueJob2
SetQueueCurrentStatus	NWSetQueueCurrentStatus2
SetQueueServerCurrentStatus	NWSetQueueServerCurrentStatus2

SAP services

AdvertiseService	AdvertiseService
QueryServices	QueryServices
ShutdownSAP	ShutdownSAP

 # Synchronization services

ClearFile	NWClearFileLock
	NWClearFileLock2
ClearFileSet	NWClearFileLockSet
ClearLogicalRecord	NWClearLogicalRecord
ClearLogicalRecordSet	NWClearLogicalRecordSet
ClearPhysicalRecord	NWClearPhysicalRecord
ClearPhysicalRecordSet	NWClearPhysicalRecordSet
CloseSemaphore	NWCloseSemaphore
ExamineSemaphore	NWExamineSemaphore
GetLockMode*	
LockFileSet	NWLockFileLockSet
LockLogicalRecordSet	NWLockLogicalRecordSet
LockPhysicalRecordSet	NWLockPhysicalRecordSet
LogFile	NWLogFileLock
	NWLogFileLock2
LogLogicalRecord	NWLogLogicalRecord
LogPhysicalRecord	NWLogPhysicalRecord
OpenSemaphore	NWOpenSemaphore
ReleaseFile	NWReleaseFileLock
	NWReleaseFileLock2
ReleaseFileSet	NWReleaseFileLockSet
ReleaseLogicalRecord	NWReleaseLogicalRecord
ReleaseLogicalRecordSet	NWReleaseLogicalRecordSet
ReleasePhysicalRecord	NWReleasePhysicalRecord
ReleasePhysicalRecordSet	NWReleasePhysicalRecordSet
SetLockMode*	
SignalSemaphore	NWSignalSemaphore
WaitOnSemaphore	NWWaitOnSemaphore

 # New calls

NWScanSemaphoresByName

 # Transaction tracking system

TTSAbortTransaction   NWTTSAbortTransaction
TTSBeginTransaction   NWTTSBeginTransaction
TTSEndTransaction   NWTTSEndTransaction
TTSGetApplicationThresholds   NWTTSGetProcessThresholds
TTSGetStats   NWGetTTSStats
TTSGetWorkstationThresholds   NWTTSGetConnectionThresholds
TTSIsAvailable   NWTTSIsAvailable
TTSSetApplicationThresholds   NWTTSSetProcessThresholds
TTSSetWorkstationThresholds   NWTTSSetConnectionThresholds
TTSTransactionStatus   NWTTSTransactionStatus

 # New calls

NWTTSGetControlFlags
NWTTSSetControlFlags

 # Workstation environment

EndOfJob   NWEndOfJob
GetConnectionID   NWGetConnectionID
GetDefaultConnectionID   NWGetDefaultConnectionID
GetFileServerName   NWGetFileServerName
GetNetWareShellVersion   NWGetRequesterVersion
GetPreferredConnectionID*
GetPrimaryConnectionID   NWGetPrimaryConnectionID
GetShellRevision   NWGetRequesterVersion
IsConnectionIDInUse   NWIsIDInUse
SetEndOfJobStatus   NWSetEndOfJobStatus
SetNetWareErrorMode   NWSetNetWareErrorMode
SetPreferredConnectionID*
SetPrimaryConnectionID   NWSetPrimaryConnectionID

➡ New calls

NWGetRequesterVersion
NWSetInitDrive

➡ New services

The following sections list the services that are new to this version.

➡ Auditing services

NWGetVolumeAuditStats
NWAddAuditProperty
NWLoginAsVolumeAuditor
NWInitAuditLevelTwoPassword
NWChangeAuditorPassword
NWCheckAuditAccess
NWCheckAuditLevelTwoAccess
NWGetAuditingFlags
NWRemoveAuditProperty
NWDisableAuditingOnVolume
NWEnableAuditingOnVolume
NWIsUserBeingAudited
NWReadAuditingBitMap
NWReadAuditConfigHeader
NWReadAuditingFileRecord
NWInitAuditFileRead
NWLogoutAsVolumeAuditor
NWResetAuditHistoryFile
NWResetAuditingFile
NWWriteAuditingBitMap
NWWriteAuditConfigHeader
NWCloseOldAuditingFile
NWDeleteOldAuditingFile
NWDSChangeAuditorPassword
NWDSCheckAuditAccess

NWDSCheckAuditLevelTwoAccess
NWDSCloseOldAuditingFile
NWDSDeleteOldAuditingFile
NWDSDisableAuditingOnContainer
NWDSEnableAuditingOnContainer
NWDSGetAuditingFlags
NWDSGetContainerAuditStats
NWDSLoginAsContainerAuditor
NWDSLogoutAsContainerAuditor
NWDSReadAuditConfigHeader
NWDSResetAuditingFile
NWDSWriteAuditConfigHeader
NWDSResetAuditHistoryFile

Data migration services

NWMoveFileToDM
NWMoveFileFromDM
NWGetDMFileInfo
NWGetDMVolumeInfo
NWGetSupportModuleInfo
NWGetDataMigratorInfo
NWGetDefaultSupportModule
NWSetDefaultSupportModule

NetWare directory services

NWDSGetEffectiveRights
NWDSAuthenticate
NWDSChangeObjectPassword
NWDSGenerateObjectKeyPair
NWDSLogin
NWDSLogout
NWDSVerifyObjectPassword
NWDSAuditGetObjectID
NWDSAllocBuf
NWDSComputeAttrValSize
NWDSFreeBuf

NWDSGetAttrCount
NWDSGetAttrDef
NWDSGetAttrName
NWDSGetAttrVal
NWDSGetClassDef
NWDSGetClassDefCount
NWDSGetClassItem
NWDSGetClassItemCount
NWDSGetObjectCount
NWDSGetObjectName
NWDSGetPartitionInfo
NWDSGetServerName
NWDSGetSyntaxCount
NWDSGetSyntaxDef
NWDSInitBuf
NWDSPutAttrName
NWDSPutAttrVal
NWDSPutChange
NWDSPutClassItem
NWDSBeginClassItem
NWDSFreeContext
NWDSGetContext
NWDSSetContext
NWDSAddObject
NWDSBackupObject
NWDSCompare
NWDSGetPartitionRoot
NWDSList
NWDSMapIDToName
NWDSMapNameToID
NWDSModifyObject
NWDSModifyDN
NWDSRead
NWDSReadObjectInfo
NWDSRemoveObject
NWDSRestoreObject
NWDSSearch
NWDSOpenStream
NWDSWhoAmI
NWDSAddFilterToken

NWDSAllocFilter
NWDSPutFilter
NWDSDelFilterToken
NWDSCloseIteration
NWDSGetSyntaxID
NWDSReadSyntaxes
NWDSReplaceAttrNameAbbrev
NWDSGetObjectHostServerAddress
NWDSAbbreviateName
NWDSCanonicalizeName
NWDSRemoveAllTypes
NWDSAddPartition
NWDSAddReplica
NWDSChangeReplicaType
NWDSJoinPartitions
NWDSListPartitions
NWDSPurgeReplica
NWDSRemovePartition
NWDSRemoveReplica
NWDSSplitPartition
NWDSDefineAttr
NWDSDefineClass
NWDSListContainableClasses
NWDSModifyClassDef
NWDSReadAttrDef
NWDSReadClassDef
NWDSRemoveAttrDef
NWDSRemoveClassDef

Bibliography

Campbell, Greg. 1993. *Developing Applications Using Directory Services: Part 2—Advanced Topics.* Presentation at BrainShare '93, 22–26 March, University of Utah, Salt Lake City, Utah.

Childers, Randal. 1993. *Developing Applications Using Directory Services: Part 1—Introductory Topics.* Presentation at BrainShare '93, 22–26 March, University of Utah, Salt Lake City, Utah.

Gauthier, Lori. 1993. *Creating NetWare-Aware Windows Applications.* Presentation at BrainShare '93, 22–26 March, University of Utah, Salt Lake City, Utah.

Getting Started with NetWare 4.0. Provo, Utah: Novell, Inc.

Herbon, Gamal B. April 1993. *NetWare Application Notes* 4 (4):21–53.

Higley, DeeAnne and Dale Olds. 1993. *Build a Network Service Using NetWare 4.0 Directory Services.* Presentation at BrainShare '93, 22–26 March, University of Utah, Salt Lake City, Utah.

NetWare Client API for C: Volume 1. 1993. Provo, Utah: Novell, Inc.

NetWare Client API for C: Volume 2. 1993. Provo, Utah: Novell, Inc.

NetWare Client Transport Protocol API for C. 1993. Provo, Utah: Novell, Inc.

Index

*****Boldface** numbers refer to art

➡ About the authors

Lori has held various positions at Novell, including test specialist, technical development support engineer, development engineer, and team leader for API development. She has been programming in Windows for three years and was responsible for the C Interface for Windows Software Development Kit and the Client Software Development Kit. She has presented on Windows and on NetWare programming for several years at BrainShare, Novell's technical conference. Currently, she is working on the Windows development team at Novell. Lori holds a bachelor's degree in Computational Linguistics from Brigham Young University.

Sue has worked with NetWare for four years. She has experience with a rich set of Novell development tools and environments, such as DOS, Windows, and NLMs. Along with Lori, Sue was responsible for the C Interface for Windows Software Development Kit and the C Interface for DOS from Novell. Sue also has had experience with chip simulation test suites and graduated from Southwest Texas State University with a bachelor's degree in Computer Science.

Other Bestsellers of Related Interest

PARADOX® PROGRAMMING
2nd Edition
Patricia A. Hartman and Cary N. Prague
With more specific programming solutions than any other book, this guide details all of 4.0's new features—the Windows-like interface, drop-down menus, PAL extensions, memo fields, and enhanced query performance. You'll cover database management techniques, from simple data entry and screen design to more complex functions like generating reports, sorting databases, and querying databases. Plus, you'll review PAL programming and script creations, screen design for data entry, multifile database systems, and more.
• 576 pages • 502 illustrations.
026978-5 $29.95

WINDOWS PROGRAMMING WITH BORLAND® C++
Jeff Mackay
You'd have to spend several hundred dollars on commercial software to match the value you'll get with this book and its 3.5-inch companion disk of professional-quality, Windows-class libraries. It's a one-of-the-kind resource that will help you get in on the Windows revolution. Covering Windows 3.1, Windows NT™, and Win325™, this guide teaches object-oriented Windows programming by demonstrating how to code an actual Windows application that takes full advantage of the Windows interfaces.
• 568 pages • 196 illustrations • 3.5" disk.
044596-6 $34.95

**PROFESSIONAL SAS®
PROGRAMMER'S POCKET
REFERENCE**
Rick Aster
An easy-to-use guide to SAS commands, functions, procedures, and syntax covering versions 6.05 to 6.07, this book's compact size, simple structure, and to-the-point solutions let you program more quickly and efficiently, without being distracted by lengthy explanations and commentary. Topics discussed include file management, the display manager, formats and informats, functions, CALL routines, statements, syntax, dataset and system options, expressions, and the macrolanguage.
• 192 pages.
001544-9 $19.95

MICROSOFT ACCESS PROGRAMMING
Namir C. Shammas
This hands-on introduction to Microsoft Access database programming is designed for anyone who's familiar with the BASIC language. It's a practical tutorial approach—complete with ready-to-use program code and professional tips, tricks, and warnings. You get information offers, how to craft the visual interface of a form, how to fine-tune the control settings to alter their appearance or behavior, and more.
• 304 pages • 518 illustrations.
No. 056850-2 $32.95

**BOOKKEEPING ON YOUR
HOME-BASED PC**
Linda Stern
Written by an award-winning personal finance columnist, this book leads you through the complete process of starting up and running your home-based business—with emphasis on the technology you need to make it work. After an overview of the attractive prospects of the business, the book focuses on how to equip your venture with computer, fax, modem, and telephone systems that fit your specific needs.
• 256 pages • 50 illustrations.
061231-5 $24.95

Look for These and Other TAB Books at Your Local Bookstore

To Order Call Toll Free 1-800-822-8158
(24-hour telephone service available.)

or write to TAB Books, Blue Ridge Summit, PA 17294-0840.

Title	Product No.	Quantity	Price

☐ Check or money order made payable to TAB Books

Charge my ☐ VISA ☐ MasterCard ☐ American Express

Acct. No. _____ Exp. _____

Signature: _____

Name: _____

Address: _____

City: _____

State: _____ Zip: _____

Subtotal	$ _____
Postage and Handling ($3.00 in U.S., $5.00 outside U.S.)	$ _____
Add applicable state and local sales tax	$ _____
TOTAL	$ _____

TAB Books catalog free with purchase; otherwise send $1.00 in check or money order and receive $1.00 credit on your next purchase.

Orders outside U.S. must pay with international money in U.S. dollars drawn on a U.S. bank.

TAB Guarantee: If for any reason you are not satisfied with the book(s) you order, simply return it (them) within 15 days and receive a full refund.

BC

Order Form for Books
Requiring Two 5.25" Disks

This Windcrest/McGraw-Hill software product is also available on two 5.25"/360K disks. If you need the software in 5.25" format, simply follow these instructions:

- Complete the order form below. Be sure to include the exact title of the Windcrest/McGraw-Hill book for which you are requesting a replacement disk.

- Make check or money order made payable to *Glossbrenner's Choice*. The cost is $7.00 ($10.00 for shipments outside the U.S.) to cover media, postage, and handling. Pennsylvania residents, please add 6% sales tax.

- Foreign orders: please send an international money order or a check drawn on a bank with a U.S. clearing branch. We cannot accept foreign checks.

- Mail order form and payment to:

  Glossbrenner's Choice
  Attn: Windcrest/McGraw-Hill Disk Replacement
  699 River Road
  Yardley, PA 19067-1965

Your disks will be shipped via First Class Mail. Please allow one to two weeks for delivery.

·· ✂ ··

Windcrest/McGraw-Hill Disk Replacement

Please send me a replacement disks in 5.25"/360K format for the following Windcrest/McGraw-Hill book:

Book Title _____

Name _____

Address _____

City/State/ZIP _____

DISK WARRANTY

This software is protected by both United States copyright law and international copyright treaty provision. You must treat this software just like a book, except that you may copy it into a computer in order to be used and you may make archival copies of the software for the sole purpose of backing up our software and protecting your investment from loss.

By saying "just like a book," McGraw-Hill means, for example, that this software may be used by any number of people and may be freely moved from one computer location to another, so long as there is no possibility of its being used at one location or on one computer while it also is being used at another. Just as a book cannot be read by two different people in two different places at the same time, neither can the software be used by two different people in two different places at the same time (unless, of course, McGraw-Hill's copyright is being violated).

LIMITED WARRANTY

Windcrest/McGraw-Hill takes great care to provide you with top-quality software, thoroughly checked to prevent virus infections. McGraw-Hill warrants the physical diskette(s) contained herein to be free of defects in materials and workmanship for a period of sixty days from the purchase date. If McGraw-Hill receives written notification within the warranty period of defects in materials or workmanship, and such notification is determined by McGraw-Hill to be correct, McGraw-Hill will replace the defective diskette(s). Send requests to:

> Customer Service
> Windcrest/McGraw-Hill
> 13311 Monterey Lane
> Blue Ridge Summit, PA 17294-0850

The entire and exclusive liability and remedy for breach of this Limited Warranty shall be limited to replacement of defective diskette(s) and shall not include or extend to any claim for or right to cover any other damages, including but not limited to, loss of profit, data, or use of the software, or special, incidental, or consequential damages or other similar claims, even if McGraw-Hill has been specifically advised of the possibility of such damages. In no event will McGraw-Hill's liability for any damages to you or any other person ever exceed the lower of suggested list price or actual price paid for the license to use the software, regardless of any form of the claim.

McGRAW-HILL, INC. SPECIFICALLY DISCLAIMS ALL OTHER WARRANTIES, EXPRESS OR IMPLIED, INCLUDING, BUT NOT LIMITED TO, ANY IMPLIED WARRANTY OF MERCHANTABILITY OR FITNESS FOR A PARTICULAR PURPOSE.

Specifically, McGraw-Hill makes no representation or warranty that the software is fit for any particular purpose and any implied warranty of merchantability is limited to the sixty-day duration of the Limited Warranty covering the physical diskette(s) only (and not the software) and is otherwise expressly and specifically disclaimed.

This limited warranty gives you specific legal rights; you may have others which may vary from state to state. Some states do not allow the exclusion of incidental or consequential damages, or the limitation on how long an implied warranty lasts, so some of the above may not apply to you.

If you need help
with the enclosed disk . . .

The enclosed double-density 3½" disk contains six self-extracting files, containing a total of 87 files, and a file named INSTALL.BAT. You need to run INSTALL.BAT to create the proper subdirectory structure on your hard drive and to copy the files into the new directories.

Put the companion diskette into the floppy drive, make the floppy drive your current drive, and type:

INSTALL *D: d:*

where *D:* is the floppy drive that contains the companion diskette and *d:* is the hard drive where you want to install the files.

INSTALL.BAT will create a subdirectory called 4498DISK on the root of the hard drive that you specified. It then will create six subdirectories under 4498DISK. Next, the batch file copies the compressed files into the appropriate directories, extracts the files from them, and removes the compressed files from your hard drive.

After running INSTALL.BAT, the files are ready for use.

IMPORTANT

Read the Disk Warranty terms on the previous page before opening the disk envelope. Opening the envelope constitutes acceptance of these terms and renders this entire book-disk package nonreturnable except for replacement in kind due to material defects.